"Joanna LaPrade's Forged in Da[...] frame for approaching, sometimes [...] descent that sooner or later we all experience during dark times. When these times come, as they will, her structure suggests a way of understanding, a mode of approach to finding one's meaning task in hours when the ego has been dethroned, and ordinary consciousness rendered powerless."

— James Hollis, Ph.D., Jungian analyst and bestselling author

"Joanna LaPrade's fine book reveals the underworld not as a mythic abstraction, but as the living reality of meaningful darkness and transformative suffering that we must all face, one way or another. She skilfully combines psychological insight and a nuanced imagination for mythic patterns with a deep feeling for human suffering and the capacity to write with an immediacy that stirs and educates."

— Keiron Le Grice, Ph.D., author of *The Rebirth of the Hero* and *The Archetypal Cosmos*

"As an integrative oncologist, I know that one of the biggest challenges for a patient is facing themselves. Dr LaPrade expertly guides folks to understand the story of their own lives and to re-establish connection, step out of damaging polarities, and engage in truly living versus being paralyzed by the fear of dying. I will return again and again to these pages and her wisdom, to help shine light on my own darkness and encourage others to do the same."

— Nasha Winters, ND, FABNO, Co-author of *The Metabolic Approach to Cancer* and *Mistletoe and the Emerging Future of Integrative Oncology*

FORGED
IN DARKNESS

The Many Paths of
Personal Transformation

Dr Joanna LaPrade

WATKINS
Sharing Wisdom Since
1893

This edition first published in the UK and USA in 2022 by
Watkins, an imprint of Watkins Media Limited
Unit 11, Shepperton House
89–93 Shepperton Road
London
N1 3DF

enquiries@watkinspublishing.com

Design and typography copyright © Watkins Media Limited 2022

Text copyright © Dr Joanna LaPrade 2022

Dr Joanna LaPrade has asserted her right under the Copyright, Designs
and Patents Act 1988 to be identified as the author of this work.

1 2 3 4 5 6 7 8 9 10

Designed and typeset by JCS Publishing
Printed and bound in the United Kingdom by TJ Books

A CIP record for this book is available from the British Library

ISBN: 978-1-78678-650-0 (Paperback)
ISBN: 978-1-78678-658-6 (eBook)

www.watkinspublishing.com

"... *facilis descensus Averno;*
noctes atque dies patet ianua Ditis;
sed revocare gradum superasque evadere ad auras,
hoc opus, hic labor est ..."

Virgil, *Aeneid*, VI, 126–9

"... easy is the descent to Avernus: night and day
the door of gloomy Dis stands open; but to recall
thy steps and pass out to the upper air, this is the
task, this is the toil!"

H. R. Fairclough (trans.)

To Ben,

for staying with us.

CONTENTS

INTRODUCTION

Entering the Underworld

I remember well the long, black corridor, the distant archway, and the shrouded figures sitting like sentinels on countless tiers. Each figure's face was hidden behind a gray fabric that fluttered in an unseen wind. Over and over, I awoke from this dream knowing intuitively it was a pathway to some kind of depth. My interest in the underworld began then.

I've never really been drawn to the surface of things. I've always pried, dug, and explored the deeper and darker layers. The thread that connects my curiosities and passions is my fascination with the inner world, particularly those places within us that are painful, confusing, yet intriguing – places I have come to see as my own underworld. Above all, I am enlivened by stories of people's lives and histories, of the human imagination and the myths we tell to explain ourselves and our place in the world. I became a depth psychologist because I wanted to engage with myself and others in complex, creative, and meaningful ways, to look beneath the surface and see and feel what is *actually* going on in the psyche.[1]

In my early twenties, I was in a public library when I randomly, it seems, took a copy of *On Jung* by Anthony Stevens off the shelf. I drained the book in a day, and in my journal I scribbled a simple question: "Do I find what I seek in these pages?" I wasn't certain, but I found the subject of Stevens's book and the question so compelling – it resonated in me so deeply – that I made a leap of faith and enrolled in Pacifica Graduate Institute to get my PhD in depth psychology – the study of the psyche through the psychologies of C. G. Jung and James Hillman.

At Pacifica, I found a world brimming with subjects I loved – mythology, dreams, history, religion, theory – and deep self-exploration. I learned from inspiring professors such as Safron Rossi and Keiron Le Grice, and, looking back, I see that depth psychology was the only path I could have taken. I'm now in private practice as a psychotherapist and writing about the underworld journey – once again walking down that long, black corridor into the depths.

Forged in Darkness is based on my PhD dissertation, "Descent and Ascent: Archetypal Styles of Consciousness in Underworld Journeys." I hope some of the tools, thoughts, and images offered in these pages might help you let the underworld move you toward a wholeness and clarity of being that simply cannot be found in daylight.

What is the Underworld?

In this book, I weave together myth, religion, history, depth psychology, cases from my practice, personal stories from colleagues, friends, family, famous people and world events, and my own inner journey to guide you – and me – toward a *remembering of* and *return to* the innermost richness of our own "underworlds."[2]

The underworld is the place of the *unknown* – the darkness, the hidden, the dead, monsters and demons, gnarly trees and cold fissures that wind deep into the earth. It's the place where we keep the discarded parts of ourselves, those aspects of who we are that our parents, educators, society, and selves deemed unfit and unsuitable.

There is no more challenging threshold to cross than that between the dayworld and underworld, between the conscious and unconscious parts of ourselves. Humans have handed down stories of the underworld for centuries – its purpose and how to get there. Whether traveling into caverns of the earth or the depths of ourselves, the underworld journey is an experience of mourning, sacrifice, unwanted and difficult experiences, danger, estrangement from the past, uncertainty, and dissolution of who we once were.

Darkness is where we go to recover forgotten treasures, and to get there we may have to cross unfathomably deep rivers, battle hostile forces, and face the judgments of the gods. In the gloom, we behold things we wish we'd never seen, horrors and challenges we'll never forget. Perhaps our voice turns into screams, our chest seizes, blood freezes, footsteps falter, and in the place where the lights go out the world stops. When we're in the submerged depths of the human mind, it can be difficult to even remember the surface.

We may find ourselves facing darkness born from a variety of triggers. Sometimes it's the result of a single traumatic event, such as the sudden death of a loved one or a physical or emotional violation; at other times it might be an illness or an accident. It can be a response to underlying attitudes implicit in our family, ancestors, peer groups, culture, or religion; or perhaps it arises from feeling unwanted, orphaned, abused, or being undermined and devalued. After years of an emotionally abusive and codependent relationship, a young woman described herself as numb, mistrusting, paranoid, and exhausted: "I'm weak from being at war for so long. All I want to do is fall on my face and lie there. I have no fight or feeling left. All I can do is be a shell and wait for the day breath fills my lungs." Her words capture what is like to find ourselves in darkness.

The underworld journey is universal, common to all cultures, religions, people, and places. In his study of burial rites, Robert Pogue Harrison notes that the word *humanity* derives from the Latin *humus*, meaning "earth" and "bury."[3] To be human means to place parts of ourselves underground and then to enter the dark places of our world to carry out rituals, predetermined ways of performing a ceremony, and sacrifices to reconnect to deeper parts of ourselves – the treasures we've hidden, the elements we've entombed. Forbidden and foreboding, journeying into the depths, being drawn into the darkness, has always been a part of the human fabric, bespeaking an ancient longing.

There are times in life we lose ourselves in the dark corridors of our minds and souls, face arduous tests of character, die to what we know, and are reborn anew. In depth psychology, the journey to the underworld is a metaphor for the *ego* (conscious awareness) coming into contact with the *unconscious* (psychic contents that are inaccessible to and autonomous from consciousness). This "journey" thus represents our encounters with the shadowed and unfathomable aspects of life – facing fears and passions we have not yet integrated and the resistances and complexes that still grip and control us. We can feel the underworld's ghostly presence in our traumas and uncertainties, our hatreds and humiliations, our sufferings and feelings of failure.

When we search within, inevitably we find the underworld – lost connections, failed enterprises, melancholy, haunting memories, embarrassing insecurities, deflation, and buried secrets. We've all walked, fallen, or been dragged into that long, dark corridor as we endure grief, self-pity, illness, and trepidation, along with the promise and threat of change. Friendships end, our sense of ourselves collapses, innocence is lost, loved ones break our hearts, and inescapably we're pulled downward to face the abandoned parts of ourselves crying out for our loving awareness. Experiences of darkness are natural and necessary markers along the path of growth and discovery – we all have them.

Life is full of stories of *underworlding*. A woman remembers being 19 and traveling utterly alone to Mexico for an abortion. Another feels her own devastating sense of failure while she watches her middle child suffer through adolescence. At three, a boy develops hearing loss, a darkness that comes to shape his sense of self for the rest of his life. In the buzz of chatter and vibrant laughter, a man freezes in place, more alone with others than when he's by himself. Thoughts of inadequacy, ugliness, and isolation stalk him like a red-eyed predator. When a woman's brother returns from the Vietnam War, he is a ghost of his former self – his soul the price of going to war. Trapped in a 24/7 underworld, tortured by visceral memories of conflict. And in a white kitchen, polished and perfect, a man tells a woman he doesn't love her anymore and is moving out – she slides to the floor and cries, wondering if she might drown in her own tears.

The *underworld* is the human experience of entering these great, powerful, destructive unknown states. It's finding yourself in gloom and mire, dread and demons. Relating underworld moments to big trauma, death, or divorce is an easy leap for the mind to make. But sometimes they aren't that big. It's about the wound in us that the experience, or "trigger," lands in. A small matter might land in a long-untended wound. And our underworld experiences might include sugar addiction, being spellbound by an imposter, hating your sibling, or finding yourself caught by jealousy. These seemingly everyday descents take us away from ourselves, away from conscious awareness and the perspective of our usual identity into the unconscious, and into the midst of the darkness, disorientation, and pain which, if we stay present to it all, offer rich opportunities for learning, deepening, and healing.

Not all underworld journeys are created equal. A lifelong wounding such as the echo of an abusive parent, pulling a dying companion off a battlefield, or feeling tainted after sexual trauma evokes a different response from being broken up with or demoted at work. There is an opaque hierarchy to darkness – it exists on a spectrum. Some experiences are challenging and painful but not to the same life-halting and -dissolving degree as a terminal diagnosis, a natural disaster, racism, the loss of a loved one, or a psychotic episode.

When I say underworld, I mean the full spectrum of suffering and darkness. The journey downward begins when we find ourselves at the gates of hell. It doesn't matter if it's a massive stroke or the recognition that the life you're living is not your own. If it's conscious and painful, and we want to or have to change, then it's the underworld. If you ask someone about the underworld, all kinds of answers arise. Someone might tell you of a sister who died when she was young. One person experienced a lifetime of societal identity subjugation. Another individual was bullied as a child and now feels ugly and unwanted. Someone had a bipolar mother or manages chronic anxiety, suffered a miscarriage, or financial distress. The litany of darkness includes everything from death to insecurity, emotional neglect to heartbreak.

Is one form of hardship more important than another? Over and over, I see people push real pain aside or even shame themselves, because they feel their issues are minor compared to the fates of others. If we put the underworld on a competitive scale, we discredit the many shades of darkness. In fact, comparing in this way is a form of denial of the profundity of the impact of even "small things" on the nervous system.

My father has lived a long and complex life – full of joy and love, but also in the presence of the underworld. When I asked him about moments of underworlding throughout his life, the first story he recalled was a moment as a young boy when, early in the morning, he carefully assembled a bowl of cereal and milk. He accidently dropped the glass milk bottle on the kitchen floor and it broke. Mortified, he rushed upstairs to his room. There, he opened the window and climbed out on the roof with the intention of making his way to the ground and running away to start a new life. Decades later, this moment, seemingly minor in intensity, lingers. It wasn't a hellish experience of trauma or exploitation, but it evoked a presence that, years after the bottle broke, he nevertheless called "underworld." It doesn't matter if it *seems* insignificant. It's how you digest it, and how deep and unhealed the wound is.

When the body of a three-year-old Syrian refugee was washed up on shore, the photo of his tiny figure gripped the world. When 300 children were shrouded in white death robes, the city of Aleppo lost a generation. An estimated 20,000 women were captured in Yazidi and sold as sex slaves to the Islamic State. In today's global world, if you compare your experiences of underworlding to those of others, you risk undermining what happened to you. All darkness must be honored, explored, and understood. The soul would not bring this, or that, to your attention if it were not, at this moment, asking to be healed.

The problem is not the degree of the underworld experience but how we meet it. Everyone finds themselves in darkness but not everyone is able to stop, look around, and notice that the presence of such pain and otherness can give our lives weight, purpose, depth, and a quality of soul that cannot be found in daylight. Generalizing, comparing with the suffering of others, is to turn your back on the message from below that is there for you, specifically.

In *Man's Search for Meaning*, psychiatrist and Holocaust survivor Victor Frankl recounts his experience of being incarcerated in Auschwitz for three years. Surrounded by barbed wire, children were torn from their mothers, barefoot men trudged across frozen fields, gunshots rang out at night, in the morning, afternoon, and evening – so frequently that soon no one even noticed them. After enduring unimaginable horror, Frankl reminds us that "suffering completely fills the human soul and conscious mind, no matter whether the suffering is great or little. Therefore the 'size' of human suffering is absolutely relative."[4] Some darkness carries more weight, has greater ramifications, consumes more of our souls. But to adopt a hierarchical vantage point is to risk invalidating your *own* darkness.

We in the West disparage the underworld. We are not a deep culture; we don't value the underground parts of ourselves. We value functioning, not introspection; doing, not being; happiness, not suffering. For us, descending into darkness is counterintuitive; it runs against the grain of our upper-world values – light, warmth, control, visibility, perfection, and accomplishment. As mythologist Joseph Campbell described this, "people resist the door of death."[5]

Many clients I work with share a sense that they cannot live up to their peers' or culture's standards. We live under the reign of positivity, and it is a burden. Comparing themselves with the varnished, Photoshopped images they see online, they think they're the only ones struggling. On social media, flawless images get "liked," and the rejected parts of our Facebook friends get buried in a shadowy underworld not visible unless you know how to look for them. We wonder if we are good enough, joyful enough, happy enough, not how we will grow from the darkness of living. We have immense pressure not to suffer. Yet our pain doesn't evaporate. When a part of us is hidden, we do not feel whole, and sooner or later, it will come up and bite us.

In ancient Greece, the dark was not only feared, it was also valued and even worshiped. Despite the terrors the Greeks encountered in the underworld, they had a profound respect for the mythopoetic, religious imagination they found there. We in the 21st century, on the other hand, prioritize the "positive." Therapy is for the sick, and the underworld is the dwelling of the pathological. Darkness is failure, or, at a minimum, bad luck. And the more we exclude darkness from our lives, the more it becomes our enemy. We think that for a happy life the underworld must be avoided. We've forgotten that darkness is the herald of transformation.

Falling into the Abyss

About six years ago, I was pulled into darkness. I was sitting on the banks of the Snake River in Wyoming when my younger brother, Ben, called me. We chatted about the dailies of life – boyfriend and girlfriend, dogs and adventures. Somehow we wandered into a conversation about God. "The faith we have in ourselves is our destiny," Ben said. "We are our own God. Believe in your existence and let it go. Let God decide." The next day Ben suffered a traumatic brain injury and was life-flighted from Santa Fe to Denver.

Ben fell off a horse, broke his femur, and marrow escaped from the bone and spread through his body, crossing his atrial wall and showering his brain in hundreds of mini-strokes. When I heard, my heart plummeted to the bottom of the ocean. The underworld was coursing through the marrow of my bones. I sobbed on the plane, held the taxi driver's hand, and stumbled into the hospital room where my beautiful and life-filled brother hovered at death's door.

I was gripped by a powerful impulse to control the situation, protect my brother, conquer any weakness of my own, and above all, deny the possibility of Ben dying. As a family, we barely ate or slept – feeding ourselves with determination and the strange willpower that's awakened when a loved one's life is threatened. I argued with doctors about what he was being fed, researched medical terminology to understand what they were telling us, and together my family and I stood vigil among the beeps, tubes, and sterile air of my brother's hospital room. Over and over we heard: he's a good person, he'll survive, he'll fight this, he can beat this, you can endure it, and, most interestingly, people would whisper to him, "Be a *hero.*"

Over time, my courageous attitude, which at first served as a powerful shield, started to crack, and deep fissures in my confidence and capacity to control began spreading. *Determination was not enough*; in fact, it was becoming counterproductive. It was beginning to break me, and once again I was stumbling down the long, black corridor, this time cutting myself with my own heroic sword.

As days turned to weeks, I became obsessed with the conversation my brother and I had the day before his accident. It seemed important that what could have been our last words together was about faith in ourselves and letting another force shape your destiny: *let God decide.* Questions about how we show up in hardship, the many faces of the underworld journey, and why we look at suffering so singularly began to percolate in my mind and heart. *Let darkness decide.*

The Hero with a Thousand Faces

Heroism requires strength and vision in the face of challenge. The hero encounters the darkest demons in service to growth, maturation, and finding one's resources. I used to think heroism meant brute force – controlling and conquering steep odds, subduing monsters, and vanquishing naysayers. While these are valid stances when faced with adversity, there are other ways to be heroic, elaborated in the world's mythic traditions, that are neither forceful nor dominating. The idea of the hero has deteriorated into a large, celebrated, and bold figure who obliterates oppressors and leaps across the abyss. Of the many heroes who populate ancient Greek and Roman myths, only Hercules, the conqueror who faces life with his sword in hand, represents the openly aggressive hero-type we value today.[6]

Hero is an essential archetypal energy, but it is not limited to the lifestyle choices of Rambo or the Terminator. As mythologist Joseph Campbell reminds us, the hero has a thousand faces. The problem is *our relationship* with the underworld and *our relationship* with the hero archetype. We're no longer actively connected to the underworld and have forgotten the many faces of the hero. We're so split off from darkness that we treat it as pathological.

The image of a hero carved out of perfect ivory, without blemish or imperfection, lacks nuance. It is not true of Aeneas and Odysseus, whose hearts broke as they reached for their dead parents, only to find empty shades. The heroes of myth, religion, and legends are much more dynamic than today's action figures. They are guides who stand with us in the currents of change, the blindness of uncertainty, and the perils of the dark night of the soul.

Some situations require Herculean might, while other moments need Orphic creativity, love, and learning from failures. At other times we channel Odysseus and use questioning, acceptance, and forbearance as sources of empowerment. And in some situations, we can embody Aeneas and use reverence, compassion, and deep listening to reclaim what has been abandoned and grow from the journey.

"We have not even to risk the adventure alone," Campbell reminds us, "for the heroes of all time have gone before us."[7]

Heroes personify the human struggle against daunting inner and outer forces – complexes and shadow material, death and rebirth, illness and violence. Exploring the journeys of mythic heroes helps us frame our own experiences of the underworld. Do we react aggressively, fail to accept reality, draw on our inner strengths, move forward directed by ego, trust powers beyond ourselves, or follow a guide? Do we embody more than one of these heroic qualities at once? However we respond, however we course-correct, between darkness and us stand the heroes ready to bring strength, flexibility, and imagination to our inevitable journeys within.

When facing the darkness, we're best served by being present with the patterns of our own journey so we can bring forth our own particular resources. Being true to our own sensibilities, we bring to the hero's journey the creativity and plurality it deserves.

Finding Our Way: Myth and Psyche

Why do I turn to myths to explore the psyche? Myths are traditional stories, many describing the genesis or early history of a people, or explaining what underlies some natural or social phenomenon, typically involving divine or mystical beings or events. Many myths and fairytales familiar to us today date back to prehistory. As theologian Karen Armstrong explained, "Human beings have *always* been mythmakers."[8]

Myths give shape and meaning to what is essential about being human, but through imagery rather than in literal terms. The monsters, gods, warriors, and demons of myths are specific expressions of the cultures from which the stories come, while at the same time the issues they explore are global, reaching beyond the personal to the universal energies that shape life. They allow us to see past our limited perspectives, investigating thorny issues through grand stories and characters.

By providing a bigger frame for personal experiences, myths initiate us into larger dimensions of life.

Heroes and gods show us behaviors, traits, and energies we can *feel into*. In this book, we'll explore how different mythic figures embody attitudes and qualities that may be present in our own journeys. If we feel the desire to be creative and vulnerable we're in the presence of Orpheus, the hero of the lyre. If we seek release from limiting ideas, we're in the presence of Dionysus, god of loosening and liberation. If we're compelled to follow guidance from a higher power, we're in the presence of Aeneas, the Trojan hero who founds Rome. When we're in flux, we may feel a longing for movement and change, entering the realm of Hermes, god of the inbetweens. Being taken into darkness leads us to Persephone, queen of the underworld and wife to Hades.

From time immemorial, myths have pointed to the deepest mysteries, revealing layers of reality through the personification of archetypal patterns. *Archetypes* are collective, recurring patterns of thought, emotion, and behavior that shape psychological life. Deriving from the Greek *arche,* "the first principle," they are the ancient and universal structures of the psyche, preexistent configurations that seem to be present always and everywhere. Regardless of epoch, location, or culture, archetypes constellate as predispositions and potentialities for experiencing and responding to our lives. We inherit, along with the structure of the psyche, the archetypal forms found in all times, among all peoples.

Take for instance, the archetypal *mother*. Like all archetypes, the mother has a nearly infinite range of aspects. She is *personal* – our own mothers, grandmothers, mothers-in-law, or any women with whom we have a relationship that carries qualities of nurturance, safety, creation, and warmth. The mother is also *transpersonal*. Christian religion and myth tell us of the mother of God – the divine Virgin Mary – who becomes mother of the

Church, the vessel from which spiritual nourishment and grace can be gained. In Hindu theology, *prakriti* (the prime material from which all matter is born) unites with *maya* (illusion or magic wielded by a god) to produce the consciousness of wholeness. All great mother goddesses are fertility goddesses – Gia, Rhea, and Demeter in Greek and Roman myth; Isis among ancient Egyptian cults; Kali for Hindus; and Ishtar amid Assyrians and Babylonians.

The mother (derived from the same etymological root as "matter") is symbolized by the earth, the sea, a garden, paradise, a cave, the womb, vessels, trees, circles, animals such as a cow or bear, or places like the kitchen or hearth linked with nourishment and transformation. To be born is to emerge from the mother's womb and to die is to return to Mother Earth. The mother archetype also carries ambivalent and negative aspects such as devouring or life-hoarding witch, dragon, serpent, grave, or deep water. The mother can stifle horizons – giving life but also entrapping her offspring. The mother is both creation and destruction: the original matrix from which all life springs that can also paralyze ego development.

Archetypes become visible through ideas and images. In their raw form, these elemental structures are invisible and unknowable, what Jungians call the *archetype per se*. To become conscious, this raw energy takes on the identity, experience, and character of a culture or an individual, becoming an *archetypal image*. An archetype is the energy that forms around an essential aspect of existence. Like iron filings to a magnet, the content and experiences of our lives are drawn to the archetypes. In the world's myths and religions, we encounter countless *images* of birth, death, love, power, magic, wisdom, and, of course, the underworld.

C. G. Jung was unique in his time for taking seriously the archetypal underpinnings of the psyche. He explored myths, fairytales, folklore, symbols, and dreams as tools for psychological understanding, believing that imagination can help us feel and bring awareness to the inner dramas of the unconscious. Jung recognized archetypal motifs as personifying dimensions of the psyche. When we examine the myths of multiple cultures, as Jung and Campbell did, we see patterns that give us deeper insight into what archetypes are, and what is going on in our lives at levels deeper than consciousness.

To explore our images and experiences in terms of archetypes, we can look to the Greek gods and recognize that we have a multitude of desires and claims made upon us. Instead of organizing these impulses under a single suite of personality characteristics, a polytheistic and mythic approach encourages living with the tensions that arise among the various aspects of ourselves. When we try to keep a singular lens, certain aspects of our nature may disappear from sight. To engage with complexity, we need to move from a literalistic, controlling perspective to an *imaginal response,* one that's more attuned to life's intricacies.

Today, myth has come to mean falsehood, and myths are often regarded as children's stories, not maps of the psyche. Jungian Robert A. Johnson asks, "On what level is it true?"[9] Myths are true on the level of psyche. Something in the psyche cries with longing and recognition when we touch the archetypal realm.

We are literal, scientific, rational, surface-oriented, and fast-paced. Yet without imagination, the world becomes arid. Mythopoetic language is magical; it brings worlds into *being.* Stories of warriors hunting the windswept plains, gods who trick and deceive, maidens transformed into sea monsters, and spiders that weave the web of life have long exerted a powerful hold over humankind. Tapping into the deeper layers of the psyche using mythic imagery is like discovering water in the parched earth. Myths are neither fanciful nor untrue. They are *ways of imagining,* maps for seeing the deeper currents that shape what it means to be human. These enduring patterns and stories help us understand the flow of the human condition. Figures such as Persephone and Hercules may belong to the past, but they evoke themes that are as important as ever.

Our lives are large and make for great dramatic motifs. The question isn't whether Hermes is real and shopping in the store today. That is not the kind of truth we're talking about. This truth entails realizing that we all experience the qualities of this lithe, youthful god – communication, connection, and deception – on a daily basis. Hermes points us back to ourselves. If we become familiar with how mythical themes move in our own experience, we can not only be present with them, we can learn to co-create the currents of our lives. This is not turning toward a bygone era. We are becoming aware of the path we're already on.

The Gods

Mythology tells us that gods and goddesses are constantly implicated in the affairs of mortals. We may have lost our connection to them and their stories, but they still meddle in our affairs – alive within our complexes, relationships, symptoms, and behaviors. The forms and powers of myth are alive in our souls and psyches. When you feel the impulse to be in nature, surrounded by pristine rivers and remote canyons, you are feeling the presence of Artemis, goddess of untouched wilderness. When anger boils your blood and steers your hand, you are feeling the presence of Ares, god of war. Myths give us an imaginal and symbolic understanding of experiences that may otherwise be incomprehensible.

There are important differences between the journeys of heroes and those of the gods. Heroes teach us how to face gods, how to be in the presence of an archetype – what to notice, how to be in the presence of these awesome realities and be affected by them. Moses, in the book of Exodus, standing before the burning bush is an example of standing in the presence of an archetype – in this case, the Hebrew God in the form of a bush.

The ancient Greek and Roman gods, despite being flawed and fickle, are distinguishable from human heroes insofar as the gods were *pre-formed*. They do not learn or change, and in that sense, they require no further development (even to resolve the contradictory aspects of themselves). Hermes, messenger of the gods, god of boundaries *and* their transgressions, and patron of herdsmen, thieves, and graves, was the protector of travelers and the conductor of souls into the afterlife. Hermes represents communication *and* silence, avian *and* stone. By observing Hermes and holding our own contradictory aspects simultaneously, we learn a critical step in the alchemy of transformation. When the tensions between different ideas and attitudes are held at the same time, something new is born. This is healing at the deepest level. Persephone was abducted *and* a ruler, a virgin *and* a queen. Dionysus represents ecstasy *and* fasting, growth *and* dismemberment. When we explore the journeys of these divine figures, we see how contradictory elements can be a pathway to wholeness.

As we explore gods, you'll likely notice aspects of the heroes in the characters and roles of the gods. This is no mistake; each hero channels different archetypal energy. The gods are the archetypal energy.

This Book as Your Guide

The figures who populate mythical stories personify styles of consciousness, archetypal motifs offering us hints for how we might engage with life. Symbolically, they represent attributes and states that embody patterns of thinking, feeling, and acting. Each mythic figure has their own motif – a constellation of images, characteristics, and tone that offers ways of processing experience. Exploring ways we resonate with these figures, attuning ourselves to the archetypal currents that flow through our experiences, is a means to understand both mythology and our own hearts.

How do you use this perspective? Our psychologies are riddled with bullet-pointed guides that approach challenges with a mechanical fix-it attitude. Working with the psyche's stories and images doesn't proffer a one-stop cure, that's not the point. The point is in *being with*, allowing the psyche's images to work with you, to have presence and energy in your life so that you can feel the deeper currents of yourself. In order to support you, the chapters on the heroes and gods end with a summary of the main archetypal qualities that each figure embodies which are shaped into reflection prompts. This distillation is an invitation to step into how the different energies are uniquely present in your experience.

First, ask yourself this question: How is this archetypal energy present in my experience? Then, deepen your inquiry with reflections such as: Why has this energy come to me? What does it want from me? How does this presence reveal a different way of being where I am?

This book is not a prescription nor a solution. It doesn't offer a timeline, promise, or a way to measure success or progress. It simply encourages turning toward ourselves in ways that are imaginative and soulful, open and curious about the parts of us not yet known or explored. This undertaking is vast. I encourage you to proceed at your own pace.

It's easier to understand something when we have an image or felt sense of it. It allows us to *be with* what arises without judgment or comparison. What does this sensation or that thought look like in your mind's eye or feel like in your body? Is it a serpent wrapped around your heart? Does it fill the world with wonder? Is it a soft, misty rain of golden flowers?

Is it a cloaked figure standing behind you, dissing you for your failures, your worthlessness, your unlovability? Do you feel it in your heart-center, your shoulder, or your back? Images and sensations are powerful tools that can help us grapple with aspects of life that might seem insubstantial or unapproachable. As you read, notice how certain images make you feel, write down a line that speaks to you, pause when needed, reflect, and get curious when an image, a song, a thought, a memory, or a sensation arises. Allow the stories and qualities of the underworld to be present in your experience.

The journey to the underworld is like this. It can be experienced as a felt sense, as an image (or series of images, sometimes one after another, quite rapidly), or in various other forms as ancient as humankind's propensity for experiencing and telling stories. All cultures have rituals that connect humans with the underworld, with the unknown, unseen, feared parts of the psyche, the gods who inhabit it, and those who guide us there and back. Greek, Roman, and other mythic systems offer a plethora of heroes and divinities who journey into the underworld and show us, if we know how to *feel into* the mythology, how to interact with the powers of the deep psyche. In these stories, each hero and each god faces the journey in unique ways, approaching darkness with characteristics that mesh their traits with the situations in front of them, resulting in a vast range of expressions of consciousness.

In this book, I share contemporary stories and ancient myth. These are the heroes and gods of your psyche. They're neither concrete nor literal. They show themselves simply through these changes of "atmosphere." Slowing down can bring awareness of messages you might otherwise miss. Use the book's reflection points to help you attune yourself to how different characteristics and attitudes may be present in what's happening for you. Whatever arises, get curious about it. Follow the threads: What associations do you have with this song or that person? These noteworthy – albeit small or quiet – clues can lead to important insights.

Awakening the Imagination

Western culture has mostly turned away from holistic healing, preferring instead to suppress symptoms. Mainstream psychology is much the same, dominated by cognitive behavioral and evidence-based therapies. We measure, predict, and standardize a person's psychology. There's security in evidence-based methods, and for some, these techniques are beneficial. Yet by choosing standardization and measurement, we gloss over some of the deep and complex dimensions of life. We cannot measure meaning, self-awareness, shame, love, loneliness, failure, relationship, fears, or our unique traumas.

Beneath the layer of literalism and rationality lies the deep psyche's innate capacity for healing. And one way to communicate complexity and whole-making is myth. *Star Wars*, one of the most popular film series of all time, follows the structure of the hero's journey, as do *The Lord of the Rings*, *Harry Potter*, and other trophies of film and literature. As a culture, despite centuries of separating body from mind, man from nature, and symptoms from their roots, we're still drawn to mythology.

Like all humans since the advent of our species, we live under the influence of myths. They shape our world, and limit our purview. Representative democracy believes that power exercised by a majority brings about freedom, fairness, and justice. Patriarchy, another myth, derives from the idea that the eldest male is best suited to rule. In the Judeo-Christian mythos, happiness used to be reserved for heaven, while on earth we suffered. Yet this myth has changed; we now expect our lives to be exclusively happy. We ask questions to gauge our happiness, not meaning. We wonder how to be positive – not how to understand suffering. This sets up the expectation for us to always be in the upper world, where happiness is a mandate.

We have so many unconscious notions shaping our perceptions. These include personal myths as well – stories of family and childhood that contribute to our identity. If we don't make the effort to become aware of the cultural and personal stories that course through us and their assumptions about life, we might miss vast swathes of who we are and what our world holds for us.

A sage response might be to turn to the power of imagination and its capacity to build new neural pathways and update our myths. Our ideas about who we are affect how we experience life. How we imagine the journey to reclaiming our wholeness matters, which is why having a multiplicity of images to choose from can be life-changing. With choice, we gain possibility. "The mask of the unconscious," said Jung, "is not rigid – it reflects the face we turn towards it."[10] How we face our life's journey can, in large part, determine our experience and its outcome.

"Everything can be taken from a man," wrote Victor Frankl, "but one thing: the last of the human freedoms – to choose one's attitude in any given set of circumstances, to choose one's own way."[11] Every day we're offered opportunities to choose how to imagine our life, what meaning to wrap around our pain, what steps to take and how to act. Even against overwhelming energies that chip away at our sense of self, we still have imagination and choice. We may have an incurable disease, lose a loved one, be the victim of cruelty, or develop limiting behaviors due to trauma and the need to survive, and the question remains – how do we be present to what's happening? It's how we meet our underworld that adds new dimensions to our personality and a broader meaning to our life.

We can begin by learning to recognize when archetypal energies are moving in us, and with awareness we have a chance to participate in our response. When we find ourselves resisting a task, acting in ways quite different from how we want to present ourselves, such as binge eating, being triggered by our mother or father, feeling worthless or like we are imposters, or any of the other ways we might lose control over our behavior or thoughts, we have "entered the underworld" and are at a choice-point.

"A psyche with few psychological ideas," explained James Hillman, "is easily a victim."[12] To take responsibility for our lives, we need to engage imaginatively with the hurdles we encounter. Our defense against darkness is *acceptance*, not denial. Our power is *imagination*, not rigidity. Every time we bring consciousness to a situation, we become a participant and not just a victim. We only need to be curious, imaginative, and open to the vast array of stories and styles of underworld journeying that we humans have been sharing for thousands of generations.

Developing an Underworld Perspective

Having an "underworld perspective" means developing a personal relationship with both aspects of darkness – i.e., that which is not yet conscious, and the many expressions and layers of suffering. The point of a mythic underworld journey is to make the unconscious conscious. It's a transformative experience that involves the dissolution and reconstruction of aspects of who we think we are and how we engage with the world. This is the danger and the lure of the underworld journey: rebirth comes in darkness. Dying to what no longer serves us affords us a chance to live fully. Letting go allows us to expand.

In the West, we run for the nearest patch of sunlight, searching for the safety and predictability, which we think can be found in the dayworld. The Austrian poet Rainer Maria Rilke wrote, "We wasters of sorrows!"[13] To create an underworld perspective, we have to give up the impulse to avoid change, any ideas we have of perfection (or any other ways we might compare ourselves to others or to an ideal), efforts to control our emotions or our thoughts, and the belief that our sense of "I" is the only force within. It's in darkness – the unknown and perhaps unknowable, in the midst of the chaos and the suffering – that the light of wisdom and our own capacity can shine forth.

When the darkness is so raw that we're not able to stay with it, it's too soon for us to begin the process of change. The journey inward can be intolerable – too painful or scary for us to walk. When that's the case, we need to pause, accept where we are, and realize that who we are right now is where we need to put our attention. For now, the doorway isn't open wide enough for us to enter. We are not yet able to tolerate the discomfort. Over time, with the help of guides – therapists, wisdom keepers, and empathic friends – we might be able to turn toward our wounds and cultivate the capacity to stay present with grief, fear, pain, darkness, and even limitations. Whether we enter the gateway or know it isn't time for us yet, we begin to cultivate an underworld perspective. Aeschylus, the father of Greek tragedy, wrote: "Drop, drop – in our sleep, upon the heart sorrow falls, memory's pain, and to us, though against our very will, even in our own despair, comes wisdom through the awful grace of God."[14] In today's world, we don't get much encouragement to process or learn from our suffering. This bias against darkness leaves us ill-equipped to face reality as it is. We fear underworlding and rush through the darkness, trying to forget our grief and keep it together. Staying in the land of dread feels like being in the wrong place at the wrong time, a failure to step up to the challenges of the dayworld.

This aversion to depth and preference for lofty heights is revealed in the ways we describe our ideals: "uplifted," not "depressed;" "spirited," not "fallen." We treat death as an enemy and gather our forces to vanquish it, forgetting that mortality for humans is 100 percent: "She *lost* the battle to cancer," "Mom didn't *make it.*"

What could be the point of feeling the suffering of underworlding? The word "suffering" comes from the Latin *suffero* and the word "relate" from *refero*. They share the root *fero*, which means to bear, to carry, to endure. These are images of going downward, beneath the surface. "Suffering," reasons the Jungian analyst Russel Lockhart, "as undergoing is a going under, a going to the underground of things, that is, to the depths."[15] The Latin root *refero* means to bear back, to return, to ascend with.

We can't avoid suffering, but we can cultivate a conscious relationship with it. We can take on the burden and learn to carry it. "And when it [suffering] comes," writes Ursula Le Guin, "you know it. You know it as the truth. Of course, it's right to cure diseases, to prevent hunger and injustice, as the social organism does. But no society can change the nature of existence. We can't prevent suffering."[16]

In *Underland*, author Robert MacFarlane weaves an alluring tale of humanity's ongoing relationship with what is under-the-land – elapsed cities, research stations and bones, deep waters and cold caverns, forgotten rites, and sacred treasures left to be protected. Journeying into the deep earth has long been a part of our relationship with life on the surface. In the dark crevasses and hollows of the earth, we place our dead, build sacred temples, document our presence by leaving cave art, face our fears, witness a world so alien, and find comfort in the afterlife. MacFarlane learns what he calls *undersight*: how to discern the subtle and disguised entrances into cave systems. To understand light, he explains, you must first have been buried in darkness.[17]

Alchemy, the medieval antecedent of chemistry, concerned itself with transmutation of matter – combination, transformation, and creation. The underworld perspective is also alchemical. It tears open the soul and exposes its depths. The caverns of those forgotten places in us harbor enigmatic ingredients that, when mixed with our dayworld selves, have the potential to make us stronger and more thoughtful, compassionate and whole. When it's more difficult to remain on the surface with its comforts and pleasantries than to journey within, we are ready to face the darkness and let its alchemical properties reshape us. This choice is rarely made consciously. We simply find ourselves "in a dark wood," as the poet Dante says in his *Divine Comedy*.

In *The Hidden Life of Trees*, Suzanne Simard's groundbreaking research reveals that fungi and trees "forged their duality into a oneness, thereby making a forest."[18] She shows that the health of the trees depends on their relationship with what grows beneath the surface. The denizens of dark soil – fungi, bacteria, and viruses – provide a seemingly invisible matrix of life. This extensive latticework of hyphae or mycorrhizal fungi weaves into the root systems of trees, passing nutrients and warnings. Just as the unconscious enriches consciousness, the biome of the underworld gives life to the upperworld.

Shamans pass between the tiers that divide worlds by means of an *axis mundi* – often imaged as a river or a great tree – a symbolic pathway that connects the upper and lower spirit worlds. In the middle realm, light and dark blend and the shaman communes with spirits of the dead – a tangible depiction of the underworld perspective.

Many of our stories, legends, and experiences contain darkness. It's time for us to give the underworld perspective the prominent place it deserves in our lives and our psychology. We need to forge a meaningful relationship with darkness. It's part of the mystery and complexity, and we need to include it for our lives and our field of awareness to be whole. We cannot know ourselves fully until we dive beneath the surface, enter the underworld of the unconscious, and explore ourselves from the inside out and bottom up. To live authentically, we need to have a relationship with the underworld. Darkness is life-deepening and soul-enriching.

We need to re-member the darkness, to re-join with it. The task is great, but the cost of banishing underworlding, even if we could, is greater. If we don't set a place in our lives for missives that come from our soul's depths, these messages that begin as whispers become shouts and then symptoms. Accepting the mystery, acknowledging the complexity and fullness of our never-linear lives brings us richness and an expansion of being. When we learn the alchemical art of holding light and dark at the same time, transformation becomes possible. To do this, we must first honor the value of darkness and then get curious about its different images and expressions. Opening yourself to the symbolism and the deeper meaning behind what is happening so darkly is the first step. Balance is to the psyche what location is to real estate. It propels our growth and stability. Equilibrium between dark and light is possible – and natural. Nothing needs to be left out.

Finding the Meaning in Darkness

Jungian analyst Edward Whitmont wrote: "The one thing we can under no circumstance tolerate is lack of meaning. Everything, even death and destruction, can be faced so long as it has meaning. Even in the midst of plenty and fullness the lack of an inner sense of meaning is unbearable."[19] Victor Frankl described how, among his fellow Holocaust survivors, a sense of meaning was the most important motivation for survival.

There is a difference between meaning and explanation – the meaning of darkness and the reason for it. During hardship, many people turn to reason, seeking to understand the explanatory basis for the torch of suffering. A friend told me:

People rationalize darkness by inferring there *must* be a reason behind the trauma. Perhaps it's a coping mechanism, a need to find balance or even reward for the endless hours of sadness that usurp your life, believing we are putting in our time and we'll later reap the benefits of some universal plan. I remember how many people, during the acute phases of my trauma, would say, "It's going to get better, it has to." But I don't think that's how darkness works. Through conversation and therapy, sadness and reflection, I've come to the conclusion that there is no reason for prolonged and personalized trauma except that darkness is a human experience – arguably the thing that makes us most human of all.

We can leave behind shame, blame, and punishment for wrongdoing, or believing we somehow *deserve* what has happened. Darkness is an attempted solution to an imbalance, a message to gain our attention. It is not a moral imperative, shameful, or wrong.

Reckoning with the underworld is not about understanding the mechanics behind why something happened, it's about finding meaning. Trying to change or suppress the reality before us is to miss the point. What is worthy of our full attention is to examine and respond to it – to place what we feel is an imposition or a hurdle within our lives in a flexible and emotionally significant way. Time heals, we tell ourselves, and we hope time will be our last fortress against this uninvited darkness. But what matters is what *happens* in time. Our task is to pay attention and discern the meaning or to "make" meaning of what happens to us, to develop a relationship with it and bring its corrective message into our life. Avoidance, fear, or clench-your-teeth determination cannot stop darkness, but they can stop life. If we put our weapons down and live with an underworld perspective, we can begin to see how precious life is and allow the underworld to enter our lives.

For thousands of years, myths have been windows into an earned understanding of the human experience. The decline of mythic sensibility has left a gaping hole in our ability to create and find meaning, a primary source of the anomie of our time. We are disconnected from the archetypal stories that provided our ancestors with meaning and purpose.

Even though films like *Star Wars* and books like *Harry Potter* are right in front of us, we don't recognize how they offer us a way in – a map to transformative experience, a path toward guidance and healing linking our ordinary lives with suffering, redemption, and the underworld. This is a sacred function of mythology.

Stories throughout world myth tell us that darkness is a source of revelation and not just a barren wasteland. Arthur seeks the Lady of the Lake, who resides in the watery depths, to reclaim Excalibur, the sword that makes him King. In the Disney movie *Beauty and the Beast*, Belle endures her father's imprisonment, her own fear, and vicious wolves to see the gentleness of her true love. These motifs appear in our own lives as well. We learn to cope with the death of a family member, a betrayal, a business failure, and we find ourselves entwined in depths of connections we never imagined.

Christianity calls the totality of divine powers *pleroma,* from the Greek *plērēs*, meaning "full." Our work is to become full, or whole. During his six-year descent into the unconscious, Jung referred to the pleroma as a dark abyss full of nothingness and fullness.[20] A paradoxical emptiness containing all opposites from which God manifests. Ancient cartographers called unmapped areas "blank space," and they invented cities, mountains, and monsters to fill the empty spaces. We have always feared the emptiness of the void. Darkness may seem bereft of light, but it is far from empty. In the blank spaces of our souls, minds, societies, and personalities rests a fullness, depth, and powerfulness hard to imagine.

Each of our lives contains dark moments, and it is through struggles, sacrifices, and suffering, if we can bear the unbearable, that we return empowered and, ultimately, actualized. These deepest, most luminous parts of ourselves are often forged in darkness.

I.

THE CONTEXT

CHAPTER 1
THE UNDERWORLD

In the ancient Greek and Roman imaginations, the underworld was the realm of the dead, called variously *Hades* (the invisible), *Erebus* (the dark), *Aïdao* (the unseen), and *Domos Haidou* (the House of Hades). The Greek word *haidou* means "unseen" or "invisible," while *domos* means "dwelling place" or "realm." The underworld was an obscure abode devoid of light, "ghastly, mouldering … and an abomination to the gods."[1] The poet Ovid described the sloping roads to the underworld as wandering through "regions mute and silent" into a "desolate spot wrapped in gloomy chill."[2] Like the unlit corridors of the human psyche, the netherworld was an antagonistic, strange, confusing, and perilous realm. Surrounded by black or frozen stone, twisted trees and blind rivers, the landscape of Hades both creates and confirms feelings of isolation, fear, danger, and numbness.

Dark and foreboding, the underworld was said to be located in the remote western reaches of the Greek world, far below ground or in a grove of black poplars beside the ocean. In the Greek poet Homer's *Odyssey*, Circe tells Odysseus that the afterworld lies at the extremes of the earth, beyond the vast ocean. Beneath the earth, where cold air replaces warmth, decay replaces growth, and blackness replaces sunlight, there is little to remind us of the human realm bustling above. The underworld is an uncharted domain that takes us to the far edges of ourselves, where beyond the boundaries of the familiar await forces beyond our power to control. The underworld keeps its secrets and mysteries well, untouched by human exploration, save the imaginal.

A long cultural aversion remains around underworld spaces, associating them with death, rotting, demons, losing our way, and eternal punishment. The abyss has never been a place we seek nor one that's easy to stand in.

The rivers of the dead – the Lethe, Styx, Phlegethon, Cocytus, and Acheron – flow in darkness. The waters of the Lethe, "forgetfulness," wash away earthly memories. Charon, ferryman of the dead, carries the newly deceased across the River Styx, offering safe passage for a golden coin. In the terrible depths, the Phlegethon burns – a river of blazing flames and boiling blood. The waters of the Cocytus, the river of lamentation, scream in pain as frozen rapids descend blindly. The currents of the Acheron, the river of woe, are placid, tenderly ushering new shades (spirits, or ghosts) into the abyss.

The deep was entered through the difficult-to-find *Pylae Hadado,* the "gate among the dead," enforcing a barrier between insiders and outsiders, integrated consciousness and the shadowy material of the unconscious. After entering the underworld, the shade or journeyer would encounter a fork in the road. One direction led to the paradisiacal Elysian Fields, where the souls of the blessed dwelled, and the other to Tartarus, a chasm of endless punishment. Many myths describe heroes and gods struggling to find their way through this maze. Aeneas required an escort. Dionysus asked for directions. The dead were shown the way by Hermes, guide of souls, and even the mighty Hercules got lost.

Utterly inhospitable, the underworld was the ultimate *other*, the place where the shades of the deceased, called *psyches*, wandered to the waters of the River Lethe where, parched, they drank and forgot their identities, remembering only their longing for life. Unable to help themselves, the dead sought guidance from Hades and Persephone, rulers of the deep. Fear of getting lost in the netherworld birthed hero cults whose function was to educate followers on the best actions and paths to take after death.

In ancient Greece and Rome, the underworld was a place of judgment and retribution. When Odysseus meets the shade of his mother, Anticlea, she says to him, "All mortals meet [Hades'] judgment when they die."[3] Virgil describes the terrifying judges and their abodes in striking detail, highlighting the penalties the gods dispensed upon the damned. And Plato describes the underworld as a place where a soul meets judges who will determine who was righteous and who was unjust.[4]

Judgment is a devious human creation. We build religious systems to organize and avoid it, craft identities and personae to feel welcomed, less umpired. "When I was a kid," a man told me, "I remember driving to a banquet for a sports team with my mom and my friend. We were all singing some Dispatch song when my friend told me I was bad at singing. The idea that judgment could be applied to me hadn't occurred to me before. I clammed up and have not been willing to sing ever since. I took my friend's harmful remark to heart, and cut myself off from whatever ability to sing I might have, or even from developing my own musical preferences."

The themes of morality, judgment, and punishment were adopted by the Judeo-Christian mythos. Ideas that have made it almost impossible not to place our thoughts and behaviors into the categories of good or bad. We judge ourselves and others, ruminating on whether we're smart, good at what we do, liked, pretty, contributing enough, or belong. Maintaining self-worth consumes all our power and inner resources. We have to prove ourselves and justify our existence over and over.

Homer is famous for the epic poems *The Iliad* and *The Odyssey*. Considered to have lived sometime between the 12th and 8th centuries BCE, Homer's writing has had an enormous effect on Western culture. In his writing, the power of the dark is bathed in the radiance of the Olympian gods and goddesses. With the Homeric preference for the Olympians, valuation shifted upward – to qualities of light, control, and spirituality – themes adopted in turn by the Western mind for millennia thereafter, culminating in the Enlightenment from the 17th to 19th centuries.

At the beginning of Dante's 14th-century *The Divine Comedy*, the poet has a midlife crisis and reads these words inscribed above the gates of Hell: "Abandon all hope, ye who enter here." The notion that the underworld is a place of alienation and despair is deeply ingrained in the Western mind. We live by this judgment every day, trying to appear upright, whole, in control, and on the mend. The therapy room is often the first place people feel permission to touch, reveal, and admit the darker undercurrents of their lives.

The underworld is not a physical place. It is a way to describe our painful experiences, unwelcome traits, and the whole of our unconsicous energies. Many of us go in and out of Hades many times a day. A young mother of two girls – a fairylike, gentle, and reflective four-year-old and a toddler who's a thunderbolt, loud and forthright – tells me how she rides the waves of underworlding hourly. A wonderful moment of drawing, listening to her daughter's imagination steamroll ahead is followed by breaking dishes, directionless screaming, and the thought that she could die of exhaustion. She goes back and forth between breaking down in tears and moments she describes as "peach blossoms."

Darkness shows up in a mélange of complex associations and symptoms. I spoke with a woman who said her underworld was the sexual violations of her childhood. Years later, she still feels numb and frozen – dissociating from her feelings and from others to protect herself. She lives in an ongoing edgy relationship with a part of herself that terrorizes her, and her days are filled with journeying in and out of the depths. Darkness shows up as the real traumata, her memory of it, her disconnection from her body, a lifetime of anxiety, cycles of abuse, and the violence of the inner figure that terrorizes her dreams.

Underworld encounters happen all the time, permeating life in thousands of ways. Whether it's self-judgment, pathos, or anxiety about the gaze of those around you, the underworld needs to be approached warily. The catacombs of the depths follow different laws of movement, interaction, and explanation than their dayworld counterparts. Darkness requires full attention. It's not a place to be nonchalant.

A Psychology of Darkness

The term "depth psychology" was coined in the early 20th century by Swiss psychologist Eugen Bleuler to describe psychoanalytic approaches to therapy that take the unconscious into account. Since the 1970s, depth psychology has come to refer to those theories and therapies pioneered by psychologists such as Sigmund Freud, Pierre Janet, William James, and C. G. Jung, and altered by James Hillman and other post-Jungians.

Depth psychology introduced the idea of an *ego-mind* that rests upon a deeper, unknowable, instinctive realm, which it calls the *unconscious*. We stand on the surface while an unseen world pulses beneath us, directly influencing our lives. Jung posited a twofold unconscious: (1) a *personal unconscious* with contents unacceptable to the ego – painful memories, complexes, personal conflicts, unresolved problems, and moral issues, collectively known as "shadow material," and (2) the *collective unconscious*, an even deeper layer that does not originate from personal experience but is transpersonal.

Many people think of the unconscious as "other" and "outside" themselves. It's important to bear in mind that the unconscious is a deeper part of ourselves, experienced simultaneously as "other" *and* "within." The metaphoric parallels between "depth" and "descent" were present from the beginnings of depth psychology, and at least as early as ancient Greek and Roman myths. Recorded dreams depict different levels of a house, underground tombs, and streams flowing in underground culverts. In the basement the unwelcome lurks, and transformation begins. Whether envisioned as a crypt, an iceberg, a fissure in stone, deep blue water, a descending staircase, a cave, or a stream flowing beneath the earth, the direction of the unconscious is symbolically downward. "The source [the unconscious] is underground," Jung wrote, "and therefore the way leads underneath: only down below can we find the fiery source of life."[5] Underworld is the metaphor par excellence for the unconscious. To arrive at the essence of things, we enter their darkness.

The word "depth" is derived from the Latin *profundum*, bespeaking the profundity and intensity of the unlimited expansiveness that lies beneath the surface. In the depths of winter, we bundle up. We are lost in the depths of the forest. We endure the depths of sorrow. When encountering the unknown, we say we're out of our depth.

Depth psychology is a psychology of darkness, a way of experiencing ourselves and life, an approach to the inner world that seeks to know what we don't yet know about ourselves. It focuses on the source of a problem rather than alleviating (or obliterating or masking) symptoms. Its aim is to *care*, not *cure* – to *dive*, not *repair*. It explores the origins of limiting behaviors, ideas, and attitudes in search of a deeper sense of self.

Today, the term "psychology," particularly behavioral and evidence-based therapies, means the study of measurable, conscious human experience. Ego-psychologies have us approach the underworld as a mechanic might. If something is broken, fix it. We're not invited to reflect, excavate, stay present with, imagine, or listen. Depth psychology, by contrast, is the experiential study, through feeling and inference, of the immeasurable, unknowable, mysterious "other" realm – the unconscious. Even if we relieve symptoms, the actual source of our suffering won't be resolved, and the symptoms will likely resurface in another form.

Freud, Jung, and Hillman

The division between ego-consciousness and the unconscious gave rise to a myriad of geographic and structural metaphors that direct us to the borderline between the dayworld of the ego-mind and its unconscious counterpart.

Freud (1856-1939) was one of the first to imagine a topo-graphic model of the psyche, seeing dreams, imagination, instincts, and repressed content as existing deep in the layers of the unconscious. In Virgil's *Aeneid*, the goddess Juno says, "*Flectere si nequeo superos, Acheronta movebo*,"[6] which Freud would later translate as the epigraph of *The Interpretation of Dreams*: "If I cannot bend the Higher Powers, I will move the Infernal Regions." Virgil's original use of *Acheronta* is a reference to the Acheron, the river of woes, and bespeaks the exploration of the hidden currents of the inner world – the shadowed waters that course beneath the dayworld, erupting upward – shaping, eroding, revitalizing.

Freud's attitude toward the underworld paralleled Homer's – hostile: the "dark, inaccessible part of our personality, chaos, a cauldron full of seething excitations."[7] His psychology focused on shining the light of awareness on the psyche's deeper regions in order to undo the injuries of repression and instinct.

Swiss psychiatrist and psychoanalyst Carl Gustav Jung (1875–1961), following in Freud's footsteps, contributed to the founding of depth psychology. Jungian psychology is the study of the unconscious in service to the ongoing process of *individuation*, Jung's word for becoming your true self.

Freud and Jung agreed that the purpose of human existence was to kindle a light in the darkness of mere being.[8] But Jung viewed Freud's treatment of the unconscious as a container for hostile repressed wishes and instincts as limited. He treated the unconscious as a geologic stratum of the psyche, a place of challenges, archetypes, guidance, and numinosity. Jung explored the underworld motif in religions, literature, anthropology, mythology, art, psychiatry, philosophy, and alchemy, seeing underworld journeys as stories of the ego's encounter with the personal and collective unconscious. Doing so, he deepened psychology's purview to explore not only passions, instincts, fantasies, and psychopathologies, but also symbolism, personification, images, creativity, dreams, religion, and the mythic imagination.

Following in Jung's footsteps, James Hillman (1926–2011) – an American psychologist who studied at and then was Director of Studies at the C. G. Jung Institute in Zürich, Switzerland – founded "archetypal psychology," a post-Jungian approach rooted in the archetypal basis of psyche. Archetypal psychology focuses on the myriad fantasies and myths that shape our psychological lives. Both Jung and Hillman saw the human psyche as grounded in the archetypal realm. Differences between them are in the context of this shared belief.

In 1975, James Hillman presented his magnum opus, *Re-Visioning Psychology,* and with it a radical reimagining of classical Jungian thought. Nomiated for a Pulitzer Prize, Hillman's first important work moved post-Jungian thought away from an analytical psychology directed toward wholeness, to psychology as a perspective.

As in the work of his predecessors, in Hillman's opus the underworld held weight. "A depth psychology," he acknowledged, "which relies upon the shadowy images of fantasy, upon deepening and pathologizing, and upon psychotherapy as a cult of soul is referring mythologically to the underworld."[9] By "fantasy," Hillman means a way of imagining, a kind of consciousness.

Reworking the term "pathology," he regarded "pathologizing" as the psyche's innate ability to create suffering, depression, and symptoms, and to imagine life through this afflicted perspective. Hillman felt darkness, sickness, symptoms, falling apart, and insanities were necessary messages that when "imagined into" brought us into deeper contact with our souls.

When used psychologically, "soul" is not a religious or moral term. Former monk and Jungian Thomas Moore explains: "It has to do with depth, value, relatedness, heart, and personal substance."[10] It is an idea of deepening. Tending the soul *includes* darkness, being present with hardship, and listening for life cues within tragedy, illness, and symptoms.

I spoke with my father about experiencing the underworld in different ways throughout his life, and he shared a pivotal journey of underworlding that helped shape his personality and life direction:

In the summer of 1975, I lived along the Skokomish River on the Olympic Peninsula just north of Tacoma, Washington. As a Forest Service Fire Prevention Technician, I drove a government truck in the woods, checked the weather station, visited logging camps, and ate huckleberry pie prepared for me by retirees inhabiting primitive campsites … as long as I told them where to look for the berries, which were thick among the fireweed down unmarked access roads. I was 22.

On August 18, 1975, my carefree days ended when I got a long-distance call informing me that my father had died suddenly of a heart attack at age 57. My dad was loved and mourned by many from all walks of life, especially my mother, brother, sister, and me. In shock, I returned home. My mother was quietly lost and stoic. My sister was broken; our father was her best friend and ally. My brother was bitter and angry. I was the middle child, the quiet one. Although I'd just lost my first, and most important, mentor, I felt it was my place to hold the center for my family. I moved back in with my mom and supported my brother and sister, who lived nearby.

Many friends reached out to our family that first year. Although their attentions were genuinely appreciated, I felt alone, as though what I was experiencing was mine alone to comprehend, endure, and integrate. I grew quieter, and my loss transformed into a sense of responsibility for my family and a diminishing expectation for my own happiness.

After a year-and-a-half, my mom and siblings were on even ground and it was time for me to find my own way. I joined the staff of a public elementary school in Western Colorado, where I found a different family and a fulfilling connection to the unfettered energy of children. A few years later, I met my wife. We started a family and a company whose mission was to empower youth to make "authentic connection to self and community."

Looking back, I realize that my innate sense of self and place was shattered by my father's death. I never grieved or despaired. I took refuge in responsibility. Now when I'm alone in Nature, I connect to those formative days. I also talk with Dad in my dreams.

The death of a family member can be a dark chasm, but for my father, it was also a chance to discover his profound care for others, and through his loneliness he found a career helping others find themselves. Darkness can be hellish and it can also be soul-building. Understanding this can help us find meaning in the darkest of nights. The anguish of underworlding can set us back, and it can also provide a sacred ingredient for growth.

Hillman believed that psychological wholeness means including all phenomena as they present themselves, not as we interpret them. Wholeness is not about balancing or reconciling of opposites, but realizing that differences are potent – that both "halves" have value. "Even should unity of personality be an aim," Hillman reasoned, "only separated things can unite."[11] Hillman is inviting us to treat darkness as part of a larger fabric that has its own meaning. He called this *soul-making*.

The modern preoccupation with consistency and containment teaches us to regard contradiction as negative. We sanitize darkness, covering it over for the sake of control. We think psychology is a way to be saved from the messiness of suffering, really the messiness of life. But suffering is part of what makes us human. If we put energy into avoiding the underworld, we miss the fecundity that can help us heal and grow.

Hillman called the archetypal perspective polytheistic: we acknowledge our relative position in an endlessly fragmented inner world. Polytheism is a preference for complexity. Like the discordant personalities of the gods and heroes of mythology, we have contradictory parts within ourselves. We can be violent and peaceful, loving and distant, proud and insecure – at the same time.[12]

To steer psychology away from psychodynamics toward perspectives (the view that perception, experience, and reason change according to the viewer's vantage point), Hillman focused on images as the most important psychological factor. He reasoned that only deep down in the psyche, beneath layers of literalization and reification, are images given their rightful due.

Descending, we dissolve our egoistic standpoints and turn to dreams, images, and even "pathologies" for guidance. Hillman called this approach *imagistic* and used personified thinking to see archetypal resemblances between ourselves and the images in myths and stories. Inventiveness, for example, takes form as Hermes, the divine messenger and creator of music. Desire and beauty wear the face of Aphrodite, the goddess of pleasure. Nation-building is embodied in Athena, goddess of wisdom, warfare weaving, and the protector of city-states.

Depth psychology is a psychology of the underworld. It looks deeper, into the dark, and mines not for clarity or relief but for enrichment, expansion, and connection. Carved in stone above the door of Jung's home in Küsnacht, Switzerland, is written *Vocatus atque non vocatus, Deus aderit*: "Called or not called, the god will be present." Bidden or unbidden, acknowledged or denied, the underworld influences us. Our task is not to ignore this harsh fact but to bring our wits and imagination to the journey within.

According to depth psychology, the theory of the unconscious means that a significant part of psychological life is unknowable. We know nothing certain about the depths. We can only infer this mysterious source by exploring the wondrous activities of dreams, symbolism, and storytelling.

In Roman mythology, the god of the underworld was called Dis Pater (*dis* meaning riches and *pater* father, another name for Pluto or Hades). Colloquially, Dis Pater was shortened to dis, and today we use *dis* or *dys* as a prefix meaning "bad" – dysfunction, disgraced, disrespect. We think *dis* is a problem to be overcome and forget that Dis, the ruler of the underworld, was also known as the Father of Riches. The *dis*-troyed and *dis*-eased parts of life are rich; they can point us to who we really are. Darkness has its genius – it broadens, challenges, and enlivens.

Opening to depth can feel threatening to our dayworld values, moving from stability to chaos, comfort to *dis*-comfort. But if we *dis*-own the underworld, we lose access to its unique recuperative properties. The wisdom of darkness can be difficult to allow in. It comes in dramatic and destabilizing guises. To learn how to be *with* our suffering is much harder than to *let it go* or *move beyond it*. To build a psychology of darkness is way harder than to remain on the surface. But there is a mysterious calling – a siren's beckoning – that entices us downward.

CHAPTER 2
DESCENT AND ASCENT

In the dayworld, we organize, identify, recognize, and distinguish, developing a sense of "I" that's essential for a mature and stable personality. Without a strong ego-identity, it's difficult to navigate even the dayworld. Yet the ego's demand for constancy of self, habits, and rationality makes conscious awareness one-sided.

Many people seek psychotherapy because of the distorted notions and perceptions of their egos. I worked with a woman who was convinced that her parents preferred her sister. Whether in friendships or at work, she felt unseen. "People don't even notice me in the grocery store. I'm a ghost," she told me. Her sense of being invisible prevented her from showing herself to others (and herself) or being recognized or validated, which limited her ability to live fully. For a friend of mine who has always been bright, popular, and talented, praise is part of her food group, a nutritional component of her diet. "My constant underworld," she said, "is perfectionism. It's sharp and guarded. I'm trapped in a prison wearing shackles of my own design. Perfection drags behind me like chains – rattling with the weight of a lifetime of feeling less than and not taking risks because I'm too afraid to disappoint or misstep." Afraid of and unfamiliar with failure, her need for perfection prevents her from doing anything she isn't already good at, inhibiting her ability to try new things.

Without connection to the unconscious – to the depth perspective – the ego can become brittle, myopic, solipsistic, and often despotic. To self-actualize, we must augment the ego's static and often trauma-based perspectives with their rich, unconscious counterparts. We need to find ways to stumble, walk, fall, and sneak *beneath the dayworld*, shedding the skin of our limited sense of self, so we can awaken to the possibilities that lie dormant within us. The descent into and ascent from the underworld is a mythic and archetypal image for this exploration.

Variations of the descent-and-ascent journey appear in stories the world over. Jesus descended into hell and was resurrected. Inanna journeyed into and returned from Kur, the ancient Sumerian underworld. Throughout Greek mythology, heroes and gods journey into and back from Hades. For centuries, bards have told stories of the heroes who leave behind their lives to embark on a great journey, and through trial and tribulation they are altered by the experience. Batman reckons with his past to save Gotham. In fairytales, the third son journeys through the enchanted wood and returns home empowered. Walking in the footsteps of these heroes, heroines, and gods allows us to "imagine into" the elemental struggles of human life.

Sometimes we undertake the journey intentionally. Psychotherapy is one kind of container in which we purposefully engage with the depths. And other times, we fall headfirst into the darkness. Entering the underworld is never easy, nor is it common for the living to make the journey. Describing his own involuntary descent in the early 20th century, Jung said, "I stood helpless before an alien world; everything in it seemed difficult and incomprehensible."[1]

Why are we so helpless when confronted by the deep psyche? There are few containers we can use to help us cope. Our culture demonizes the unfamiliar. There's a stigma in admitting things aren't going well. We value composure; seeking help is for the weak and troubled. Yet everyday failures and frustrations, doubts and shame are far more common than so-called normalcy. Despite the pervasiveness of darkness, we have a deep-rooted conviction that ease is our entitlement and darkness is a failure. Driven by this belief system, we do everything possible to remove the pain.

For centuries, humans told a different story about darkness. Our ancestors' relationship with the underworld was symbolic, ceremonial, imaginative, balanced, and honoring. Journeys into the abyss were recognized as important moments of spiritual growth. By turning to our past, we reconnect with the parts of us that "know" that descending into and ascending from the underworld are not only a natural part of life but necessary for expanding and deepening our lives.

Initiation

Mythic stories and religious rites have the power to guide us through both personal and collective change. The most common of these is the rite of initiation – a psychospiritual enactment of transformation through a highly choreographed trial and task. In ritual, we act out a myth on a personally significant level in front of the collective – communities come together to bear witness to the initiate's life change. The Eleusinian, Bacchic, and Orphic cults of ancient Greece, for example, had rituals in which journeyers descended into Hades, confronted the powers within, and returned transfigured by their encounter with the darkness. On what level was this true? Did they really enter Hades? Is Hades "within" the earth or "within" ourselves? These kinds of questions (and answers) are present in the potent field of a ritual.

Initiation is, therefore, a rite of regeneration. The spirit of life is reborn in the land of death. Michael Meade, one of the leaders of the late-20th-century men's movement, explains that in initiatory rites, "death is the opposite of birth, *not* the opposite of life."[2] For a transformation to be meaningful, it must honor the aches of sacrifice and wonders necessary for restoration. Mind and soul *feel* the death of the old personality and the birth of change.

As part of a lengthy ritual of becoming warriors among Brazil's Sateré-Mawé people, boys as young as 12 are stung by bullet ants, whose venom can cause disorientation, hallucinations, and muscle paralysis for hours. In Liberia, novices are "killed" by a forest spirit and resurrected into a new life, tattooed, and given adult names. In many oceanic cultures, neophytes are secluded in remote cabins shaped like a marine monster. They have been swallowed by a Leviathan and in its belly, they will die, be digested, and begin the process of being born into society as adults.[3]

The fear and terror so skillfully built into these ritual scenarios create strong emotions that strip the initiate of their old being. The blows, mutilations, insect bites, and burns symbolize the death of the immature personality and the emergence of the adult. Although these rites of initiation are conscious and intentional recreations of darkness's great challenges, sometimes we just "fall into" an initiation. Every darkness can be called an initiation as you are in something that has the potential to – by trying to get out of it – transform you.

In modern times, the influence of religious initiations of this nature has dwindled. Without some form of ritual and spiritual structure, we lose the opportunity to process symbolic death and embrace life change, especially at developmental stages when it will happen one way or another, with or without our consciousness. This lack of meaningful acknowledgment can breed a host of symptoms, both physical and psychological.

In retelling the Brothers Grimm fairytale "Iron John," poet Robert Bly observes how modern males are damaged by the lack of rites and role models.[4] He believes that young men, when ritually initiated into adulthood, are welcomed by their ancestral fathers, and without this, men isolate, rage, and eventually become numb. The military may initiate youths into the warrior complex, but a drill sergeant's role is to desensitize young men and women so they can cause harm without remorse. Bodies are toned, teamwork is learned, but the life of the soul is not embraced or included.

Contemporary masculinity is modeled by cinematic roles played by the likes of Jason Statham, imparting Herculean toughness, stoicism, and emotionlessness. This leaves many unable to transcend adolescence. Outside the warrior training our society offers in boot camp, gangs try to fill the gap, but rather than seeing men with cultural bearings we witness suffering youths hurling their own woundedness at others.

In ancient Greece, the goddess Artemis presided over female biological transitions – from maidenhood to childbearing. In Attica in the city of Brauron, young girls gathered to dance for their goddess. In a rite called Arkteia, girls imitated she-bears, *arktoi*. The little bears of Artemis learned the ways of the bear – dancing and running, wearing saffron robes and amber jewels. They learned to honor the final years of their maidenhood and prepare to become mothers.

Ritual is a way to keep the doors of perception open to the sacred. It could be setting a new intention when moving into a new home; crossing a threshold as a newly married couple; or pausing under a tree to place a flower and thank the spirits of nature for nourishing your soul.

Rites celebrating life's transitions that are still practiced – from Bar Mitzvahs to baby showers – have often become somewhat superficial, failing to call forth their psychologically transformative power. The mythic sense of birth and rebirth has been sanitized away for our modern sensibilities. Instead, we worship the anthem of the Enlightenment, believing that *reason* removes our need for magical and instinctual explanations of the world, and in doing so, we cut ourselves off from our own impulses and unconscious. Something essential to making meaning of our lives is lost as we skim over these important levels of reality.

A client I worked with was grappling with the awesome change in his life of becoming the father of twins. He didn't know how to process what he was feeling. I advised him to go to a place of stillness, where the simple things lie – rock and wind, branch and soil. "A ritual is needed," I told him. To make this life transition emotionally satisfying and properly embedded, something had to be given up for new waters to flow.

Initiation includes a descent into death and an ascent into rebirth, the altering of one's identity, the old, now departing, to the new, being birthed in plain sight. It marks the beginning of a new self and the freeing of potentials not yet realized. Every crossing of the threshold is a funeral for the old and birth of the new. We need rituals of loss and renewal in order to retain the capacity to experience the range of sorrow and joy that is so vital to feeling fully human.

Why is it important to ritualize darkness? Because without a ritual to hold and process life's wounds, meaningful change can be blocked and suffering arises in its stead. Uncontained, the underworld flows into life, its black rapids coursing over everything we do.

Ritualizing darkness doesn't have to follow a formalized ceremony. Jung recalled a time in his early school years when a teacher accused him of plagiarism, demanding that he confess who wrote the paper he submitted. Jung protested his innocence but to no avail. The experience was excruciating; he felt branded as a cheater. Unable to share his torments with his strait-laced, religious family, he began a ritual in which he created a little figure and stowed this away carefully in the attic. The thought of this manikin, tucked away safely, reassured him whenever difficulties arose at home.[5] When darkness descended, Jung's ritual took care of him, unifying his fragmented sense of self by preserving a secret that protected a vulnerable part of himself. Locking it in the forbidden attic saved his young soul from unbearable woe.

Death as Transformation

There is no more profound metaphor for change than death. Death symbolism – skulls, suicide, falling off of a high mountain, murder, corpses, cloaked figures, and tombs – allows us to imagine into the parts of ourselves that we need to release, or let go of, for rebirth to be possible. "When the death side of life is denied," writes Michael Meade, "the birth side becomes obscured and some of the importance of each life is lost."[6]

Death – literal or symbolic – is challenging to hold in the psyche. An encounter with darkness is often experienced as the demise of what makes us recognizable and safe. Despite the pain that letting go engenders, inner death is a prerequisite for rebirth. The forest burns before it grows, the fields lie fallow before spring, and the caterpillar dies to its old form before becoming a butterfly. "Only birth can conquer death," Campbell tells us, "the birth, not of the old thing again, but of something new."[7]

The underworld has a mysterious capacity to transform us. My father recalled moving at the age of 25 to a remote town where he didn't know anyone. He had a teacher's degree but had never taught. He got a job at a brand new school, 35 students in a self-contained sixth grade with no desks, books, or curricula. Alone and unconfident, he found himself in what he has since described as "a lesser underworld journey." This uncomfortable and scary situation forced him to discover what he was made of.

Throughout our lifetimes, we die over and over to what we have been, becoming something else, each time more actualized. A woman emerges out of the maiden, a man separates from the boy, and the comforts of childhood come to an end as maturity and independence begin. No myths tell us the journey is easy. There are always tests – demons, confusion, and conflicts – challenges the ego-mind faces when turning toward the unknown.

In horoscopic astrology, a Saturn return is an astrological transit that occurs when the planet Saturn returns to the same place in the sky that it occupied at the moment of our birth. It occurs in our late twenties and can be felt into our early thirties. In later life, it strikes again when we're between the ages of 57 and 60. Saturn, the god of time, tradition, manifestation, and order, begins to choke out youthful vitality. "Choose," Father Time demands. "Pick a path." A Saturn return is a wake-up call to many painful realities, the end of youthful freedom and infinite possibilities. At this crossroads, the soul needs a different diet; discipline and sacrifice replace being footloose and fancy-free. A Saturn return may be painful, for it's a time that marks the end of a life cycle. Yet it's also rewarding; maturation builds a different type of internal satisfaction. This is a cosmic rite of passage.

As our lives go forward and we enter different stages of life, our insights and attitudes require reimagining. We need new perspectives to handle these new situations. If we remain a child (*puer aeternus* is the name of the complex "eternal child"), it's impossible to function as an adult in the world. If we long for maidenhood (*kore*, the virginal archetype of youthful purity), it's difficult to be with a life partner. If we aren't aware of our father complex (needing external approval, protection, and guidance), we'll seek substitute fathers everywhere. We can't evolve without change, and we can't change without evolving. From an analytic perspective, we won't come into wholeness until we move beyond a state of potential to an integrated, actualized life. Your first middle-school dance requires a different attitude than your wedding. Going to summer camp requires a different stance than going to college. Caring for a doll requires a different perspective than raising a child.

During the year leading up to my wedding, I had a series of dreams in which I slowly buried a body. At first, the body was alive, but over time it began to decay. A month before the wedding, the body was so frail and putrefied that I knew it was finally dead. It was time to put it to rest. After interring the body, I pressed my dirt-caked hands into the soft ground and small golden bubbles escaped from the dark soil. I knelt and peacefully watched the bubbles rise to the sky.

A part of me was afraid to let go of my identity as a girlfriend, not a wife. To move forward consciously, certain aspects of my personality needed to be put to rest. The dreams pointed to parts of myself – freedom, self-reliance, and youthful identity – that needed to die so I could be present for the next phase of my life.

If underworlding offers potential for growth, why is facing our darkness so daunting? It's in part because the ego leans toward stability and control while the unconscious includes the full range of experience, including shame, love, fear, lust, evil, and power. Facing the vast darkness of the unconscious can be overwhelming and even distressing. The ego-mind feels overpowered by the forces unloosed.

And there are risks. We may find ourselves revisiting trauma – afraid, alone, shamed, misunderstood, and abandoned once again. But if we only try to protect ourselves from darkness's dangers, we lessen our ability to heal and to grow.

To feel safe enough to journey into darkness, we need a sense of self that reflects reality and that we feel comfortable with. Otherwise, veering from familiar spaces can disintegrate edifices we've built and leave us adrift. A client once told me that if she were to make the changes we were talking about, she wouldn't know who she was. If we undergo a journey that transforms us, the first challenge is making peace with who we are becoming.

A second challenge is finding whether we are accepted for who we've become among family and friends. Our old community has probably not transformed with us. One of the tasks of the hero is honoring how the journey changed us. A metamorphosis can threaten the stability of old relationships and patterns, and so a part of returning from the underworld is withstanding loneliness and forging new ways of connecting with ourselves and those we love. Can we accept the new, deeper, and more real sense of self? And can others?

Confronting the Shadow

The *shadow* is the repository of the disowned aspects of our identity. It is the negative and unwanted side of the personality – the sum of all rejected possibilities in life. A part of descending into the depths is facing this neglected and unkempt part of ourselves.

The development of culture divides personal characteristics into two categories: those deemed acceptable and those we must disavow to be part of civilization – ego and shadow, right and wrong, good and bad. Each of our shadows is unique. For some, freedom is threatening, while for others morality or responsibility threaten the sense of "I" that we maintain. Despite the trepidation engendered by the idea of facing the shadow, doing so is of utmost psychological importance; for it reveals what's holding us back, what we don't own (or even know) about our core self and the ways we limit expressing ourselves.

The process of division and subjugation that creates our shadows happens because we wish to be seen in a certain way. It isn't a matter of preference; for most of us it's a matter of survival. Our caretakers, when we are young, want or need us to be a certain way, and it's critical that we respond to that. We become this way to be accepted by those who nurture and support us, and abandon elements of who we are. This idealized image is called the *persona*, the outward identity, or mask, worn by the ego.

The ego has its own ambitions and defenses, and everything that inhibits this aim is relegated to the shadow. Robert Bly likens the shadow to carrying a sack on your shoulder, and every time a parent, teacher, or you yourself identifies something unacceptable, you put it in the bag. And after a while, you are carrying an increasingly heavy burden on your shoulder.[8]

Shadow characteristics have an energy as great if not greater than the ego. The parts of our personality we suppress do not go away; they gather in the dark places of the unconscious. They fester, erode our confidence, and send their dark tendrils deeper and deeper until they take over. Those of us who put too much of our self-worth in the shadow are plagued with crippling doubt. "I've always known self-esteem was a challenge for me," a friend told me. "I have terrible personal boundaries." Tell me why, I asked. "Because I'm constantly seeking approval from other people – my coworkers, my boyfriend, even my dog." For this woman to know self-value, she must bring the hidden gems of her personality, banished and neglected, back to life.

The individual we choose to be has a dark double: the person we choose not to be. In Ursula Le Guin's *The Wizard of Earthsea*, the protagonist, Ged, unleashes his shadow (gebbeth) into the world. In Earthsea, each being has a true name that holds immense power. When it is revealed that the gebbeth knows his true name, Ged is stripped of his power and abilities. As the story unfolds, it becomes apparent that the gebbeth knows Ged better than he knows himself. Finally, after much running and hiding, Ged faces the shadow and begins to learn what it is. At the edge of the world, he meets the gebbeth and discovers that its true name is his very own.

This is a story about becoming whole. The shadow cannot be transformed unless the ego-mind recognizes it as its counterpart. We are all tasked with integrating our shadows and thereby regaining our rejected qualities – the parts of ourselves that do not fit with what our family or culture finds acceptable. At some point, we must journey to the edge of the world, descend into darkness, and name and recover the lost part of ourselves.

A young man in his late twenties came to see me because he felt disconnected from the world and was retreating into himself in ways that limited his relationships. When not actively engaged in his life, perhaps while resting, watching a movie, or sitting quietly, he would feel fear and anxiety around rejection.

He grew up with emotionally neglectful parents. They wanted to correct the rage experienced during their own childhoods by emphasizing balance and stability, but in the process, they unintentionally crushed my client's expressiveness. Although they provided all the food, shelter, toys, and opportunities any child might need, they didn't see him for who he was or even notice his emotional needs. So he retreated into a vibrant inner world.

In the beginning of our work together, he reported two dreams. In the first, zombies rose out of a dark lake and brainwashed people sitting in a bar. In the second, zombies attacked him in a tower. There he died, was reborn, only to relive the attack repeatedly.

Zombies symbolize a state between the living and the dead, an image of existing without true life. The zombie, human in appearance, lacks consciousness and so symbolizes debasement, not noticing the world go by. It's a blank state of being, a vacuous interiority that makes it impossible to connect with life or even affirm our own realness.

When parts of us aren't mirrored and tended by our original parents or caregivers, we may disown the parts of ourselves that are felt as unacceptable. We abandon our own essential potential and morph into who we think we should be. Who we really are, all our wondrous creativity and identity, is regulated to the shadows.

These dreams were windows into the young man's longstanding feeling of distance from real-life events, not being able to think for himself or have agency in his life, like the walking dead. The zombie represented the shadow of his personality – unintegrated wounds desiring life, and not assimilated into his personality. This zombie energy was attacking him, increasing his lifelessness and his inability to engage with the world. "I'm either in the present moment," he said, "or I just kill time." The zombie looks at the world through deadened eyes. It has hidden the spark of life, unable to wake up to its own authority and identity.

The zombie dreams helped my client explore the roots of his "mindless inactivity" and the importance of his life spark. As the Greek philosopher Socrates reminded us, the unexamined life is not worth living. From the dream's point of view, it was time for him to wake up, and not surprisingly, the zombie dreams foreshadowed a rich period of growth.

Unless we shine the light of awareness on the shadow, usually with the help of a psychopomp, a guide, it will be projected onto someone or something outside of us. This is the way humans learn. When a characteristic of someone else has a voltaic charge, it's a good guess we are seeing our own shadow in the form of a projection, the unconscious expulsion of subjective psychological content onto an external object.

The natural world lives in polarities – death and rebirth, light and dark, female and male, winter and summer. The psyche follows a similar dual structure – unconscious and conscious, ego and shadow. According to Jung, ego and shadow both come from the same matrix of psyche, the unconscious, and together they offer wholeness. We cannot know ourselves without knowing our shadow. Light cannot exist without darkness.

The Treasure Hard to Attain

Like initiatory rites, the underworld journey is both perilous and life-changing. Hades was also called *Ploutos* ("wealth-giving") and *Torphonios* ("nourishing"). To journey into Hades and experience the unconscious is to infuse our life with wealth-giving treasures and nourishing depth.

Jung called the prize hidden in the inner world "the treasure hard to attain."[9] He believed that the descent-and-ascent journey was more about *completeness* than *perfection*; not about returning flawlessly formed, fixed, or cured, but about collecting something of ourselves that had been hidden in the depths. He said that to develop as an individual "the 'thorn in the flesh' is needed, the suffering of defects without which there is no progress and no ascent."[10]

Quick to emphasize the relationship between darkness and progress, Jung claimed that only through an encounter with darkness, with the shadowy parts of the psyche, can we deepen life's meaning and expand our sense of self. I'm reminded of the words of Shakespeare: "Sweet are the uses of adversity, which like the toad, ugly and venomous, wears yet a precious jewel in his head."[11]

In Genesis (32:22–32), Jacob spends the night alone beside a river on his journey back to Canaan. There he encounters a "man" with whom he wrestles until daybreak. Finally, the man touches Jacob's hip, wounding him and ending their clash. He then tells him he will no longer be called Jacob, but *Israel* from the Hebrew *sara* – "he fought, contended" – and *El*, "God." Israel is the one who "contended with God." In response, Jacob says, "I have seen God face to face, and yet my life has been delivered." In Hosea (12:4) the man is described as a *malakh*, "angel." Either way, this story is about encountering an archetype and struggling with its touch. Jacob is wounded by the encounter, bearing his injury as a sign of being touched by God. Yet through the clash, his life was delivered. Direct, affective experience of the *Self*, the encounter with the archetypal ground of being, the transpersonal, leaves a scar. Darkness wounds but it also delivers connection with the Self, the seat and source of our being. To wrestle with an angel and be wounded is to gain the treasure of life.

We humans have long placed what is most valued underground. Legends tell of dragons who hoard glittering jewels in the bowels of the earth. We tuck what is precious into dark corridors, imagine treasures hidden on desolate islands, entomb our dead, and carve out entire hillsides to find diamonds, today's symbol of love and commitment.

Over 5,000 artifacts were buried with the Egyptian Pharaoh Tutankhamun in an enclosed and protected tomb for nearly 3,500 years. These were painstakingly unearthed, and millions of visitors now visit the tomb to see treasures once unimaginable to the living.

In France's Chauvet Cave humans wandered into the earth 36,000 years ago to immortalize their lives on stone walls. "Hide them in caves and cellars," declared Winston Churchill in 1940, as the National Gallery sent its collection of masterpieces into a Welsh slate mine to protect them from the Luftwaffe bombing.[12] And in Svalbard, Sweden, deep in the ground is a seed bank; the potential for renewed life is quieted into dormancy by the otherworldliness of its womb of ice. We journey downward toward darkness to *hide* what is of most value, but also to *find* it.

My mother grew up with an emotionally distant father, a Vietnam veteran with PTSD who suffered episodes of violence and withdrawal. When her father was in his late eighties and dying, she flew to Florida to say goodbye. When she arrived at the hospital, her family was frozen, unable to see how ready her father was to pass. She made the call to unplug him from life support.

In his last moments, she said to him, "You've been the best dad you could be." He gently shrugged his shoulders. She understood this to mean, "Really?" That was the first time her father recognized he hadn't been the father she needed. She described this underworld moment as one of the heaviest of her life, yet also a healing gift – the pearl within the darkness that opened up a final understanding between generations.

Entering the underworld reveals priceless treasures that seem to be visible only in darkness. All her life, my client's father was critical of her. A helicopter pilot in Vietnam, his exposure to napalm eventually caused leukemia and prostate cancer. Near the end of his life, she underwent a craniotomy to assess her own recent brain cancer diagnosis. "I felt like someone had tied a tire to my head," she recalled, "but when I left the hospital, I had a friend drive me to see Dad." On his death bed, he finally said everything she needed to him to say – death gave him the permission to be someone different, the father she always needed: "He had a love in his eyes that he'd never had before."

Underworlding must never be taken lightly. Elie Wiesel survived the Holocaust before having the depth of understanding to write his moving memoir, *Night*. Nelson Mandela served 27 years in prison while becoming the world's moral compass. There's nothing easy about facing our inner demons, yet in the end, the rewards almost always outweigh the risks.

When a beloved dies, when adversity grinds, when we're victims of violence, depression, mood disorders, or abandonment, we may find ourselves stumbling toward a powerful darkness. If we allow ourselves to *feel* the anxiety and discomfort, the fear and the rage, the journey offers the possibility of insight and expansion. Jungian Marion Woodman confessed that she'd forced herself to make the long and painful journey within motivated by the "fear of coming to my death bed and realizing that I had never lived *my* life."[13]

Sacralizing Darkness

The ancient Greek cosmos encompassed both the dayworld and the underworld, the *telluric* ("upper earth") and *chthonic* ("under earth"). In accord with this vision, the divine pantheon was separated into gods that belonged to the deep earth, *cthonioi*, such as Persephone, Hades, and Hecate, and Olympians such as Athena, Apollo, and Hera, who were of the high, sacred mountains.

This cosmological distinction began when – in a mythical drama known as the Titanomachy, a ten-year series of battles – the younger Olympians achieved dominion over the elder Titans, and thus over the universe. When Zeus overthrew his father, Cronus, he banished the Titans into Tartarus, and "the old powers were cast down into the abyss by the new society of gods."[14] After that, the elemental and primitive powers were seen as separate from the glory of the Olympians.

The enlightened and humanistic Olympians, characterized by lightheartedness, sanity, and order, were separated from their dark, repressed, and feared Chthonian counterparts. Apollo, Lord of Light, was unable to contact the dead. His sister Artemis could not pollute her eyes with the dying. And Hera, queen of the Olympians, had to "brace herself" to enter the underworld.[15]

The notion of Olympians being incompatible with Chthonians governs the mythic Greek cosmos. Olympians were worshiped in daylight, garbed in festive attire, cups brimming with ambrosia, their hair adorned with garlands. Chthonians, on the other hand, were worshiped at night, in silence. Hades, the dreaded god of death, was not to be looked upon. Those who sacrificed to the beings of the lower world did so with their gazes averted.

The gods of the underworld were terrifying and unwelcome, but they were still gods, an intricate and important part of a balanced cosmological vision that worshiped *both* the light and dark aspects of the divine. The underworld was a complement to Olympus – differentiated but not cut off, remote yet treated with respect.

In the modern West, we perpetuate the Greeks' fear of the underworld but have lost their reverence for it. Neuroses are repressed, not worshiped; depression is "treated"; and "negative" experiences are cut off and contained. Instead of divinizing darkness, we repress it.

Scientists believe that more than 68 percent of the universe's total mass is dark energy, a mysterious force that seems to be driving the expansion of the cosmos. Baryonic matter, the mass of our tangible world, is 5 percent. And the remaining 27 percent is dark matter, particles that do not interact with baryonic matter. Dark matter and dark energy may be invisible, but they are the architects of the cosmos, binding and drawing all things together. It is believed that without the presence of dark matter, galaxies, planets, oceans, humans, lions, ferns, bugs, and soil would not exist. On a cosmic level, darkness makes life possible, yet we think that on a psychological level, darkness is unessential, to be avoided as unnecessary, even though it's a building block of life.

The connection between the mysteries of darkness and the mysteries of life were not lost on our predecessors. The image of death and our relationship to it was the beginning of mythology; the earliest evidence of mythological thinking is associated with graves and the belief in an afterlife. In ancient Greece, Hades, Persephone, Hecate, and other powers of the deep were feared, but still sanctified. The underworld – the dark and unworthy aspects of human nature – was honored as part of a holistic religious system.

The underworld is a powerful unifier; it can bring the world closer together. Like dark matter, darkness has an invisible gravity that pulls things together. Suffering reaches across time and division, culture and tradition – between the survivors of barbed-wire concentration camps and the survivors of veiled prisons within homes, between those separated by generations and continents, gender and languages. Devoured by unremitting exposure to the horrors of trench warfare, the soldiers of World War I shattered the global illusion of honor and glory on the battlefield. Confined in rivers of mud and blood, rendered helpless, and forced to witness the death of friends without hope of reprieve or escape, men broke down in unparalleled numbers. They called it "shell shock." We call it PTSD now. World War I veterans brought the battlefield home with them, entering the polished veneer of civilian life. These soldiers wept, froze, disappeared into silence, and lost their capacity to feel. The world watched as combatants from all countries fell into darkness; the underworld of the soul was introduced on a global scale and our understanding of the true cost of war changed forever.

"The realm of the ancient gods," Walter F. Otto wrote, "is always tangential to the religion of the dead; in that, indeed, life is a sibling of death."[16] Depth psychology shares the belief that the unconscious is a necessary part of life, seeking to differentiate not divide, building wholeness through connection. To use the word coined by Zen master Thich Nhat Hanh, they inter-are: they're inextricably interrelated. Without a storm, there is no rain; without moisture, the forest cannot grow and the animals cannot eat. The storm is essential for animals to exist, so they inter-are. Light and dark, depth and heights, death and rebirth follow the same patterns of interweaving.

Today we support those going through hard times with cognitive behavioral therapy or meds to make symptoms disappear, but this is not integration nor worship. We rarely come together to pay homage to the instinctive realms or recognize the possibilities that come from facing life's challenges. We've all but forgotten that darkness is the sibling of life, that it's a treasure trove to be both feared and valued. When we suppress darkness, we lose aliveness and fertility.

The desire to lessen or avoid pain is understandable. Freeing yourself from anxiety, overcoming fear, re-finding yourself after illness, stabilizing a mood disorder, and healing from acute trauma are important goals. I'm not encouraging anyone to let darkness consume them. Rather, I'm saying that underworlding, difficult as it may be, is a part of life, and ignoring the material that arises from the depths does not make it go away. Taking a pill or mastering a technique does not heal the wound at the root of our distress. Filtering life through perfection and control prevents us from discovering the meaning and opportunity conveyed by these ghostly teachers from the depths. Rather than masking symptoms, staying present with our woundedness to the extent that we can, can be whole-making.

Ascending

Throughout the world's myths and religions, there exist tales of underworld descents and ascents. These stories remind us that it's essential to experience the unconscious and equally vital to return. The word "return" dates to the 16th century, meaning "giving in repayment" or "restoring." To "return from the underworld" is to give, repay, and restore our connection to the unconscious. Return is not just about coming back up; it means integrating, being truly affected by our experience of darkness and attempting to use what we've learned in our life going forward. What is required of us during the ascent is immensely challenging. It's tempting to seek easier solutions, quick fixes. But if we truly want to heal and access our fullness, we have to undertake the tasks of repair and change, integration and ascent.

Ascent (*anodos*) derives from the Greek *ana* (upward) and *hodos* (path), meaning to go up to the next stage. The Greeks called *athanaton hodos* the way of the immortals. By returning to daylight transfigured by our experience, we evolve as individuals and enter the next stage of our growth.

Falling into darkness usually happens *to* us – depression grabs us, accidents ensue, emergency surgery repairs the body but upends the psyche, and complexes grip us. We are taken to our depths without having to *do* anything. In these cases, it's ascent and integration that present the greater challenges. After experiencing the worst that life can offer, the task is to pick ourselves up and let the wisdom of darkness reshape us.

Despite the importance of returning from the underworld, many Greek myths go into intricate detail regarding the descent and time spent in Hades and then skim over the ascent. Odysseus described his whirled flight back to his ship in a single sentence. The descent is formidable, the ascent brings relief. Yet the ascent can take a lifetime.

It's my observation that ascending can be even more difficult than the journey downward. Integrating changes to our identity, learning to live with what was revealed and experienced in darkness, takes time and patience. Campbell called this "the labor of bringing the runes of wisdom … back into the kingdom of humanity."[17] Reading the classics, it appears that the Greeks gave short shrift to this important challenge. In this move, we see the beginning of the Western mind's preference for the dayworld.

My friend's father suffered a massive stroke, and ten months later her mother-in-law died of cancer. "The darkness lightens over time," she reflected, then went on to express the challenges of integration. "After the acute phase subsides, you button your shirt, put on your makeup, discuss wine varietals, or laugh with colleagues, charging forward through the months, presenting a foolproof façade of professionalism and, dare I say, happiness and contentment. But barely beneath the brave face lurks the darkness. And for me, it sits at the very edge of my holding it together, requiring only the smallest prick of a needle to pop the entire balloon that is my presented sanity."

Many who are in the heart of darkness visualize relief, closure, meaning, and normalcy. They imagine that if they can get themselves back up, everything will be normalized, the burden will be over, and they can "move on." Of course, we want relief from darkness, but the truths of underworld experiences don't just disappear. They're either integrated or they go back underground. If the experience isn't "metabolized," we're likely to face a similar challenge again. And next time around, the whispers might become shouts, discomforts might become symptoms, and the forgotten and neglected will slip past our barriers again.

Naturally, relief from the acute stages of trauma is necessary, so we can both function and have the strength to face the darkness. But simply moving on does not value the depression or loss, the soul's message in bringing us into the underworld, or the ongoing process of integrating the experience through staying present with it. Relief alone is often not a true ascent. Integration is.

I know of no one who has experienced tragedy, depression, divorce, attempted suicide, violence, shame, or trauma who does not continue to live with the impact of these events. It isn't about *getting rid* of them or even overcoming them. It's about making a meaningful relationship with them that informs us in an ongoing way.

Poignantly, veteran Tim O'Brien's celebrated book about the Vietnam War, a masterpiece of the redemptive power of storytelling, is called *The Things They Carried*. "I remember the white bone of an arm," he writes. "I remember the pieces of skin and something wet and yellow that must've been the intestines. The gore was horrible, and stays with me."[18]

If we understand inner work as tending not fixing, re-ascending throughout our lifetime, our psychologies would change substantially. We might become curious about the messages revealed in our turmoil, believe problems offer opportunities for reflection rather than hurdles to be overcome, and accept life's unanticipated and unplanned changes.

With every breath, my brother has to learn to live with the changes his brain injury forced upon him. Each morning, my father lights a candle for his father, who died 50 years earlier, and for his mother who passed decades later. Dad's ritual is how he remembers and brings his parents into his life every day. Sipping on her coffee, my colleague drives to work where she helps adolescents who are suffering from sexual trauma, each morning confronted with the violations of her own past as well. These are windows into the daily lives of people who live with an underworld perspective – living in a state of ritual that is continually integrating the darkness.

Valuation of order and light only requires a denial of darkness. We cannot risk revealing that we are still in relationship with the underworld while others around us seem so together. "I don't want to attend a grief group," a woman told me. "My grief is not tidy like that of others."

We overlay morality onto darkness. Shadows are evil, instincts are sinful, dying is a kind of failure. This perspective misunderstands ascent as *ascendance* – rising above the conflicts and messiness of life. The idea of a single, heavenly ascent comes from the Judeo-Christian myth, which despises darkness. We repress underworld experiences and control our instincts so we can rise above matter and be closer to God. In my opinion, this isn't helpful.

Roundtrip Journey

Life is filled with movements of descending and ascending. The Greeks called ascending *palingenesia*, "the recurrence of birth." We never *fully* ascend from the underworld. We're in a constant process of descending followed by integrating, and each roundtrip affects the rest of our lives. There's no need to overlay morality onto it. Our continuous relationship with the underworld is beyond shame, suppression, or sin. It is simply being alive and learning to handle the challenges of life as best we can.

Poet Robert Graves reflected on how the undigested underworld of World War I pervaded his life. "I was still mentally and nervously organized for War," he explained. "Shells used to come bursting on my bed at midnight … strangers in the daytime would assume the faces of friends who had been killed. When strong enough to climb the hill behind Harlech and visit my favourite country, I could not help seeing it as a prospective battlefield."[19] Once you've seen the underworld, you can't unsee it.

Hillman believed that ascending feeds the ego's addiction to meaning and development, critiquing Jung's concern with interpretation, meaning-making, and integration. For the ego to ascend, Hillman reasoned, it artificially bifurcates the psyche. There must be a realm to ascend from and a realm to ascend to, and he objected to this idea. This psyche, he said, is not a cookie cut in half; it's a smashed cookie with hundreds of crumbs. For Hillman, the journeyer doesn't descend and return on a definable path, bringing with him a missing piece of himself. The psyche is too complex for that, too fragmented to be contained or experienced in such a singular way.

At first glance, Hillman's approach might seem unrealistic – why wouldn't we strive to ascend, integrate, and return to normalcy? Why wouldn't we seek meaning and understanding? But Hillman's perspective is less about descending into an underworld *never to return* and more about creating an imaginal consciousness that is accepting of underworld conditions. It's a preference for the gerunds – *descending* and *ascending* – as active, ongoing, and familiarizing processes of constantly engaging in a relationship to the underworld. Hillman's sensibility views the underworld as *part of*, albeit peripheral, our everyday lives, allowing the darkness to have a seat at the table.

"Darkness is a polarizing experience," my friend whose father had a stroke shared with me. "It became glaringly clear that there were people with whom I wanted to lament my tragedy and people with whom I didn't. The people I chose not to turn to seemed to have no idea what I was experiencing. They had never seen that level of darkness themselves. One friend jokingly said, 'At least now your family will *have* to slow down!' Another wanted only to hear about the saddest details. Some didn't want to 'bother me,' so they never reached out. Many showed up at first and never again. The more distant the acute phase you're experiencing is from everyday reality, the less people want to dive into the darkness with you."

Her words point to an essential component of ascending. We need support and many people reach out during the acute stages of darkness, gifting food, companionship, motivational literature, flowers, photos, and phone calls. But after this initial embrace, they treat the pain as if it's gone, as if we no longer need their presence. As if we've ascended instead of are still ascending. Being with someone in the thick of their suffering is difficult. Everyone wishes life would go back to "normal." Time softens and often lessens the acuteness of suffering. But even time is not a magic eraser that leaves no trace. Years later, we may still need a nightlight. Perhaps, if we practiced ascending, we could understand the necessity of continuously supporting others and ourselves – witnessing our continued and mutual relationship with darkness.

If we view symptoms as only negative, we lose the capacity to see them as mentors, as pathways toward a life of self-exploration. Convincing ourselves that the underworld doesn't permeate all of life is a grave mistake. I'll never be *rid* of my brother's accident. Parents who lose a child never *fully* heal. Trauma victims don't *overcome* their experiences. Veterans never *forget* combat. Moral and physical injuries inform us for a lifetime. Psychiatrist Elvin Semrad once said, we "often think that the best way to deal with any difficult situation is not to deal with it – to forget it. But … the only way you can forget is to remember."[20]

If we do this, we begin to see darkness as a vitamin of growth. If we ignore the labor of integrating its wisdom, even if it takes a lifetime, we miss the opportunity to expand. When someone comes to me with a seemingly unsurmountable underworld experience or a small hint pointing to a large wound, it is just life manifesting itself. We need frameworks imaginative enough to hold these experiences and begin to process what we've encountered. We need the necessary digestive enzymes.

Whether we look at the journey as a forerunner of individuation, soul-making in real time, or the ability to withstand and eventually embrace life's upheavals and hardships, the essential point is that valuing the descent-and-ascent journey in combination with a reverential vision of the underworld can provide a model for us to treat darkness not only as alien and terrifying but also as potentially enriching. This is to develop an underworld perspective that appreciates the richness of our depths and weaves underworlding into our being without being naïve about the challenges of integrating the lessons learned. Ascending, whether once or repeatedly, is a part of our ongoing journey to wholeness, which is very different from a quest for perfection. If we strive to live an unblemished life, nothing changes. The vexing nature of the journey is itself the price of rebirth. We'll look at a panoply of mythic descent-and-ascent journeys to show what it looks like to cultivate an imaginative relationship with the underworld.

CHAPTER 3
THE EVOLUTION OF THE HERO

Of all underworld journeyers, no other figure has captured the mythic imagination – East and West, North and South – as much as *the hero*. For tens of thousands of years, we have told stories of great heroes who journey into unimaginable darkness, battle monsters, and return transformed and empowered.

Cave paintings in Europe, Indonesia, and Australia dating from 30,000 to 40,000 years ago show that storytelling about heroism has been going on for a long time. Myths in many cultures tell of the trials, tribulations, and triumphs of powerful figures who faced great odds. Some of the earliest known stories, such as *Gilgamesh*, *Beowulf*, and *The Odyssey*, are of heroes who grow profoundly from facing adversity. And in the last 1,000 years, William Wallace battled the English, striving to unite the Scottish people; James Bond faced evil masterminds; and Wonder Woman with exuberance, integrity, and strength followed the path of virtue. Average people are also called heroes when they bring forth exceptional courage and sacrifice. The ways the Western mind imagines the hero have changed over time, and in this chapter we'll explore the hero's evolution through history – focusing on developments in the Western worldview that have shaped the character of this captivating figure. Heroes are relevant to our own experiences because they are images of human transformation.

Hero Worship

In the ancient world, heroes helped bridge the weakness of humans with the awesome power of the divine; they stood between the gods and us. Heroes were most often demigods, born of both mortal blood and immortal ichor. Hercules was son of Zeus, ruler of the gods, and Queen Alcmene of Thebes. Aeneas was son of Anchises, a member of the royal family of Troy, and Aphrodite, the goddess of love, pleasure, and procreation.

It was sacrilegious and dangerous for a common mortal to get too close to the gods, who were remote and omnipotent, but demigods were an exception. Demigod heroes such as Orpheus and Hercules, though half-human, were worshiped for having the appropriate relationship with the divine, guiding religious experiences that connected worshipers with their gods.

Hero cults rituals marked the end of isolated, mortal individuality and the emergent connection to the gods. The Greeks called this being "born into spirit" or *epoptes*, literally "he who sees." Heroes were embodiments of the possibility of rebirth, expansion of being, and the ability humans have to face life's great unknowns – including death and divinization.

In a society that feared the underworld, people relied on rites to prepare for death. Alone among those with mortal blood, demigod heroes could guide individuals into the underworld, serving as gateways between the mortal and the divine. Having already traveled into the abyss themselves, heroes such as Orpheus and Hercules knew the correct path to take and how to appease the powers of the deep. Classicist Walter Burkert called heroes a "chthonic counterpart to the worship of the gods."[1] To make peace with darkness, to enter the underworld, required relying on those heroes of myth that had journeyed into Hades.

Of all the Greek heroes, Orpheus was the most widely worshiped, and the cult of Orphism elucidated an elaborate system of posthumous rewards and punishments. To achieve ideal placement in Hades after death, cult followers outlined a daily didactic regime, not unlike the Judeo-Christian mythos that living a certain way means receiving favor upon dying. As descendants of Titans, humans were inherently sinful, and to overcome their titanic DNA, they sought the favor of Hades and Persephone. With such divine approval, they could be purified of the negative aspects of humanness. Orphic eschatology offered a detailed explanation of the afterlife, which could be followed by receiving guidance from a hero who knew how to appease the powers of the deep.

The poet and playwright Aristophanes described the consequence of not receiving favorable placement in Hades as spending eternity in "a mass of mud and ever-flowing filth."[2] To prevent this fate, the dead were buried along with golden tablets engraved with directions describing important landmarks and warning of mistakes others had made along the way, such as: "There is a spring at the right side and standing by it a white cypress. Do not go near that spring. Ahead you will find the Lake of Memory, cold water pouring forth; there are guards that will ask what you are seeking. Say, 'I am a son of Earth and starry Sky, quickly grant me water from the Lake of Memory.'"[3]

Cultural historian Richard Tarnas described the characteristics and virtues of ancient Greek heroes as being about "courage, cunning and strength, nobility and the striving for immortal glory."[4] I would add posthumous guidance and initiation. Over time, the ancient Greeks' vision of the hero receded and merged with characteristics of our time, resulting in a change of purpose.

Christianity

The first major shift in the heroic character was brought about by the rise of Christianity. With the declaration of the one true God, the worship of a pantheon of many gods and goddesses became blasphemous. Although monotheism predates Christianity, the latter's ascendency is a primary factor in the rise of a singular, monotheistic hero – Jesus Christ. Christ as hero is associated with *resurrection* and *redemption*. With the rise of the Christian faith, heroism became a story about participation with Christ.

God rescued Christ from the underworld, for it was impossible for the Son of God to be held by the power of death. For three days and three nights Christ descends into the abyss – the *tis katabesetai eis ten abysson* – before – the *ek nekron anagagein* – rising from the dead. Christ is a hero who overcomes the underworld so his followers can overcome the limits of the human condition and be closer to God. By descending into hell, he relieves his disciples from having to do so ("He died for our sins"). They only have to believe in him. And so, the Christian worldview modified the spiritual function of the hero from one associated with the chthonic, initiatory death and rebirth, and funerary rites to a figure who *annulled the underworld*, transforming it into the abode of those who were evil.

The Fall of Man alienated humanity from God, portraying human nature as sinful. Instincts such as lust, greed, jealously, and power were associated with the Devil and forbidden. The Christian moral objective to avoid sinful impulses means that humans need to be mindful of their thoughts and actions. Consequence becomes the priority of rational consciousness, along with repression of unconscious instincts and desires. This creates a theologically driven worldview that pits the rational against the instinctual.

The Christian vision posits a Godhead that rules over humanity and the cosmos, yet despite God's omniscience, the divine is also potentially available to everyone. God gives humanity the capacity for free will and the capacity to transgress his sovereignty, setting up the need for Christ's sacrifice to redeem humanity. By granting value to the individual soul, Christianity prioritized the growth of personal conscience and moral responsibility.

In the Christian myth, each human life is significant to God, a sensibility that differs from the Greek belief that placing humanity on an equal footing with the divine would be a grievous act of hubris – from the Greek *hybris*, meaning excessive pride or self-confidence associated with defiance of the gods. In the Christian paradigm, mortals seek to stand next to God, whereas in Greek religion, only the half-divine hero could do so. And so heroism began to focus on the individual ability to rise above darkness and ascend toward God.

Viewing the underworld as a container of sin that disconnects us from God inspired the repression of darkness. Christianity brought dramatic moral division to the inner world. God and his associated qualities of purity, morality, and prudence were seen as good (light); and human nature as sinful (dark). Western civilization focused on the dayworld – light, spirit, reason, and goodness – and instinct, nature, passions, sexuality, and the body were seen as evil. We began to believe that in the deep places, where light does not reach, lurks a panoply of demonic terrors and temptations.

Modern Western Worldview

The Greeks' connection to the underworld as a way of offering guidance toward transformation metamorphosed first into redemption through Christ, and then slowly into our modern notion of "hero" as one who is hyper-individualistic and death-defying, exercising free will through might. Hero figures lost their chthonian nature, then their redemptive nature, and became *solar*, personifying personal achievement, ascendency, and individual strength.

By 1300, the rise of the Renaissance marked the beginning of the modern era and a fundamental change in the Western mind. The modern personality, writes Tarnas, is "marked by individualism, secularity, strength of will, multiplicity of interest and impulse, creative innovation, and a willingness to defy traditional limitations on human activity."[5] The new personality was expansive, inventive, individualistic, inquisitive, and self-possessed – qualities projected onto the evolving face of the hero.

By the early 17th century, the modern era had ushered in a whole new expression of the heroic attitude. Today's hero, Campbell explained, symbolizes a combination of "the democratic ideal of the self-determining individual, the invention of the power-driven machine, and the development of the scientific method of research."[6] As the Western worldview congealed, the face of the hero adopted the personality of the emerging individual.

Secularization, the rise of democracy, freedom of will, self-determinism, and extraverted action combined to create the Enlightenment tradition. The new zeitgeist inspired a sharply defined individualism. The modern personality is assertive and self-reliant, willful and independent, very much like Hercules.

On the one hand, individuality supports free expression and the ability for each of us to independently pursue our unique personality and desires. On the other, individuality burdens each of us with the responsibility of choosing our own path. We are accountable for shaping the conditions of our lives – what university we go to, what vocation we follow, what faith we believe in, the partner we choose, where we live, and where we will be buried. While these ideas inspire an enriching degree of personal agency, they also create obligation and responsibility, often without guidance or resources.

Our cultural predecessors were much more supported by the spiritual practices and rituals of their religious and mythic worldview. Untethered from religion and stable communities, it's up to us to determine the course of our lives – answering for ourselves the great questions of purpose and meaning. This divorce from traditional systems of connection, which were rich with symbolism and animism, adds to the pressure on the ego to distance itself from the deep psyche. The Norwegian artist Edvard Munch's painting *The Scream* becomes a representation of the plight of modern man – alone, sky ablaze, trapped within a bolt of suffering.

"The hero myth," psychologist Keiron Le Grice explains, "carries the individualism of the West to its logical conclusion, fulfilling the Western spiritual ideal, leading the individual self to its own transformation through the inner encounter with the depths of the psyche and spirit."[7] Adapting the character of the Western mind and culture, the image of the hero became more about the accomplishments of the self-determined individual than those of the collective, a twist in a mythic portrayal of a figure originally concerned with teaching entry into the underworld.

Science

In the 15th and 16th centuries, the Cartesian–Newtonian worldview emerged, alongside the idea of the modern self. The work of French philosopher, mathematician, and scientist René Descartes (1596–1650) laid the foundation for 17th-century rationalism by hypothesizing that there is a sharp distinction between inner, subjective reality and the objective dimensions of experience. This created a dichotomy between the psychic and the physical, mind and matter, known today as the mind–body split. Cartesian dualism believes that humanity inhabits two distinct realities, one accessible through sensate experience and the other through self-examination. Theories of dualism combined with the work of Isaac Newton (1643–1727) to create a divided cosmological vision that could be understood through mechanistic causes and effects.

The new scientific paradigm brought about a colossal shift in the Western mind's relationship to instinctual life. The prioritization of consciousness, spirit, rationality, and extraverted "masculine" energy led to the exclusion and repression of other, opposite qualities: the visceral power of nature, the feminine and body, sexuality, irrational urges, and uncivilized desires.

Religion, myth, and creative expression were seen as within the purview of the subjective inner world, while explanations of the external world were the exclusive domain of science. Science and religion were separated, and the cosmos stripped of enchantment. Where once stories of myth had provided meaningful portals into the collective undercurrents of the mind, now they offered empty truths and childish hopes. Freud used this type of reductive thinking, viewing myths as pathological and fallacious, and dreams as infantile fantasies. For Freud, religion provided comforting delusions for those who couldn't face reality. Instead of rites and religion, smoke and talismans, symbols and ancestral knowledge, we began to worship measurement and replicability. Labs became our temples, and science proudly eradicated primitive, animistic, and magical explanations for the world and our place within it.

By the 17th century, the Western mind saw nature as lifeless matter – a dominion to be controlled and conquered. Knowledge no longer came from religious systems, myth, or symbols, but from experimentation, predictability, and tools of the rational mind. Logic replaced faith as the governing explanatory force. Yet the barbarism, conflict, psychopathology, and suffering that populates the underworld did not go away. It continued to thrive in the shadows of polished, rationalized, civilized society.

In the 18th century, widespread economic development drove large portions of the population into cities, and the Industrial Revolution created a mass society in which individual experience was less important than collective production. Standards of uniformity blurred personal uniqueness, fueled by science that favored statistical averages over uniqueness.

The National Institute of Mental Health estimates that nearly 47 million Americans experience mental illness, of whom 11 million live with serious psychosis. Industry reports that depression alone costs the economy nearly $200 billion annually. Statistics indicate that mental health in young people is deteriorating, with an increase in caseloads of more than 4 percent in the last six years. Chain reactions such as suicidal ideation have jumped to more than 10 million adults.[8]

As these norms imply, the mystery and complexity of the human mind is being translated into statistical averages. Less attention is given to tending the distinctiveness of each person's life, let alone their soul. We live in an age in which people feel trivial and deficient, swept into piles of statistics. Something is lost in approaching life this way. Without connection to the depths, we lose access to wellsprings of inspiration, connection, meaning, and self-awareness. We label this disconnect "neurosis."

Depth Psychology and the Western Mind

Depth psychology arose in the 19th century as a response to the religious, scientific, and personal changes in the Western mind and way of life. Reacting to the Enlightenment's emphasis on empiricism, individualism, and reason, depth psychology sought to balance exploration of the inner world with scientific inquiry. It used the methodology of the Enlightenment – observation, hypothesis, and rationality – to understand the terrain of Romanticism: ancient religion, passion, art, and an animistic worldview, the belief that all things, including animals, plants, rocks, and rivers, have a spiritual essence. The intent was to find a middle ground between rationality and science, on the one hand, and the more ineffable dimensions of life, on the other.

Jung was concerned about the impact the modern zeitgeist has on the psyche. The modern individual, he wrote, "wants to live with every side of himself – to know what he is." The individual has broken with tradition, he added, in order to "experiment with his life and determine what value and meaning things have in themselves."[9]

Jung observed many people afflicted by feelings of insignificance, rootlessness, inadequacy, and meaninglessness, and saw this as a spiritual problem. The decline of traditional religions forced many to face life's existential dilemmas without symbolic or religious support. The combination of authority of the individual ego, the rise of mechanistic, empirical science, and the de-animation of the world discredited spiritual orientations; consequently, the gods, goddesses, and even God no longer held psychic importance for large numbers of people. The mysteries of the depths and symbols of traditional religions no longer interested vast swathes of modern society. With the secularism of the Enlightenment, gods, demons, and spirits were rationalized out of existence.

All previous ages of human history believed in gods of some form. "Only an unparalleled impoverishment of symbolism," argued Hillman, "could enable us to rediscover gods *as psychic factors*, that is, as archetypes of the unconscious."[10] Jung called this impoverishment of symbolism a *Kairos*, an opportune moment for the gods to metamorphize from principles and powers *outside* of us to *inner* psychological factors.[11]

Cultures of antiquity had mythic, visionary, and religious systems that gave meaning to humankind's relationship with the unknown. Today, these approaches are seen as primitive, irrational, or even delusory. Descartes's famous statement, *cogito ergo sum* ("I think, therefore I am") sums up the modern individual – I exist because I am consciously aware of and capable of intellectually understanding my reality. It's all about the neocortex, with the rest of the triune brain relegated to the back of the bus. We banish the ineffable in service of clarity, avoid the unexplainable in favor of what we can engage with tangibly, and neglect the symbolic for the concrete.

A psychology of depth sits uneasily in the Western mind. Mainstream psychology deals with the surface, treating symptoms without diving deeply to discover their source. Yet despite repression, neglect, or quick "fixes," the demands of the inner world insinuate their way into our lives, expressed as symptoms, compulsions, depression, and neuroses. Surface techniques often ignore the deeper, unknown parts of ourselves, the realm of meaning, spirituality, imagination, emotion, soul, dreams, and darkness. To access this well of knowledge, we must turn our attention to the inner world, inclining toward the journey to the underworld. We turn to the parts of ourselves willing to leave the comforts of the dayworld behind in search of a greater life story – the parts of ourselves we call heroic that can withstand the battlefields, even in the darkest of nights, and take the next steps into the darkness.

The Hero's Journey: Setting Out

Despite these formidable shifts in Western culture, the hero remains the prototype for enduring challenges, whether navigating the death process, as it did for ancient Greeks, or mustering the courage needed for personal development. In a culture in which religion, science, and identity all buy into a bifurcated cosmology, the unifying and balancing role of the hero is all the more vital. If we believe that essential aspects of ourselves lay buried in the depths of our being, sorting out how to reengage and rebuild a relationship with them is critical for self-growth.

In 1949, Joseph Campbell published *The Hero with a Thousand Faces*, a detailed study of the archetypal pattern of the hero. By distilling a wealth of cross-cultural myths and combining culturally specific hero traits, he identified archetypal phases of the hero's journey, calling it the *monomyth* of the hero.[12]

The hero's journey tells the story of the trials of individual growth. The "effect of the successful adventure of the hero," Campbell explained, "is the unlocking and release again of the flow of life into the body of the world." In this way, the hero's path conducts people "across those difficult thresholds of transformation that demand a change in the patterns not only of conscious but also of unconscious life."[13] The ardor of personal growth has inspired hero myths that tell of the inner strength needed to move forward, abandon the security of the known, and face the perilous death-and-rebirth experience required to transform. It's a story about stepping out into the rushing current of life, where anything can happen next.

The hero's journey begins when psychic energy becomes stuck, limited, or restless. It can be triggered by a collision with a person or an idea, uncontrolled emotionality, or an eating away from within when we notice our restrictive patterns and recognize the need for a new perspective. Perhaps we've reached rock bottom and the ways we've coped are now obsolete. Maybe we've passed from one stage of life to another, and this new stage requires something new from us.

The hero's path is a metaphor for the energy and resources that actively challenge our attachment to self-preservation and control, meet the hurdles of life head on, and stay present with the burdens of self-growth. The inner capacity to sacrifice stability and comfort in order to pursue self-growth is *heroic*.

The Hero's Journey: Death

When we know that our old ways no longer serve us, the journey begins. We journey into the underworld, encountering terrible, destructive, combative energies, as well as unexpected and magical ones.

The heroic deed is about overcoming resistances and challenges. It could be overpowering identification with archetypal figures, complexes, or fantasies that rob us of our individuality. We need heroic energy to face these challenges of the lower world. "A genuine claim to self-confidence," Jung wrote, "comes from facing the dark ground of ourselves and thereby gaining ourselves."[14] Without contact with the depths, there can be no fundamental change in consciousness.

In the underworld, the lights are out. To journey within is an unsettling choice of *volunteering to die to our old selves* "in order to beget a new and fruitful life in that region of the psyche which has hitherto lain fallow in darkest unconsciousness."[15] In darkness, the old parts of ourselves – scripted voices that tell us we have to act this way and not that, edifices built on pain, violations, mistakes, or fears that have become complexes running wild – have the chance to bid farewell, to perish.

We step into the abyss because we know, deep down, that doing so we gain the possibility of accessing a deeper well of potential, a long lost freedom. Our conscious awareness must connect with the Self, the larger psychic totality – not unlike what religious people call God, or Soul – that embraces and, at the same time, is bigger than both the conscious and the unconscious.

My father told me about his experience of "dying" over a year-long period. For the past five years, he has thought about stepping back from the daily responsibilities of running his company. To help with this change, he hired an individual to manage his transition from leader to elder. Smiling sadly, he recounted:

This past year was a slow death for me. I felt actively banished. I lived in exile watching decisions and choices unfold at my company that, at the time, I barely understood and felt powerless to stop. My family and staff were gaslighted. When the money from a trustee's grant ran out, our manager resigned abruptly. We looked into the books to find that our savior had stolen more than $200,000 from the company, hired all of her friends and paid them huge wages, and left us in dire straits.

Although our other employees have rebounded, my connection to my work was deeply ruptured, possibly dead. The staff treat me as an outsider, someone to manage. I go there now because I have to, because I own the company. I have financial and legal responsibility for its operations. Instead of a gracious path to Elderhood marked by celebration, gratitude, and respect, my last years were marked by a sense of loss and a deep failing.

I asked him to tell me more about how this underworld journey was a death. "My journey toward this death," he said, "was marked by sleepless nights, cold sweats, despair, depression, weakness, fury, disappointment with myself, and failure to handle responsibility well for the first time since I was in my twenties. I allowed myself to be wronged. I feel like a victim.

"Perhaps, my love of and attachment to my business had to be trampled in the mud for me to 'let go.' But I don't think that's true. I've been ready for a while to 'let go,' to see what lies ahead. I just haven't known how to extricate myself from the responsibility. I still don't."

My father's reflection shows the complexity, layers, ebb and flow, and pain of inner death. Worn thin, he has yet to ascend from this underworld journey. He's still in the process of letting the death of his old life and identity work him. And to ascertain the deeper message from what still feels like a betrayal by the other person.

We don't often bring enough imagination to our treatment of death. We take death literally and look for literal solutions. Psychological death is not the same as physical mortality. If we bring the same lack of imagination, we risk holding on to old patterns that no longer serve the betterment and wholeness of our development.

Death is the ultimate *other*. It's natural for the ego to defend against the otherness of its presence. This is a common reaction of the ego in dreamwork. The ego jumps on satisfying interpretations of itself that fit its existing view. What it doesn't understand is that dreams are from the otherworld, translating the messages of the unconscious through symbols and feelings. Dreams are not given to us to fortify the agenda of our usual ways of thinking.

We seek conclusions and compartments, tidy destinations to wrap up our quest for meaning. The ego wants to identify with the hero, but *a true hero is from another realm*. As we'll see in later chapters, what all heroes have in common is encountering and facing death so that regeneration is possible.

The Hero's Journey: Return

The final sequence of the hero's journey – the return – is about returning to the dayworld and integrating the new ego-attitude into the personality.

Integration is the connective tissue between the hero's journey and individuation, because both focus on the activation and channeling of psychic energy toward personal development. Individuation is neither a goal nor a destination: it's the *process* of becoming who we really are – discovering our unique identity by connecting to the deeper and more complete aspect of our being, the Self. Jung once said he had never met an "individuated man." Becoming yourself is an ongoing process; there isn't a "stopping" or "arrival" point. The sun rises and sets. The washer rinses, washes, and repeats. Life brings us a constant stream of hardships, developments, and changes. The hero personifies our ability to weather this onslaught, facing the great unknown in service to life. The hero holds the tension between avoiding danger and confronting darkness.

Integrating unconscious content in a way that leads to greater wholeness is called "assimilation." It's tempting to try to return to the comforts of the old world – familiar patterns, automatic thoughts, well-worn pages – but that door has closed. It won't work, but it nonetheless takes strength to resist the temptation to regress. To *return* means to accept being irreversibly changed and to focus on incorporating the changes that are already well underway into your life.

The Shadow of the Monomyth

Joseph Campbell uses the term "monomyth" to describe the commonalities of the hero archetype throughout times and cultures. He is correct to deduce that the hero's journey varies little in its essential plan – courage, integrity, and strength. However, by focusing on the commonalties and not the nuances of each hero we have overly simplified the hero's journey. How we leave the security of the known, battle monsters, and claim inner treasures can take a multitude of forms. Mythical heroes battle their monsters on mountaintops, in distant caverns, and on islands in the far reaches of the world; real people like us have to take our monsters back home and integrate our shadows and treasures into our own personalities. And each of us does this painstaking work differently.

Heroism wears a thousand faces. Hercules faces darkness differently from Orpheus, who is distinct from Aeneas. Just as we share common human emotions and experiences – the need to be loved, dealing with hardship or aging, wanting to be seen – we each have our own traumas, identities, and histories that make our journeys distinct. We don't and cannot respond to all of life's hurdles in one way.

The myths of Hercules, Orpheus, Odysseus, and Aeneas show us different ways we can engage in underworld journeying. Are we dragged into the underworld? Do we enter voluntarily? Are we witty or compassionate? Do we do it hubristically, sacrificially, for love, for society, or to listen, question, and learn? Do we seek personal gain? Do we fail? Are we transformed, dismembered, or barely affected?

Sometimes we need to be Herculean – conquering, proving, accomplishing, vanquishing, and subduing the powers of the unconscious. At other times we'll be Orphic – charming, persuasive, and even faltering in our quest. Sometimes we may act Odyssean – refusing the call, making intentional changes, and accepting the reality before us by acknowledging what is beyond our control. Perhaps we're Aenean – listening, moving reverentially, and following an inner guide toward finding our true power.

No circumstance, adversity, force, or person can take away your ability to reimagine and find meaning in the dark. Expansion of being and, thus, wellness comes from psychological choice. One way to attain this is by using many mythical patterns to bring imagination and diversity to our psychological life. An underworld perspective is about being conscious in our suffering, open to its full intensity, knowing that if we stay with it, we will almost certainly grow. We can choose to relate to our suffering rather than try to escape from it.

II.

HERO TO HEROES

CHAPTER 4
HERCULES

Hercules, the mightiest son of Zeus, worshiped as *heros theos* – hero god – was the most celebrated of Greek heroes, invoked as he who "takes all" and remains "unconquered."[1] The "Hymn to Herkales" illustrates a vivid picture of his character:

> Herakles, stout-hearted and mighty, powerful Titan,
> strong-handed, indomitable, doer of valiant deeds,
> shape-shifter, O gentle and endless father of time,
> ineffable, lord of all, many pray to you, all-conquering and
> mighty archer and seer, omnivorous begetter of all, peak
> of all, helper of all, for the sake of men you subdued and
> tamed savages races.[2]

Hercules confronts the world. From infancy to death, his life is a series of adventures, battles, victories, and tragedies. The Herculean hero faces life with the strength of will to overcome and control the unfamiliar, rise strong, and destroy all the beasts that lurk in the depths. He represents the part of us that is unrelenting and powerful, confident and brave, full of extraordinary power and superhuman intensity. He wields a combative sword and sees victory even in destruction. Hercules represents our ability to accomplish the seemingly impossible.

We all know him. He lives in our fight, our resistance, the moments where we use sheer determined willpower to get through what's happening. The Hercules part of us goes to battle. This could be wrestling a terrible memory, resisting our pain by forcing it into the shadows, or never giving up on a dream or a value.

During the siege of Sarajevo, snipers rained invisible death on residents who courageously risked their lives to cross streets to collect water, firewood, and food – 1,425 days of hell. Herculean courage manifesting on war-stricken cobblestone streets.

When William Ayotte opened his front door in Alaska, he saw a polar bear mauling a woman. He grabbed a shovel and ran toward the bear, hitting it in the eye. The bear turned on him. With his ear gone and many staples later, newspapers worldwide called Ayotte a hero.

When Zeus' wife, Hera, heard that one of her husband's mistresses was pregnant with Hercules, she flew into a rage. Determined to destroy the baby, Hera prevented him from becoming heir to the kingdom of Mycenae and sent two snakes to kill him in his crib. The babe strangled both snakes. When Hercules grew into a man, Hera cast a spell that caused him to murder his beloved wife, Megara, and their two children. After recovering from his madness, he went to the Delphic Oracle to ask how he could atone for the murders. The Oracle told him to go to his cousin King Eurystheus of Mycenae and complete 12 labors. In return, he would be rewarded with penance and immortality.

Hercules' twelfth and final labor was to kidnap Cerberus, the three-headed hound of Hades. Hercules said that King Eurystheus "made me hunt this one time to get the watchdog of the dead: no more perilous task, he thought, could be; but I brought back that beast, up from the underworld."[3]

Preparation

During his fourth task, killing the Erymanthian boar, Hercules came to the abode of the centaur Pholus, who had a cask of wine from the god Dionysus. Pholus begged Hercules not to open the cask, but Hercules ignored him. The wine's fragrance attracted other centaurs, who besieged Pholus' home and, in their frenzy, killed him. Hercules drove them away, but the fleeing centaurs rushed to the home of Chiron, the centaur who trained heroes (including Hercules). While pursuing them, Hercules accidently wounded Chiron. Overcome with grief, he tried to relieve his mentor's suffering. But Chiron was an immortal, and as such he was fated to suffer his wounds for all eternity. Hercules beseeched his father, Zeus, to lift the centaur's immortality. His father granted Hercules' request, and Chiron died.

For ancient Greeks, unsanctified violence had to be ritually purified before journeying into the underworld. To honor this belief, Hercules prepared for his journey to Hades by going to Eleusis to be purified for his murder of the centaurs.

Purification is the symbolic removal of contaminants – getting rid of unwanted or limiting behaviors and thoughts. Hercules' purification suggests that sometimes aspects of the ego-mind, in this case its vicious nature, need to be washed away for further growth to be possible. In Christian myth, purification requires descent into hell and passage through the lower world. In

Dante's *Divine Comedy*, sinful desires and instincts are exposed and purified in Purgatory.

Purification is about releasing the past in order to move forward, "washing yourself of sin." When a relationship, job, or friendship is finished, when something needs to be left behind, when we want to break a connection, we "wash our hands of it." A prerequisite for change and going forward can be washing away attachments and narrowing ideas. Acceptance replaces self-pity; acknowledgment weathers away not feeling valued; being less judgmental creates space for compassion. Purification is not about offloading or numbing, but forgiving, atoning, and releasing.

Rituals of ablution are present in all religions. Sometimes the body is washed (the Jewish *mikveh* or Hawaiian *hi'uwai*), clothes are changed, or an individual is smudged with sacred smoke – burning sage or incense, frankincense and myrrh. Sometimes a prayer or incantation is recited, or an object is anointed with a pure substance such as oil, rosewater, or wine. In the Hindu ritual *abhisheka*, the *murti*, or image of the god or sacred mortal, is bathed with water, curd, milk, and honey. In many traditions when you enter a home recently visited by death, you bathe or wash your hands at the door.

Water is the substance most often used to wash away the past. Many rites begin with handwashing, or sprinkling water to remove old thoughts and commitments, reminding us that the psychological need for renewal and release cannot be ignored. "To cherish secrets and restrain emotions," Jung wrote, "are psychic misdemeanors for which nature finally visits us with sickness."[4] Sometimes we need to take ownership for past wrongdoing so we can remove shame, anxiety, or fear that could otherwise calcify. This could take the form of reparation, recognition, or honoring remorse. If we don't wash ourselves of inner grit, we might lose the chance for redemption and transformation.

Ritual preparation can take many forms. In World War II, Japanese *kamikaze*, "Divine Wind," pilots drank sake infused with "magic" to provide "spirit lifting" before boarding their planes and plummeting to their deaths. Norse warriors earned the glorification *berserker* after living in the wilderness and being possessed by the soul of a boar, a bear, or a wolf. The warrior then drank the blood of the chosen animal, becoming more beast than man.

Sometimes we pause and take a conscious breath to be present for what lies ahead. Inner preparation might include setting goals or intentions, entering therapy, or performing rituals like lighting candles, journaling, visualization, or going for a walk. It could be mindfulness, breathwork, creativity, prayer, or meditation. Preparation is about setting an intention to use your time well. Doing so may enable you to face your next steps with acceptance, stability, and strength. Hercules' preparations tell us that his journey to Hades was purposeful.

Overpowering the Underworld

During the journey, Hercules violently and reactively challenged a host of underworld figures. He wrestled Charon, the ferryman who delivers the dead across the rivers Styx and Acheron. Wanting to provide the shades with blood, he butchered one of Hades' sacred cattle. He wounded the herdsman Menoities, tampered with Hades' enforced punishment by freeing Theseus, and rolled away the stone placed on Ascalaphus, the gardener of the abyss who Demeter punished for telling Hades that Persephone had eaten six pomegranate seeds.

In the underworld, Hercules did as he pleased, the "the terror and controller of the ghost-world."[5] He reorganized the rhythms of the deep to fit his desires, journeying to Hades and harrowing it to his will. He faced darkness with a goal-oriented approach — proving his valor and worth by accomplishing tasks. It's difficult to tease out his aggressive style from his task-oriented purpose, because he accomplished his goals, but violently. Before kidnapping Cerberus, he subdued Hades by brandishing a stone at him. In some accounts, he wounded Hades so severely that Hades fled to Olympus to be treated by Paeeon, physician of the gods.

Hercules faced life from the vantage point of the ego-mind – the desire to control and beat the unknown into submission. His ego was so dense he almost sank Charon's ferry. This organized, muscular, masculine, self-determined, individualistic attitude is familiar to us today; it's about conquest. When we want to accomplish something from an egoistic place, we rise, gather our strength, make with a plan, and exert our full effort. And we have pickup trucks with huge tires to take us there. When our task is seemingly insurmountable, we're told that it will take a Herculean effort. Hercules represents the ultimate victor, letting nothing happen to him except the goal-oriented, self-proving tasks he accomplishes at will.

Hercules' nature is primal and bloody, progressive and developmental, always making mistakes and always fighting. He drew his sword against the shade of the Gorgon Medusa, whose head was covered in snakes and who turned all who looked upon her to stone, blindly attacking Medusa until Hermes reminded him she was only a phantom. Despite formidable strength, Hercules is not omniscient or perfect. He's raw, flawed, and human, yet focused and determined.

History is full of Herculean heroes. When a Thai soccer team was trapped inside the Tham Luang Nang Non cave, oxygen diminishing, darkness descending, a rescue effort involving more than 10,000 people charged into the submerged cave system. Oskar and Emilie Schindler saved over a thousand Jews from horrific deaths in concentration camps, risking everything for their beliefs. And police officers, firefighters, nurses, and doctors are called heroes – "essential workers" – when they battle the unimaginable to save us from the unbearable.

The power of the deep psyche does not frighten those with a Herculean perspective. He is a conqueror who muscles his way through every barrier. In the *Aeneid*, Virgil said that for Hercules "the lakes of Styx have trembled and the guardian of Orcus as he huddled within his bloody cave on half-chewed bones. No shape could panic you, not even tall Typhoeus, bearing arms; the snake of Lerna, its host of heads surrounding you, could not rob you of reason."[6] Herculean moments occur when we stride into darkness with the force of our own determination. No challenge is too great, no enemy too strong, no situation unsolvable. It takes perseverance and willingness to suffer the unknown in ourselves and in the world.

The Herculean experience manifests when we aren't ready to give up, although aches lace our bodies, fear grips our souls, we keep going, willing ourselves onward.

During World War II, British Prime Minister Churchill was very Herculean: "You ask what is our aim? I can answer in one word: Victory. Victory at all costs. Victory in spite of all terror. Victory however long and hard the road may be. For without victory, there is no survival."[7]

Hercules divides the world into good and bad, alive and dead, victory and failure; and his moralistic clarity allows him to advance toward victory despite all odds. Herculean thinking is black-and-white. Reducing the complexities of life enables him to attack anything perceived as threatening or even unknown, earning him the epithet *Aretos* – warlike.

Reflecting on trying to finish school after recovering sufficiently from his brain injury, my brother told me, "I was driven by something in me I couldn't touch. It was on some level the only way I saw forward, and I knew that no one could do it for me. Finishing school had to happen one way or another. Some invisible part of me knew that life would ultimately be more streamlined if I did what I could in that moment to make it happen. It was just moment-by-moment, simple things. It was hard enough to get through the day, let alone rewrite my script the way I wanted to. I just focused on little actions that allowed me to see my predicament with optimism, even opportunity." Basketball star Kobe Bryant famously responded to a question the same way: "So, I start chopping the problem into smaller pieces, and I focus on them."[8]

Breaking complexities into bits allows us to face them one at a time. Sometimes we aren't able to make the grand gestures we desire. When this is the case, daily steps are important. We must first to go to the bathroom to take a shower. We cut the larger picture into smaller pieces so that life is more digestible. Someone who's been traumatized cannot immediately sit with returning memories. They have to begin by regaining safety – practice conscious breathing and grounding themselves in their bodies; then after a while, they can connect to their grief and anger and change their relationship to their experiences.

Either/or thinking has its place; however, it also limits the value that can be gained from failures and mistakes. The polarization of grand fantasies of success or consuming feelings of failure blocks our missteps from teaching us. Belgian therapist Esther Perel once asked a client, "Are you here to listen or to be right? If you want to listen, you'll have to be less right."[9]

It's easy to ignore the underworld perspective when we leap ahead to solutions. When we divide life into simple high-minded categories, we lose opportunities to hang out in the gray areas, and it's there that the intricacy and majesty of life reveals itself. Reduction limits possibility – if we look for just one color, we miss the rainbow.

The Herculean hero meets life's challenges head on, overcoming toils and gaining the approval of the gods. Hercules' mythology tells us that invincibility and brutality are not only distinct from the spirited and idealized mind, but also favored by it. Hercules is primitive muscle, "defeating snakes in my cradle."[10] As early as the 5th century BCE, Hercules was worshiped at

Eleusis as a figure who broke the terrors of death and could protect initiates from the dangers of the underworld. He was not born immortal; he *earned* the honors of the gods through blood, sweat, and toil, reminding us that there are great rewards for boldly facing the unknown.

Every time someone walks into my office, a part of them is Hercules. At the doorway they bravely step across the threshold to expose themselves to another person – to display their woundedness and secrets, to admit their insecurities, and to take the next steps, no matter how painful, toward self-discovery.

Hercules personifies fighting the underworld and resisting its wisdom, and he also represents the strength needed to overcome the destructive power of the unconscious – to tame Cerberus, the three-headed watchdog of Hades. It takes profound courage, willpower, and determination to face unconscious content, turn toward our traumas and our embodied memories, and remain steadfast during the upheavals of hardship and change.

Slaying the Imagination

Hillman believed Hercules used his sword to slay the imagination – to separate the imaginal from the rational discernment typical of ego-consciousness. Instead of metaphor we literalize, diminishing our ability to imaginatively engage with ourselves and lives.

Hercules' warlike nature is symbolized by his sword and his club. The sword is the mortal expression of divine power. Unlike his father, Zeus, Hercules doesn't fight with a celestial thunderbolt but with a weapon forged from the metal of the earth. The sword is a symbol of discriminating wisdom – sharp edges of polished metal that divide skillfully. The world is simpler and easier to navigate if it's divided in two: worthy and unworthy, this and that, us and them, yes and no, victory and failure.

If I were to battle a real beast, I might have to kill it. But a psychological beast can be faced with imagination. Often the greatest of monsters are the ones we create. For some people, inner fiends conjure thoughts of worthlessness and the lack of ability. For others, it's the beast of self-image – am I thin, pretty, or strong enough? We are all prey to the many monsters of mind.

This is the Herculean dilemma: Do we slay our inner demons, or do we meet them with the same mythopoetic imagination that created them? Without imagination, it's easy to regard the unfamiliar as something to overpower or slay. This is the *Herculean error* – destroying the unfamiliar and unanticipated. The strong-willed pursuit of stability can stand in the way of substantive transformation. Brandishing a weapon at the unknown won't help us grow. Making a relationship with it will.

My initial reaction to my brother's accident was Herculean. I was *determined* to control the situation, sleep in the hospital, attend all the doctors' meetings, learn their language, care for my parents, and overcome the possibility of his death. I entered the hospital sword in hand, ready to do battle. I wanted a simpler world in which my role was clear, and I could show up in "the right way." I found comfort in believing that if I resisted the facts on the ground, reality would never catch up, my brother would be fine, and the nightmare would end well.

My healing began when I realized that wherever I looked – at family members, staff, pretty much everyone – I saw Hercules with his dense energy and ramrod determination, which was no longer serving my brother's recovery, or, if he was not going to recover, his transition from life. I saw Hercules in the nurse who told me to be strong, the doctors who tried to prolong his life at all costs, even my friends who called with wishes of courage, and above all, me – the sister and daughter who fought to protect everyone around me (including myself) from feeling the full array of what was going on. Herculean energy had been immensely empowering. Its single focus and denial of darkness helped us survive. However, as time went on, carrying such a heavy club was preventing us from tuning in more deeply to what Ben needed. Being a hero continued to be lifesaving, but being Hercules no longer served the cause.

Our society is solution-oriented and many of us feel charged to fix our world. In therapy, many people want to be "fixed" and have bought into the fantasy that there's an easy solution to what they feel is broken. The harsh truth is there is no Wizard of Oz, no vending machine of magic potions that will rid us of suffering. Quick fixes are fantasies of the ego; the soul has eternity, it isn't rushed.

Hercules enters the underworld to *take* something, and there, as Hillman points out, he "wrestled, he drew his sword, he slaughtered, and was confused about the reality of images. Each of us tends to be Hercules in ego when we begin to engage imaginal figures."[11] If we view the unconscious through the Herculean perspective, we create a problem-making attitude that appeals to the Herculean ego – facing the ambiguous with the tools of combat.

In the West, illness is generally approached with a Herculean attitude: complexity is simplified and morality is included in our understanding of disease. Survival and health are seen as good; death and illness are bad. Oversimplification has its place, but the inner journey of psyche includes more than genetic and environmental factors; it has a symbolic dimension that is not just imaginal but expresses in matter, the body. To activate our healing potential, we have to move beyond the restrictive paradigm of blame and logic and distinguish *meaning* and *cause*, *symbol* and *symptom*. When we approach suffering as single-minded fighters without considering the meaning hidden within our darkness, we limit our capacity to find lasting solutions.

Limits

Persephone gave Hercules permission to take Cerberus *only if he could do so without weapons*. Despite his unparalleled strength, Hercules was subservient to the rulers of the underworld, reminding us that unconscious "cares" little for the ego's agenda. Even the strongest among us meet their limits and have to bow to deeper authorities. Inner work has no shortcuts — we all, to a greater or lesser degree, end up taking a knee to the unpredictable forces of the psyche and the dark moments of life.

Hercules meets his limits again with the ghost of the hero Meleager. At first he tries to force his will on the shade, and Meleager tells the story of killing his uncles, in response to which Meleager's mother burned the stick that represented his lifespan, and he died. Saddened by Meleager's fate, Hercules promised to marry his sister Deianeira.

This moment shows an uncharacteristic flash of empathy and reflection, a crack in Hercules' veneer that ultimately leads to his downfall. Later in Hercules' life, the centaur Nessus tries to force himself upon Deianeira. Defending his wife, Hercules shoots Nessus with a poisoned dart. In death, the centaur persuades Deianeira that his blood would deepen Hercules' love for her. Convinced, she soaks a tunic in the centaur's blood and gives it to her husband. But the blood is poisonous and causes Hercules so much pain that he begs for death. The gods heard his cries and allow the mortal part of him to perish.

Hercules enters the underworld with strength and conviction, but not reflection. There he encounters a larger story — a fate that takes his mortal life. No one is immune to an underworld experience. No matter how strong our systems of protection, our determination, or our goodness, we can never predict how darkness will impact us. Even when we feel in control, we're not. The unconscious always has the last word.

Cerberus

At the entrance to the gates of death, Hercules captured Cerberus, the demonic dog that prevents shades from escaping the land of darkness. Persephone told Hercules that he could only take the beast if he overcame it with brute strength, not with composure, thought, or refinement. It wasn't the strength of his weapons but his own raw physical capability.

Hercules is a warrior. Honoring who he is means honoring his physical prowess and his ability to rely on force when encountering adversity. We each have our own inner strengths that sustain, yet when faced with darkness we often struggle to find them. Summoning what supports us is an important practice. If walking or running is our release, we can do that. If connecting with others heals us, reach out. Knowing and activating our unique strengths can help us weather great storms.

Leaving Persephone, Hercules returned to the gates of Hades where he found Cerberus and choked him into submission, chained him, and hauled him up to the surface. The ancient Greek scholar Apollodorus said that during the fight, Hercules "never relaxed his grip and stranglehold on the beast until he had broken its will."[12] Cerberus doesn't meekly follow Hercules: "The dog struggled, twisting its head away from the daylight and the shining sun. Mad with rage, it filled the air with its triple barking, and sprinkled the green fields with flecks of white foam."[13] At the gates of death, Hercules encountered unrefined instinct in its own realm, a confrontation with what lies beneath the surface.

Imagine facing our inner monster with so much strength and confidence that we break its hold on us and choke it into submission, throttling self-doubt, subduing shame, and strangling the life out of our inner critic. Hercules is the part of us that's strong enough to challenge our most formidable monsters.

Conquering Cerberus and dragging him to daylight is a metaphor for forcefully bringing the unconscious into conscious awareness. Overthrowing the three-headed dog of instinctive energy and coercing its unconscious content into consciousness takes Herculean might. When we journey into the unconscious, we face the scary and painful process of bringing what has been neglected and even unknown in us to the surface.

The viciousness of Hercules' battle with Cerberus shows us how difficult it is to drag what we don't yet know about ourselves into the daylight. There's nothing peaceful about engaging with shadow figures, fighting the grip of a complex, or working through inner conflict, trauma, grief, illness, or loss. It's like encountering a rabid dog, and it takes all our strength to stay present with it, not to mention control or subdue it.

A woman was shamed as a child. Whenever she expressed her emotions, she was made to feel somehow at fault. Laughter and tears, excitement and disappointment were all squashed and ignored, and in time she learned to dissociate from her emotions. The child's joy and curiosity were blocked off by a protective shield, and she became a stoic and distant shadow of herself. Over time, the shield calcified, and although designed to protect her, started limiting her life. By the time she was in her thirties, her friends called her an "ice queen" – removed and distant. In therapy, she began to speak about and attend to her wounds, returning that broken and afraid child to life. Every step back up the rocky slope felt like dragging lead, pulling Cerberus to the surface.

Hercules and Theseus

While in the underworld, Hercules frees the Troezen hero Theseus from punishment inflicted by Hades. Theseus and his friend Pirithous had journeyed into the abyss to kidnap Persephone and make her Theseus' bride. Upon reaching the throne of darkness, the companions explained their intention to Hades. Full of self-importance, they expected him to forfeit his wife. Hades invited them to take a seat and called for refreshments. But upon sitting down, Theseus and Pirithous were bound to their chairs by serpents, chains, and their own flesh. In some accounts, it is said that they sat upon chairs of Lethe (the river of amnesia) and lost all recollection of who they were. Full of pride not long before, they found themselves stuck fast to the underworld.

Theseus' journey shows his hubris. His torment occurs because of his misplaced promise to follow Pirithous, a human and thus a personification of ego. He believed he was beyond the reach of the powers of the deep, descending to kidnap the queen of the lower world, a grave violation of the respect a mortal should show a god. Just because our ego desires something doesn't make it ours, nor is it necessarily in our best interests to claim it.

The unconscious rarely celebrates the ego's achievements. If we lead from ego, even our greatest successes are ephemeral. In the Persian fable "Solomon's Seal," a sultan asks King Solomon for a phrase that will always be true. Solomon responds, "This too shall pass," which has become a popular saying about life's impermanence, reminding us that dayworld longings hold little weight in the deep psyche.

Being chained and bound by Hades' chair is a powerful image of psychological bondage, a sensation that often parallels the activation of a *complex*, a collection of personal images, associations, and ideas clustered around an archetypal core. When a complex constellates, it creates intense emotion and sensation. We use words like "stuck," "trapped," "spellbound," "glued," "frozen," and "consumed" to describe what it feels like to be in the throes of a complex.

Imagine you're the driver of a bus filled with passengers, each sitting quietly in their seat. You pass something on the road that triggers a memory, desire, or thought in one of the passengers, and they begin to yell, get out of their seat, rush to the front of the bus, and grab the wheel. The bus is swerving down the road, out of control, and you're unable to stop the crazed passenger. This image gives a sense of why we say complexes "have" us in their grip – that they behave like autonomous beings.

Most complexes are unconscious, and they burst into consciousness to wreak havoc.[14] In the grip of a complex, it feels as if you're trapped behind an invisible pane of glass – wishing you could stop acting a certain way and regain control. Often you can't, because, like Theseus, you're bound to an unconscious constellation of associations. It's like sitting on the chair of Lethe, forgetting who you are, shackled to the thoughts and emotions of the complex.

Complexes feed on their own stories, warping reality to align with the internal narrative. Someone's genuine apology feels like an attack, agreement feels like discord, support feels like rejection. The interpretation of what is going on changes to fit the inner story. Old memories, behaviors, and ideas, thought to have been resolved and put to rest, raise their heads once more and sniff the air, enlivened and back in control.

Take, for example, an inferiority complex in which one struggles with feelings of inadequacy. The individual needs constant validation, and it's never enough. The internal invalidator outmaneuvers any praise or validation from the outside, so external attempts to show us our strengths are, at best, respites. Complexes maintain control by mining for their favorite ingredient in the bag of trail mix. They don't even register what else is there. People who have been degraded or treated as insignificant, such as prisoners, neglected children, unseen partners, or those shunned at work, often suffer from some kind of an inferiority complex. The individual is chained to an inner narrative that tells them they are fundamentally valueless.

When life darkens, it's easy to get stuck in a time machine. The underworld can be sticky. Time stops, and over and over we relive the details of the day we were thrown into darkness, watching the horror movie repeatedly. The present moment rests on the surface, and we're stuck underground remembering life 5, 10, or 20 years ago. We might still be standing at our loved one's death bed, frozen on the battlefield, or hearing bad news. We might be stuck at an accident or in a childhood fight still waiting for the next blow to come. Replaying the past may be more comfortable, even if it was terrible, than choosing to be present in a world where the unknown seems even more terrifying. Stuck in the underworld, we refuse life. To be chained to the acuteness of darkness is to get swept up in the undertow of the past – as if we too are sitting on the chairs of Lethe, forgetting that life continues on.

While Theseus sits bound in darkness unable to save himself, Hercules storms past on his way to capture Cerberus and frees him. It's easy to get trapped by unconscious energies and regress into old patterns. Shadow material and complexes exert powerful lures over our sense of agency. Breaking unconscious patterns that shape our personalities and understanding of the world can require Herculean strength. When we feel helpless and overwhelmed, the willful determination of Hercules serves a critical purpose: it holds the sky up.

Breaking the patterns of past traumas (rerouting neural pathways) takes tremendous effort. So much of our lives is cyclical – days and seasons, death and rebirth, stars and planets. Our minds echo these rotations, carving deep loops that are nearly impossible to resist. It can take Herculean effort to disrupt old patterns, complexes, behaviors, and shadow energy. To convince yourself you are enough when you've always felt flawed. To force yourself into social situations when you've always felt you have nothing to say. To find the balance between work and home when you've always struggled to support your family. To take risks when you've always preferred predictability. By breaking these automatic cycles, we create space for new choices and perspectives to enter. Making the conscious decision to live, not just be alive, after the pain and confusion that darkness heralds can be a feat of Herculean strength.

Overcoming Darkness

The Herculean hero gives it all they've got to encounter and contain the contents of the unconscious. Herculean *metis* (wisdom, skill, craft) is of the fight, resistance embodied. Hercules is said to have "struggled hard and he did many fantastic things, really extraordinary tasks! Now on the other hand he lives on the beautiful top of snowy Olympos."[15] In death, Hercules appealed to the gods for reprieve, reasoning that he deserved relief because he "faced unflinching, these tripled-bodied monsters."[16] Remembering his strength and great deeds, the gods took pity on him and made him immortal.

Some things in life are worth fighting for. Struggling against the grip of a confining complex, wrestling anxiety, or facing off the shadow can lead to greater freedom. Some aspects of ourselves need to be battled, separated from, and overcome. If we see Hercules only as a destructive action figure, we'll miss his courage to charge toward the dark crevasses of life, his bravery to enter the unknown, and his strength to meet the challenges of overcoming what no longer serves. His energy represents the willpower and self-developing instinct of the ego. The fragile flame of progress must be protected at all costs. Old patterns, regressive longings, and instinctual desires threaten to extinguish this delicate spark. Sometimes Herculean force is needed to fight for conscious selfhood.

The darkness of mere being can become habituated. The Herculean hero represents the ability to face terrifying moments with force when the personal "I" is threatened. Bringing light into darkness, overcoming the underworld's powers, Hercules symbolizes the victory of ego-consciousness over the unconscious – the light separated from the dark, *sol invictus* – rebirth as the victorious sun.[17] We don't want the literal death of the ego, that's psychotic. We want to develop flexibility and consciousness, and attaining that goal sometimes takes Herculean effort.

Hercules personifies the archetypal motif of slaying the dragon – destroying an evil that guards a long-forgotten treasure. Slaying the dragon, or any underworld power, parallels fighting the unconscious when it has you in its grips. To overcome attachment issues, convincing yourself that people aren't going to leave you, requires Herculean focus. If you find validation only in others, generating self-acceptance requires Herculean determination. If you seek healing from addiction, discovering what actually needs nurturance requires Herculean tenacity.

The inner world is not an easy place to stand. Recognizing and facing the unlived and uncivilized aspects of ourselves is exceedingly difficult. When I first began analytical work, I dreamed that I entered an ancient building that was on fire, and dancing around the flames were grotesque and demonic creatures. I felt that these figures represented the shadowy energies of the deep psyche, the monsters who dwelled in an arcane and forgotten place of my unconscious. Repeatedly exposing yourself to these kinds of powerful shapeshifting energies requires the contained and determined energy we see in Hercules.

Moving beyond anxiety and sharing your voice in a group can be an act of bravery. Surviving trauma, illness, divorce, or a sense of failure requires strength. Even admitting you need help can be an act of Herculean empowerment. As anyone who has been to the depths and then returned to the light will tell you, there are moments in life when we are confronted by obstacles, and that meeting them with a warlike, Herculean stance is an arrow worth having in our quiver.

Destroying the Threshold

"One had better not challenge the watcher of the established bounds," Campbell warned, for it "is only by advancing beyond those bounds, provoking the destructive other aspects of the same power, that the individual passes ... into a new zone of experience." *Crossing the threshold* is a stage in life in which the mystery of transfiguration begins – "a rite, or moment, of spiritual passage, which, when complete, amounts to a dying and a birth."[18] When we outgrow a familiar horizon – a habit, an emotional pattern, values that no longer fit – we know it's time for crossing the next threshold. When something we've relied on is ready to let go of us, we need to be fully present. Like a baby tooth, it might just fall away. But it might take standing steady in the midst of an aftershock.

Hercules journeys to Hades to take Cerberus, who safeguards the threshold into the abyss. By challenging the threshold guardian, he willfully acts out the drive to prevent personal change, which is possible only by crossing the threshold into the lower world. Hercules represents the hero who is *unaffected by the journey*. It's as if his famous lion's skin protects him from external threats and also internal development.[19]

As we fall into darkness, we have to die to the old ways of being and change our attitude first and then our outer life accordingly. Even if we have all the insight and treasures of the depth, if we don't embody them, our efforts have been in vain. To free ourselves from life-denying behaviors, we have to wrestle our demons, make them conscious, *and* relate to them.

After dragging Cerberus to the surface, Hercules returns the demon to the underworld, reminding us that Hercules isn't a permanent denizen of Hades, nor does he desire to keep what he takes from the depths. The Herculean hero may battle a complex or face shadow material with awe-inspiring courage, but he or she does not build a long-term relationship with it, doesn't integrate the experience in a lasting way, and so in time the demons return.

Hercules was famed for his many battles. Since he never integrates the lessons of his labors, he is tasked with constantly fighting the monsters of the world. We do not want to spend a lifetime battling the same types of beasts. If we don't work to learn from what we find in the depths, it won't matter what monsters we drag up – we remain unchanged. When the world is erupts, we long for a return to stability. Hercules reminds us to not mistake the return of stability with the return of the old. If we try to bring ourselves back to who we, and others, remember we risk not recognizing how we've changed. Personal growth requires living *in relationship with* Cerberus – integrating our shadows, instincts, and complexes.

In the period following my brother's accident, I learned through adversity that a long and happy life is by no means promised us. No one can foresee the coming of illness, tragedy, or death. By living so intimately with the possibility of my brother dying, I came to see the value of living my own life more intentionally, aware of its impermanence. Now when I feel myself moving too fast or not appreciating my life, I think: "One day I'm going to die, and that day could be today." This simple practice helps me focus on what's really important to me – my husband, family, dog, career, health, time in nature, and friendships. I don't always get it right. It was more vivid when my brother was holding on by a thread or during other moments of death I have experienced. Time has diminished the intensity of the lesson; it's all too easy to let even hard-earned wisdom slip back beneath the surface. I therefore consciously practice allowing darkness to have an ongoing and meaningful place in my life, and in so doing, I'm building a relationship with Cerberus.

Here we begin to see the paradox of Hercules. Rescuing ourselves from darkness by getting involved in life in a forceful, protective, and active way prevents the wisdom of the depths from affecting us. Our pain calcifies, our fear freezes, and we collapse upon ourselves, unable to stand tall and take the next steps forward. Still, Hercules does personify the struggle to *face darkness willingly* and the strength of character and determination to undergo and be impacted by whatever hardship we're faced with.

It all belongs, but it has to be integrated. Neglecting to integrate both dark and light experiences prevents growth and destroys the passageway between our old and new selves. Hercules is not just about the repression of darkness, although that is a part of his character. He is also an image of the conquering and progressive energy that mobilizes individual willpower, an energy that is required for growth and change. Hercules is more dynamic than we give him credit for. It takes awesome strength to stand in your suffering, to let darkness work you.

Hercules focuses all his energy on controlling and combating the unknown. There are moments in life when Hercules' energy is exactly what we need – when power, confidence, extraverted action, and goal orientation help us endure extreme challenges. Herculean journeying in pursuit of our inner treasures includes the same traits – action, courage, and willpower – that are the defining characteristics of Western consciousness. We mustn't underestimate the strength it takes to face the unknown.

Welsh poet Dylan Thomas wrote, "Do not go gentle into that good night. … Rage, rage against the dying of the light."[20] This is a Herculean image, to *rage* against the dying of consciousness, against inner monsters, against the boundary between old and new. Hercules, who pummels, wrestles, or slices whatever he wants to overcome, represents an important aspect of the hero archetype. There are others.

Reflections

Hercules is about willful strength and victory. He slices life into small pieces and attacks what threatens him with force and forward focus. Sword in hand, conquering, and striving for perfection, Hercules pertains to the monster-slayer within all of us.

Reflect on how Herculean qualities may be present within your experience in:

- Bringing intention to your attitudes and behaviors to help prepare you.
- Removing what holds you back so you can present for what lies ahead.
- Facing your hardship with a goal-oriented mindset.
- Simplifying things so you can fix them – facing darkness like it's a mechanical issue.
- Feeling the desire to control and beat the unknown into submission. Muscling your way through barriers using determination, bravery, resistance, and surviving through sheer will.
- Facing suffering combatively. This could be positively challenging yourself or negatively limiting yourself by always reacting with a sword.
- Boldly facing darkness and being rewarded for your fortitude.
- The strength needed to break old dynamics.
- Refusing to be affected or learn from your encounters with darkness and thus remaining unchanged.

CHAPTER 5

ORPHEUS

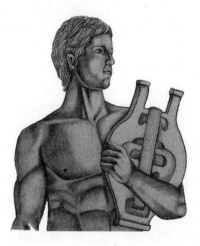

While wandering in a meadow, Eurydice, the beautiful bride of the Thracian poet Orpheus, was bitten by a snake and fell to the ground lifeless.[1] Orpheus mourned her loss so profoundly that he decided to descend into the underworld to return her to life.

Orphic heroism is completely different from Herculean heroism. Orpheus' strength does not come from warlike exploits but from love, song, grieving, and persuasion. While Hercules was victorious in his task, Orpheus failed to retrieve his bride. He entered the gate of Taenarus and when he reached the throne of Hades and Persephone, he implored them to allow him to speak his truth. He confessed that he had hoped to endure the grief of Eurydice's loss, but was unable to do so. His love and longing were too much for him. Prostrating before them, he convinced Hades to consider Eurydice merely "on loan" to him: "If the fates refuse [Eurydice] a reprieve, I have made up my mind that I do not wish to return either. You may exult in my death as well as hers."[2] Struck by his conviction, the rulers of darkness called Eurydice.

They agreed on the condition that Orpheus lead Eurydice to the surface without looking back at her. Hermes was their guide. When the surface was near, Orpheus began to worry that Eurydice hadn't followed him, and he looked back. Because of that, Hermes was forced to return Eurydice to the depths. Consumed by sorrow, Orpheus abandoned civilization and retreated to the secluded forest to play his lyre.

Music

Instead of bludgeon and muscle, Orpheus was armed with a lyre and his musical gifts. In the tombs of the deep, he wove an enchanted song that confessed his unbearable need for his wife. He sang of a consuming love, a grief that ate away at his heart. He was not combative or aggressive but vulnerable, creative, and expressive.

Orpheus' song was a powerful weapon. With it he subdued Charon and Cerberus, brought tears to the Erinyes' eyes (the Furies, female goddesses of judgment and vengeance), and caused those condemned to eternal suffering – Tantalus, Ixion, Tityus, and the daughters of Danaus – to pause and forget their torments. Ovid wrote that as he sang, "the bloodless ghosts were in tears" and "weapons would have been rendered harmless by the charm of Orpheus' songs."[3] Orpheus didn't attack the powers of the deep but *broke their hearts open*. He faced the same instinctive, destructive, and chaotic forces of darkness that Hercules did, but he met them with music and longing.

On a cold winter's night, my brother called to tell me that a friend of ours had died in a skiing accident. After I got off the phone, I found myself sitting at my piano for hours, playing "The Ludlows," composed by James Horner, while the haunting melody echoed the sound of my tears, the loss of a bright life, and a new emptiness in my world. It was a ballad for my soul and the unlived life taken so prematurely. In moments like these, when the heart is heavy and creative expression arises, the essence of Orpheus is there.

It takes heroism to lead with the heart, to speak the truth of your soul, your wounds, your fears. It takes heroism to travel deep within oneself and face the greater energies of life, begging them for renewed life and energy.

Orpheus' success in persuading Hades and Persephone to release Eurydice highlights the power of sincerity and self-expression in the face of darkness – the pathos of vulnerability. We can be heartfelt and authentic through drawing, painting, singing, dancing, writing, sculpture, and playing music, to name a few. These tools help us express and thus know our own experience. Paintings, songs, poems, and movement are ways of coming to know who we are and what we are feeling so deeply.

"When I was really depressed," a woman shared with me, "I could only paint in reds and blacks. I didn't realize how sad I was till I looked at my art." A man told me he built a table after his grandfather died. He sanded the wood, polished its smooth surface. Without his grandfather, who had always been there for him, he felt a void around him. And so he crafted a table – a place to nourish himself, to come together with those he loves, to celebrate milestones, and to share food and thus life.

Many people release pain, complexity, imbalances, and darkness through cathartic artistic expression. Suffering and creativity go hand in hand. Some of the greatest artists in history led agonizing lives. Jackson Pollock lived a reclusive and volatile life in which he struggled with alcoholism; Virginia Woolf endured the deaths of close family members while struggling with her own psychic breakdowns; Anne Frank channeled her trauma and fear into her diary; and in the Czech work camp Terezin, Rafael Schächter composed and conducted an adult chorus of over a hundred Jews who sang of their misery.

In 1913, Jung separated from his mentor, Freud, after reaching a fundamental disagreement about the structure of the psyche. After the break, he suffered a self-declared mental collapse that lasted through World War I. It was not just a breakdown. The experience turned out to be a highly inventive period of self-reflection and discovery. He would later say that his psychology originated from this "creative illness." During that time, Jung experienced episodes in which he vividly encountered fantasies of the unconscious. He named the record of his dialogues, writing, and art *The Red Book: Liber Novus*. Unpublished in his lifetime, the book is now considered his magnum opus and an important work of analytical psychology. There are Orphic elements to *The Red Book,* because it communicates inner turmoil through conversations, prose, and vivid illustrations of a vibrant, alluring, and terrifying inner landscape. It's a creative expression of navigating the underworld.

My husband is a reflective and introverted man. When his mother was diagnosed with cancer, his fear and helplessness were difficult for him to process and express verbally. Throughout his life he's digested inner turmoil through music, whether by himself, in a band, or just listening to favorite musicians. "It has always been easier," he shared, "to communicate with myself and others through music than talking. Music offers solace and catharsis. I can't express in words what I can in song and sound." In the pain of his mother's illness, he turned toward song and melody to channel and relate to the many dark feelings.

Orphic expression isn't limited to music. It's about creative release and using our artistic instincts to process and understand suffering. When my brother was in the hospital, I often sat by his bed and imagined him as a great bear hibernating in a winter cave. Wise from his ancestors and full of nature's patience, he slept. "Rest now," I would say, "just as the forest sleeps under its blanket of snow. Nature is dreaming, just as you are." And I would pour this message – half-image, half-song – into his cells, reminding him that even the greatest of bears hibernate to rest, renew, and be born again in the spring. I would use this image to assure him, and me, that it was okay to sleep but soon he would need to wake up. Spring would come, fresh air would return, dark berries would ripen, and sunlit mornings would sparkle. "Soon," I'd say, "the forest of life will call for you."

This soothing practice led me to write and illustrate a children's book about the lessons learned by Bunny as she planned a party to celebrate the springtime return of her best friend, Bear. I channeled my love, hope, and despair into this story, allowing the sweet images to comfort me. This is an Orphic way of navigating the underworld – less aggressive and more reflective, using imagination and creativity to connect with, process, and express the darkness we encounter.

Unity

Orpheus' song has power in the realms of the living and the dead. In the myth, mortals, shades, gods, animals, and trees alike listen to his music as one. "We are told concerning Orpheus," classicist Karl Kerényi explained, "that the endless flocks of birds flew about over his head as he sang, and the fish leaped high from the dark-blue sea to meet him, we know that this was the effect of his song."[4] All beings, regardless of their different natures, are enchanted by his music. His ballad dissolves divisions, and the world becomes one. Our experiences of self, nature, darkness, and grief are conjoined.

The world of Orpheus is interconnected. Darkness is woven into light, passion into suffering, love into creativity. In this narrative web, everything belongs – suffering and joy, anger and gratitude, relief and pain, death and birth. Life can be easier to face when simplified and boxed into categories. Holding the interlaced matrix of life is overwhelming. But unlike Hercules, Orpheus doesn't divide the world into parts. His is the heroism of facing the interbeing of life. While the sword cuts in two, the lyre weaves together.

The nexus of darkness becomes a tangle of emotions, ideas, and actions. Take for example, the COVID-19 pandemic. By March 2020, the whole world was experiencing a rise in fear and isolation, a descent into darkness, confusion, insecurity, shortages, grief and loss, and constraints on independence and connection. Domestic violence skyrocketed, unemployment surged, political divisions increased, protests increased – people struggled to pay the rent and feed their families. Businesses closed as the underworld rose to the surface on a global scale. The consequences were profoundly interconnected and complex; it's impossible to process and understand the butterfly effect of the situation – intricacy gives rise to overwhelm.

There's a difference between treating the fragments of life as separate, as Hercules did, and as interconnected, as Orpheus did. We have to hold the interconnectedness of trauma and challenges to move beyond them. We may approach our journeys step by step, but to create lasting change we need a broader and unified understanding of our destination. We have to give ourselves permission to feel contradictory emotions and eventually bring the fragmented pieces of ourselves into relation with one another so we can reclaim our wholeness.

Prayer

The Papal Audience held in Saint Peter's Square on Sundays has 80,000 attendees, on average, and thousands more make the pilgrimage to Rome every day hoping the Pope will hear their prayers. Standing before the throne of Hades, Orpheus prayed for Eurydice's resurrection, a *petitionary prayer*, a request from the divine.

The desire to pray in hardship is an archetypal response to the human relationship with the divine. There is a universal need, constellated by suffering and uncertainty, for support from a higher power. "Those last days in our race with death," remembered Victor Frankl, "the words of our prayer asking for peace, were as fervent as any ever uttered by the human voice."[5] People pray to the divine for many reasons – praise, thanks, apologies, forgiveness, relief, guidance, and help.

Everyone has stories, whether or not they align with a specific faith, of asking for support from something or someone beyond themselves. When my brother was in the hospital, a family friend went to the banks of the Mississippi and drove poles into the hard sand, attaching a prayer flag to each pole. Dancing in the breeze, their blessings traveled across rivers and mountains like clouds in an empty sky, finding their way into my brother's hospital room.

I don't identify as a religious person but every night I slept in my brother's hospital room, I would repeat the same silent prayer: "Please, let him stay." At night, when everything was still and my hopelessness unbearable, I prayed to a God I didn't believe in. "May it be a light to you in dark places," Lady Galadriel tells Frodo in *Lord of the Rings*, "when all other lights go out."

All over the world people light candles to honor the sacred, prayers fill synagogues, chanting reverberates on stained glass, and five times a day the sound of the adhan fills rooftops, calling Muslims to prayer. Does it matter to which divinity or sacred figure we pray – Yahweh, the prophet Muhammad, Allah, Buddha, Yama (the Tibetan god of death), religious leaders such as the Pope or Dalai Lama, the spirits of nature, or a dream image? A Jungian answer to this question would be *no*, it only matters *that we pray*. Romans 8:26 says, "The Spirit helps us in our weakness.

For we do not know what to pray for as we ought, but the Spirit himself intercedes for us with groanings too deep for words."

The hero, Campbell tells us, is one of "self-achieved submission."[6] To rest in your insignificance, to feel the numinosity of the divine, to surrender to what you cannot control, to beseech the mysterious powers of the world for guidance, support, and reprieve is heroic. It requires a profound act of courage to surrender.

What matters is that we put our faith and hope in the guidance of a force larger than ourselves. To grow, we sometimes have to feel something beyond ourselves. Without a connection to the divine, we alone are responsible for enduring and understanding our suffering, a weight that sits heavy in the soul.

Journeying for Love

Orpheus understood Eurydice's untimely death to be a grave mistake, so he journeyed to Hades to correct this blunder of fate. The ancient poets tell us that Eurydice was restored to him because he showed *extraordinary proof of love*. Orphic love is both shamanic, journeying for the redemption of another, and self-serving, journeying to requite his own desires. When we cross the boundary between the known and the unknown, the upper and the lower realms for love of our self, another, cultural traditions, values, or religious beliefs, we are enacting Orphic heroism.

People do astonishing things for those they love and what they believe. Often our desire to be the best we can for ourselves, our partners, communities, families, and children is inspired by a mysterious depth of love. Loving and being loved is an overarching human experience that can impel us into unimaginable territory.

A friend told me she never understood love until she had children. Of course, she loved her parents, her friends, and her husband. "There are different types of love," she shared. "What I feel with my kids is soul-stretching love, nightmare love, give anything and do anything love." She laughed. "It feels like insanity." Love is perhaps something we can't ever fully grasp, but that we need nonetheless. We love our children, parents, traditions, and hopefully ourselves, our bodies, and our livelihoods.

Orphic love is shamanic because Orpheus crosses between realms to retrieve the lost pieces of a soul. Through fasting, meditation, substances, or dancing, the shaman goes into an altered state to perceive the spirit world and channel its transcendental energies into this world. It's not a journey for personal advantage, but for the well-being of others. The shaman takes the soul of another into the great abyss, ushering them past the threshold into the beyond.

We have all stood in dark places for another, endured hardship, loneliness, sacrifices, and fear so someone has a chance to heal and survive. Soldiers are awarded medals of honor – the Purple Heart, Wound Stripe, and Croix de Guerre – for heroism and achievement under fire. Rushing across death fields to save a friend, dragging their wounded brothers to safety – acts of military distinction born out of the courage of the heart.

I stood in the underworld because my brother needed me to be there, to be present with his suffering. On his first night in the hospital, I slept on the floor of his room, my mother on the coach, his girlfriend by my side. All night the nurses flew in and out of the room, trying to stabilize his seizing body and his wounded brain. We were glued there because what we loved most was in that room.

I walk with my clients into the underworld because they need someone to witness and be with them during their journeys. We become caregivers when we make changes in our lives to support the well-being of a family member or friend. As we see someone we love descend into darkness, the desire to protect, support, help, and even rescue is often sparked. Our love makes being in the underworld not only meaningful, but important.

Orpheus did not journey just for the sake of Eurydice's soul. He journeyed because of his *great longing*. His intention thus had a self-focus, the desire to return to his old life and the joy his bride had brought him. There's always an element of self-serving in inner work. Our desire to expand and deepen ourselves is perhaps the most important commitment we can make. At some point, if we desire to live more consciously and more authentically, we will have to face darkness *for our own betterment*.

How can we love others if we don't love ourselves? Self-love begins by nurturing our souls and having compassion for ourselves – feeding ourselves with the things that bring us joy, accomplishment, passion, and energy. Self-nurturance gives us a greater capacity to care for the ones we love. It's not easy to see our own value and release the conditions we place on our love for ourselves and each other. Our society and our families lean toward conditional love – we are expected to show up in a certain way to get the reward of being loved. Unconditional love for ourselves and others is rare.

People fear self-focus, associating it with narcissism (pathological self-absorption) and feel guilty about being selfish if they prioritize themselves too much. If this belief engenders negative feelings, you may miss the expansive consequences of focusing on yourself. Self-love is different from inflated self-worship. To repress the former for fear of the latter limits our ability to face our inner world and stay present with the challenging work of becoming self-aware. If you are not willing to journey within for yourself, you may never know your deepest potential.

The Song of Solomon says, "Set me as a seal upon thine heart, as a seal upon thine arm: for love is strong as death … the coals therefore are coals of fire, which hath a most vehement flame. Many waters cannot quench love, neither can the floods drown it."[7] The human capacity to endure suffering because of love is a wonder of life. In Victor Frankl's view, love allows us to endure suffering honorably. He recalled spending hours, days, and months reflecting on the image of his beloved wife, a practice that gave him solace, hope, and the will to live. Whether we journey to the underworld for love of another, for ourselves, or a combination of the two, love resides in a mysterious and powerful corner of the human soul – *et lux in tenebris lucet*, the light that shines in the darkness.

Nothing but Yielding Air

As Orpheus returned to the surface, he looked back at Eurydice. With his glance, Eurydice's right hand touched his shoulder in loving farewell while her left hand took Hermes'. Straining to grasp her, Orpheus touched "nothing but yielding air."[8]

The Orphic ascent tells us that our choices as we integrate an underworld experience make all the difference. Hades told Orpheus not to look back or the gift of her return would be lost. All Orpheus had to do was trust that the powers of the abyss had been swayed by his musical plea. Orpheus needed to trust his deep self and his music is a symbol of this intrinsic selfhood. Yet at a critical moment he was unable to rely on his true Self, and he looked back. The great lesson of Orphic journeying is to *trust in our innate* sense of who we are. Here we see the consequence of not doing so.

"So much fluff was paired away," my brother said. "I was skeletonized and left with what characterizes me most deeply. It was never easy or natural to identify those things, especially when I was exhausted and overwhelmed, but my TBI experience highlighted parts of me, like my caring, compassion, and the passion to make good of what happens to me. I had to trust these deeper levels of myself."

The word "weird" comes from the Latin *wyrd*, meaning "personal destiny." The Greeks told the story of the three sisters of fate, the Moirai or *Wyrd* sisters. The sisters, Clotho, Lahkesis, and Atropos, were responsible for sewing each individual's destiny into his or her soul. Whatever in you is *wyrd* – unique to you – is your soul's unique gift. Mozart's *wyrd* was being a musical prodigy, a racehorse's *wyrd* is running like the wind, and Bobby Fischer's was to become the youngest chess grandmaster.

Some people possess the gift of caring for others; others are gifted with clear and honest communication. Some of us have a baked-in capacity to bring humor to hardship, to act steady in times of volatility, to be patient, or to act tenaciously. When you find yourself in a life-stopping darkness, when you hear the old tug of negative inner stories or begin any kind of self-exploration, relying on what is authentically *you* is an act of heroism.

In the science-fiction novel *Dune*, author Frank Herbert calls the ability to amplify or empower oneself "weirding." What is unique to us empowers us. One way to endure life's darkest moments is to call upon the power that comes from what makes us "weird," distinctly ourselves. Facing darkness with knowledge of our own strengths and capacities provides strong footing.

Owning our gifts and learning from our failures are important steps in integrating unconscious energy and dark moments. If we succeed in channeling the turmoil into new ideas, traits, and behaviors, we grow more and more whole.

Although Orpheus relied on his musical gifts, in the end he did not trust that his song was enough. When aspects of our identity are new (to us) and thus seem foreign and unconvincing, old patterns return. It's easy for the emerging personality to slip back underground.

After Orpheus returned empty-handed, he was consumed by grief. Instead of striving to move forward, he retreated, preferring the company of nature and animals. We have to trust the parts of ourselves we discover during the journey, traits that may seem insubstantial and unfamiliar – like holding the hand of a shade – but if we let them slip away, back into unconsciousness, we risk retreating from being ourselves.

Letting Go

Orpheus journeyed to the underworld to restore the past – to relieve his own pain and reclaim his identity, rather than recognizing Eurydice as more than just his beloved wife. He was unable to love her in her own right, whatever form she took.

Relationships get into trouble when one person tries to change and the other tries to stop them. One of the hardest things to do is let your partner's destiny unfurl. It's easier to demand that they conform to what we want: "Why can't you be more expressive," "not procrastinate so much," "not lose direction"? We want to expand the people we love, rescue them from "negative" habits, and help them see hidden parts of themselves, or the hidden parts of ourselves projected onto them. There's a line between encouraging what's incipient in another and trying to reconstruct them. Love requests of us an openness to the best and the worst in others, letting their journeys be their own.

Many people project their hopes, potential, and unlived lives onto another, putting value (positive and negative) on their partners rather than focusing on their own journeys. We burden them with our fantasies, shadows, and expectations, at the expense of our own development. Orpheus projected his ability to live a happy life onto Eurydice, and he journeyed to Hades to reclaim what she awoke in him.

We always project our shadows onto others. It's the way human development works. When we do, our partners relieve us of the burden of having to become complete, as they carry these undeveloped and unlived parts of ourselves "for us." By projecting our shadows onto them, we wrap our partners in the fantasy and responsibility of being our life-source – giving them the power to uplift or destroy our lives. To create healthy and lasting relationships, we must make the effort to reclaim our shadows or we weigh our loved ones down with godlike expectations that are impossible for them to meet.

It took me a long time to understand that by trying to rescue my first boyfriend I was really rescuing myself. He was abusive and an alcoholic, and he always chose self-destruction over me. No matter what I did, I was never more alluring or valuable than whiskey, and so I blamed him for making me feel worthless. It took years of analysis for me to accept that I drew this broken man into my life to shine light on the part of me that already felt valueless. The healing question wasn't what was wrong with him, but what I was trying to save in myself by saving him. He was charming and magnetic, people were drawn to him like moths to a flame. He mirrored the part of myself that others turn toward, and by loving him I magnified those qualities in myself.

In extreme situations, reliance on another for validation and happiness breeds codependency and enmeshment. We can become so disconnected from ourselves and so merged with another that we lose the ability to tell where we stop and the other begins. Their life becomes our own, a lifeline to feeling alive and connected. If we define ourselves through others, we are unable to touch our own inner reality.

Orpheus paid a high price for not accepting Eurydice's independence. What he failed to understand was that the part of himself that had a life with Eurydice was gone. Instead of facing this harsh reality, he descended to correct the "mistakes" made by the natural order of life.

We can't control someone else in life or in death. Nor can we expect them to be responsible for our creativity, potential, or life force. All we can do is be responsible for how we show up in our own lives. No one else can rescue, reverse our fate, or live our lives for us. In every dark crevasse of the underworld there is the potential to be confronted with fate, with the chance of evolving through our own suffering. As the old saying reminds us, "You can lead a horse to water, but you can't make him drink." You can support, mentor, and lead someone by example, but *that person is responsible for their own life*.

Eurydice transcended her attachment to life. In his poem "Orpheus, Eurydice, Hermes," Rainer Maria Rilke describes Eurydice as transformed by darkness and filled with a depth she did not previously have. In death, Eurydice individuated. She no longer *belonged* to her husband, but to the underworld. Blinded by his own agenda, Orpheus was unable to see her transformation.

I asked a man who tends to seek relationships where he protects his partner if he'd ever had an experience where he couldn't protect someone – or perhaps shouldn't? He nodded. "I have a tragic flaw of caring too much about people, which means to take care of their feelings and tell them what they want to hear, rather than being honest. It weaves an ugly nest of lies and duplicity. When I try and prevent them from feeling bad," he continued, "I'm not sure who I'm really taking care of. Intent and consequence don't always align. Even if my intentions are good, the consequences are out of my hands. Perhaps it's just a matter of recognizing that consequences can be different from intentions."

Loving someone in their own right means letting another's life happen to them, not protecting them from the circumstances of their lives, even when they are painful. In the words of Kahlil Gibran:

> Love one another but make not a bond of love: let it rather be a moving sea between the shores of your souls … Give your hearts, but not into each other's keeping. For only the hand of Life can contain your

hearts. And stand together yet not too near together:
For the pillars of the temple stand apart, And the oak
tree and the cypress grow not in each other's shadow.[9]

In the journal I kept during my brother's recovery, I made a
list of guidelines for how I wanted to interact with him while
he was waking from his coma: my brother is not broken, just
wounded, he needs respect; repeat myself with patience, as if I
know nothing; slow my energy down; make eye contact to let
him know I understand that he is still there; ask him questions
with specific answers so he can hunt for his words; break every
action into smaller steps; believe he can relearn and celebrate
his successes; focus on what he does, not on what he doesn't
do; and finally, this is about Ben, *not me*.

It may feel more secure to impose our beliefs rather than
let others make their own choices. To surrender to our
helplessness, to not feel seen, heard, or loved, are challenging
parts of underworld work. It takes a hero to let another person
follow their own path, even when we want to protect them.

It can take superhuman strength and self-transcendence
to give space to another's life journey. This difficult act can
save a bond or it can break a heart. Love rests in a world of
togetherness and separateness. For a relationship to succeed,
neither person can be robbed of their freedom to develop
their own independence. We can live side by side, closely and
intimately, while allowing enough distance to see the other for
their unique wholeness. If we abandon ourselves to rescue
another, we both disappear, as Eurydice did.

Life is full of moments when we pause and then choose not
to act, because we realize our agenda is not in the best interest
of others. This boundary is elemental to any therapeutic
work: when do you say or not say something, when is certain
information appropriate, and how do you know if you are the
best conduit for that information? Holding back may be harder

than acting out our impulse. Orpheus didn't hold back – there was no restraint or reflection. After journeying to the farthest realm to reclaim his bride, he panicked and she vanished.

Orpheus' choice to repossess Eurydice was a betrayal of the natural order, as if the rules of the universe didn't apply to him. If he loved Eurydice, she couldn't die. I sat in my brother's hospital room for days without quality sleep or food, determined, by the very impossibility of the task, *to stop his death*. When a friend passed away earlier in my life, I refused to believe it – not engaging with the grief because it simply didn't seem possible. These are Orphic moments, *ignoring the realities before us*.

The human mind draws on the past to navigate the present. As former Buddhist monk Cuong Lu explained:

> If you have a beautiful photo you want to archive, you can scan it and save it on your computer or you can print a copy. Consciousness functions the same way. It photocopies experiences, and then the next time you encounter something similar, it shows you the copy and you think your earlier experience is happening again. But it's a copy, not the original. Reality has changed – *it's always changing* – and we're living in a photocopy.[10]

"In robbing the present of its reality," Victor Frankl reflected, there lies a "certain danger. It became easy to overlook the opportunities to make something positive of camp life, opportunities which really did exist."[11] Frankl warned that, for those who closed their eyes to life before them, choosing instead to live in the past, life became meaningless. They forgot to take their inner strength and present moment difficulties seriously. A fantasy world replaced reality, protective and comforting but also alienating and eventually meaningless.

"Revisiting our past," explains psychotherapist Bruce Lloyd, "is a gateway to a new life only if we do not become stuck in our past and defined by it."[12] Remaining in the past is not recovery, we cannot change the events of life – the snake lying in the field is out of our control – but we can take control of how we repair our lives.

Eurydice's response contrasts starkly with Orpheus'. Although she came to the underworld unwillingly and he willingly, she consented to her death while he suffered the lot of one who resists destiny. The difference is in accepting or resisting reality. Novelist and philosopher Iris Murdoch wrote, "love is the extremely difficult realization that something other than oneself is real."[13] This is the wisdom Orpheus lacked. He saw Eurydice as a part of *his* life and *his* sense of self. He doesn't see *her* reality, *her* independence, *her* "otherness."

In darkness and the terrible process of the ascent, the plot lines of the life we'd envisioned are undone – the life that was and the future that will no longer be are destroyed. We're pummeled by a long, dark rain that drowns us in the impossibility of what was taken from us. There's wisdom in letting go of circumstances beyond our control. We cannot keep the past intact nor can we control fate. Jung believed Orpheus' story hinted at a reality "where one is united with everything that was dear to one and yet can't enjoy the happiness of reunion because it is all shadowy, unreal and devoid of life."[14] Life moves on; when we cling to what has passed, it can be devoid of life, a shade in the underworld.

For those who have felt the unique grief of losing a loved one, the mourning of the life lost is a delicate, painful, and essential process. Orpheus was unable to go through a full grieving process. Psychiatrist Elisabeth Kübler-Ross identified five stages of grief: denial, anger, bargaining, depression, and acceptance. She does not see these stages as bus stops on a linear timeline of grief, but as tools to help us frame and identify what we are feeling. Orpheus got stuck in denial, refusing to allow Eurydice her fate. He tried to resurrect the past, unable to accept the never-again-ness of death. After he lost her a second time, he chose to retreat from the world, perhaps intending to recover, but as the story tells us, he did not change. He was subjected to grief for the rest of his life.

It's tempting to hope for a life free of darkness. To wish a loved one hadn't died, that we hadn't made a certain consequential choice, or that the living nightmare we're in the midst of had never befallen us. Fantasies of white knighting and living in bygone eras may be relieving and hopeful, but they stall psychological growth. Too much regressive longing puts life on hold, freezing our potential to grow and participate in the changing currents of life. *No one escapes darkness.*

Orpheus' disregard for Eurydice's fate did not improve his life. In fact, it destroyed it. Grief took her place as his partner in life. Memories of what we once had or who we once were can provide reprieve in dark times, but there's a difference between taking the essence of a lost person or experience as a touchstone, and clinging to them. The myth of Orpheus challenges us to remember that the vestiges of lives past are not warm and animated, but cold, lifeless shades in the land of death.

Our only choice is to let go. After my mother-in-law passed away, I had a dream in which I was in my office and found a drawer full of her papers. I had a distinct sense I had to throw away the papers. This dream was about mourning; the mortal remains have to be let go of. It isn't the papers and details of life that leave an impact, but the essence of our loved ones. It's not about forgetting but about not holding on too tightly. Death can interfere with life, removing us from our potential and our path forward. Those we love gift us with lessons learned, attitudes we can adopt, and perhaps above all, feeling the preciousness and fragility of life. My mother-in-law was an extraordinary woman – loving beyond imagination, present in the lives of those she loved, positive and encouraging – the first person to tell you she believed in and was proud of you. She used to call me just to say she was thinking of me and wanted to hear my voice. If love is a magnet, she was it – pulling people together, encouraging them to see themselves as she did, always there to give the extra touch. It's important not to hold on to the wrong things. Her daily presence had to be let go of, but her essence remains in my heart.

We don't want to get stuck in the past, living more in relation to the shades of yesterday than to the life of today. Darkness entangles past, present, and future. Are you still at your loved one's deathbed? Are you still at the funeral or fighting in the kitchen? *Where and when are you?* It's easy to wander in past memories, some meaningful, others empty and regressive. To linger on the threshold between life and death is to be nowhere at all. To fuel ourselves too much with longing for the past is to remove ourselves from life.

Healing is an active process, time alone will not transform us. When in the underworld, each of us must decide whether or not we want to return to the surface and continue on living. Living is not the same thing as being alive. Orpheus retreated from the world, denying life on the grounds of its unfairness. His hair grew, his body needed food, and he fell asleep at night, all signs of life. But he wasn't *living*. The underworld perspective is about *being present for life*, no matter how painful the moment is.

We can gain new perspectives on traumas, failures, and pain, not be in the throes of complexes, and grow as individuals. But we cannot go back to where we stood before we found ourselves in darkness. Part in the past, part in the present, we end up *nowhere at all*. We have to let Eurydice slip back into Hades. What else can we do?

Dismembering Grief

After Eurydice returned to Hades, Orpheus was "completely stunned." Once more, he attempted to cross the River Styx, but this time he was blocked by Charon the ferryman. Consumed by his loss, he wandered "unkempt and neglected ... without tasting food: grief, anxiety and tears were his nourishment."[15]

I used to work with a college student whose brother died mysteriously during a drug trip. My client was frozen in time, plagued by questions of whether his death was by suicide or an accident. What was he thinking in his last moments? Uncertainty dissolved the barriers between worlds, and his brother pressed through the thin divide. Questions from the other side became a partner to his life, more real than the toast he ate in the morning and the sheets he slept upon at night (which reminded him of a burial shroud). His confusion turned to frustration, which became anger.

"When I was really suffering," my brother Ben told me, "it was impossible to see how any good might come from this. I was lonely and absorbed in my suffering. It limited my ability to engage with the opportunities that were in store." Ben was feeding the part of himself that was grieving, desolate, and angered by all the confusion, loss, and helplessness. In place of a vibrant young life, he nourished himself on the suffocating reality of his own pain.

Orpheus distracted himself from his loss by setting forth to correct fate's mistake. Many people act similarly, trying to divert their pain, choosing to avoid rather than engage with the darkness. They busy themselves, filling time and the void within, with overwork and mundane tasks.

Years after Eurydice's death, Orpheus remained so absorbed with his grief that one day while playing his lyre, he failed to notice the arrival of the Maenads, female followers of Dionysus, the god of ecstasy. The wild cadence of the Maenads' horns and tambourines drowned out his music and "the stones grew crimson with the blood of the poet, whose voice they did not hear."[16] Unmoved by and unable even to hear his sorrowful music, the Maenads tore him apart.

As devotees of Dionysus, the Maenads were worshipers of life force. In the forested glen, two responses to existence clashed. Orpheus' rejection of life was met by their unrelenting call to vitality, and he was dismembered.

The presence of Dionysus in this part of the myth tells us that underworlding, here in the form of grief, can be a wild beast – roaring, tearing, disconnecting. We've been torn from life and forced into an unmediated archetypal state, where psyche is most raw. When the organizing principles of life are gone and we feel intensely wild, the Dionysian experience is underway.

We don't often honor the need to create space for dis-sembling experiences. We don't let ourselves fall apart, and we don't have practices of re-coagulation, relearning, and accepting the "new normal." Too often we are Orpheus, descending to reverse suffering or retreating from life. Death, loss, illness, and change will inevitably visit us. The question is not how to avoid them, but what to do with the life we have.

The presence of Dionysus reminds us that in the process of grief and mourning, life leaves the world, but eventually it has to return. We have to answer the call back into life. To combat the desire to remain withdrawn, we turn to the god of life force who holds the ceaseless energy of emergence. Eventually, we answer phone calls, exercise, stop avoiding people, return to work, and begin to live again. Even in the darkest night of the soul, Dionysus has the capacity to bring us back to the living, to pull us out of the realm of the dead.

A young woman experienced the death of her best friend, followed by the death of her college roommate, and she was haunted by survivor's guilt. Every time she felt joy or connection, she felt ashamed for reentering the world. Moving on felt like a sin, a disregard for how important her friends were. Each new friendship and relationship inspired a fear that they too would leave her. Reentering life was not easy for her, but she forced herself to make new friends, take risks, and live in a way that honored her two friends.

Although we have to find our own way through the underworld, the stories tell us that we aren't alone. We don't have to disappear into the wooded glen. There are small lights in the oppressive darkness that guide us toward a communal experience of human underworlding. Robert Romanyshyn experienced this feeling of suffering beyond his own sorrow:

> I felt touched by a still deeper grief, a grief older than mine, a sadness at the very heart of things, where the ocean itself seemed like the tears of the world, mingling with my own, forging a bond of kinship rooted in sorrow. For so long I had lived with my grief as if I were a ghost, an invisible presence haunting the outer margins of the world. But now in this moment, in the very darkest hour of the night, I felt witnessed by the world, seen in my sorrow, no longer completely alone.[17]

A Buddhist parable tells of a woman who lost her child. Stricken with grief, she asked the Buddha to restore the life of her child. The Buddha told her that he would if she could bring him a handful of white mustard seeds from a house where no one has experienced tragedy. The woman went from door to door, eventually returning to the Buddha without a single seed. Tragedy is shared by all.

Our responses to some tragedies take us so far out of life that we fuel ourselves only with misery and a longing for the past. Frankl divided his fellow Auschwitz prisoners into those who believed that life still expected something of them and those who didn't. For those that had a reason to endure – an unpublished manuscript that needed finishing, a wife who needed strength, a child who needed their father – living through the unimaginable horror was possible. Without this *lifeline of meaning*, we cut ourselves off from our own life force and its ability to regenerate. Healing cannot come from abandoning or denying what has happened to us. There's a dismembering consequence to denying life.

Grief is something we can avoid, but at a cost. The price tag is avoiding love. Grief and love are interwoven. To spare ourselves from one we must detach ourselves from the other, refusing to love anything that can be taken from us. Our bodies will fail, so we avoid hiking, swimming, biking, or other activities we love. Relationships end, so we must avoid intimacy and connection. Our suffering arises because we have risked love; our grief is the mark of loving even when we know death awaits. The only way to protect ourselves from dismembering grief is to avoid life.

Failure

Campbell said that the hero is "one who knows when to surrender and what to surrender to."[18] Surrender is the conscious act of letting go. It's not the same as giving up; it is saying yes to leaping into the unknown to experience our full potential and our exceptional, authentic life. Rarely do we willingly surrender; many of us must be brought to the brink of despair by a force greater than ourselves – trauma, grief, or illness – before we surrender.

Orpheus paid a high price to learn the importance of surrendering to fate. By not trusting that his musical gifts had persuaded Hades and Persephone, he failed to return with Eurydice. By not relinquishing his attachment to a specific life, he lost everything about himself. Failure is often seen as the opposite of the heroic ideal. Heroes are the great and powerful among us who don't give up or misstep. We're taught not to surrender to our failings and encouraged to get back up and keep fighting.

But Orpheus reminds us that failure can spark heroism. Learning from what defeats us may be painful, but it builds resilience, confidence, and wisdom. The ideas of Apple founder Steve Jobs were originally scoffed at; Walt Disney was fired for lack of imagination; and J. K. Rowling was rejected by 12 publishers before *Harry Potter* was published. Failure doesn't mean we're weak, untalented, mistaken, or worthless. Blunders can be floods that cleanse and motivate us to pursue our dreams with renewed vigor.

Unexpected Transformation

When Eurydice died, Orpheus went from being a young man with dreams of a future with a beautiful bride, to a grief-stricken hermit. His life pivoted, putting him on the tragic course that led to dismemberment and death. A part of the Orphic journey is the fantasy of regaining our old lives, retrieving the past. Yet along the way, an unanticipated transition happens. Although Orpheus returned defeated, a widower at a young age, in time he became a prophet of the Orphic religion, showing us that the darkest moments of life can transform us in ways we never thought possible.

Life is full of unexpected circumstances that plummet us into darkness. Accidents, sudden death, panic attacks, traumatic memories, and violence all unleash the underworld. Mathematician John Nash didn't expect his life to be derailed by schizophrenia, nor did Steven Hawking anticipate contracting Lou Gehrig's disease. Humans have an incredible capacity, though, to meet the unexpected. Nash's work revolutionized major mathematical theories and Hawking's contributions to physics, relativity, cosmology, and our understanding of black holes are unparalleled.

In his lifetime (insofar as myth tells us), Orpheus did not come out of his suffering and teach others how to journey into the underworld. The Orphic cult was a later development based on Orpheus having gone to Hades and then back up to the dayworld. His failures became their lessons, his endless grieving their call to life. The Orphic cult made him into a mythic hero who could teach the living how to prepare for death, the ultimate underworld journey.

Orphic doctrine in ancient Greece believed that life was a painful burden and suffering could be alleviated by following a disciplined lifestyle. It's the precursor of Christian morality. Both Christ and Orpheus suffered and then taught their followers how to alleviate anguish in the afterlife.

In Orphic rites, the journey to the underworld was symbolically enacted to prepare initiates for their deaths. Since Orpheus resisted Eurydice's death and suffered for it, he was believed to have developed the skills that could help followers submit to their own mortality and know what to do after death. In the formula of the hero's journey, the returning hero is tasked with teaching humankind the wisdom learned during the adventure. To do so, the hero must translate the mystery of the depths into the language of the dayworld. Although Orpheus failed to conquer darkness in his (mythical) life, he became a hero who taught others how to journey into the underworld, a prophet of darkness.

It is tempting to try to avoid suffering by learning from the mistakes of others. But I wonder if escaping misery should be our primary aim? Eluding Orphic pain and failure might feel like relief and even seem positive. However, it was through torment that he became a prophet and teacher and ascertained his higher calling. Learning from darkness and avoiding darkness are different. The wisdom and experiences of others can be supportive and educational, but avoiding darkness altogether engenders stagnation, not growth.

The Wounded Healer

Sometimes darkness inspires a personal transformation that uniquely qualifies someone to teach and guide others. This archetype is called *the wounded healer* – an individual who works with a specific clientele that has experienced the wound that this healer treats. Wounded healers are guided by an authority inside themselves sourced from their own direct experience of darkness and what they learned along their journey of healing. They are known to be calm, present, and contained within the storm and can thus help us navigate the waves that are still crashing upon us. A wounded healer turns their own suffering into health-giving power.

I spoke with a woman who was the victim of extreme sexual abuse at a young age. Years later, she specializes in trauma therapy. She shared her journey toward identifying as a wounded healer:

> The childhood trauma forced me to kill off a part of myself to survive. Through the dissociation and splitting a part of me was left in that experience. When I first started working as a clinician, it was my own dissociation that made me calm in the face of my client's pain. I stumbled into being able to contain people because my work triggered my own trauma wounds which would make me go numb. Looking back, I wasn't really containing my clients; I was just so dissociated that, unlike everyone else, I wasn't freaking out.
>
> I've been in therapy since I was 16 and have done it all – inpatient treatment, group work, family therapy, and, of course, my own work. For years, everyone I worked with focused on the solution – solving the problem – up and out. People were afraid to dive into my story. About seven years ago, I began working with my current therapist. She wanted to go with me into the horrific moments of the trauma. At the time, I had never told

my whole story to anyone save the police, and even then I'm not sure I shared all the details. Trauma creates isolation and for healing to happen the healer has to break into and share the trauma space.

My work with her helped me start reintegrating the part of myself I had killed off to survive. Slowly, I was able to bring that woman [the part of me I had killed off] into my own practice. Instead of going numb I called upon the soul of my wound. I know what it is to have to leave a part of myself behind, and how hard the process of reconnecting with that piece is. Taking that part of myself into the transference is what really helps my clients heal. I allow "that woman" to be in the space with us, letting go of techniques and tools and bringing my own wounds. I walk with my clients into the deep darkness of their stories because I know the importance of someone joining you in that place without trying to solve or fix you.

The wounded healer sees their pain in others and heals from this shared wound. They embody the capability to be "at home" in the darkness of suffering and find there the seeds of healing and recovery. An essential piece is that the healer is no longer in the throes of dismembering darkness – they have come out the other side with the capacity to stand in dark places for people going through something similar. Through healing others, the wounded are gifted the opportunity to make meaning out of their suffering, standing for something bigger than themselves.

Mythically, the wounded healer is associated with the god Asclepius. The mortal healer Asclepius, due to immense zeal and skill, sought to resurrect the dead. Taking this as a crime against the natural order of the cosmos, Hades felt he'd been wronged and convinced Zeus to destroy Asclepius with a lightning bolt. In the underworld, Asclepius learned his lesson, so Zeus forgave him and made him immortal.

A temple dedicated to Asclepius was called an Asclepeion, where the sick came and after much purificatory preparation (baths, fasting, and sacrifices) were permitted to spend the night. While asleep, it was believed that the god would appear to the patient in a dream and give them healing advice.

During his underworld experience, Asclepius learned that true healing recognizes that a part of health is a relationship with inner death, with what in us has died in the underworld. We accept the "dying" of worn-out attitudes and behaviors in service to expanding, or we stand with another as they feel the death of their old lives, sense of self, or even of their wounds.

Jungian Rafael López-Pedraza believed Asclepius' rejection of Hades has "led to the concretization of rescuing life from death and an artificial prolongation of life as medicine's chief goal."[19] This attitude dominates the Western allopathic medical ambition of conquering illness and preventing death. We see this intention in language like "cancer survivor" and the "fight against Alzheimer's." Instead of Orpheus or even Asclepius, mainstream Western medicine adulates Hercules.

This approach to healing builds barricades between symptoms and soul. In Asclepius' mythology, we see the importance of connecting healing and darkness. This does not mean we shouldn't strive to enjoy long, healthy lives and battle illness. It means that when it comes to exploring the many facets of darkness, our aim shouldn't only be to *cure* and *remove*, but also to *tend* and *accept*. The wounded healer is an archetype activated in darkness, born from pain, who reshapes the unbearable into empathy, understanding, and the capacity to go with others into the abyss and let them be there for as long as they need.

Reflections

Orpheus is about facing darkness with vulnerability and self-expression. He embodies the challenges of letting go, journeying for love, and using the lessons of suffering to teach others. To be Orphic is to rely on imagination, creativity, and to be unexpectedly transformed by failures and missteps.

Reflect on how Orphic qualities may be present within your experience in:

- Moments when you call upon creativity or vulnerability for support.
- Speaking your authentic truth.
- Requesting aid from your sense of the sacred.
- Facing darkness out of love of another or for yourself.
- Ignoring the reality before you.
- Slipping back into old patterns.
- The inability to let go.
- The challenges of letting another's life be their own.
- Projecting your potential or unlived life onto another.
- Letting darkness pull you from life.
- Learning from what defeats you – the wisdom of failure.
- Teaching others through your own suffering – the wounded healer.
- Being unexpectedly transformed by the journey.

CHAPTER 6
ODYSSEUS

Odysseus, King of Ithaca and hero of *The Odyssey*, sought to return home after the Trojan War. While sailing homeward, he landed on the island Cyclops. With his men, he entered a cave filled with provisions. The cave belonged to the cyclops Polyphemus, who captured Odysseus and began to eat his companions. Odysseus tricked the giant into getting drunk and, after he fell asleep, drove a sharp stick into his only eye. Polyphemus was the son of Poseidon, the sea god. Learning of his son's fate, Poseidon was enraged and obstructed Odysseus' journey for ten years. Destiny is often expressed in a name, and Odysseus' name is from the Greek *odussesthai* – to "be wrought against" or "at odds with someone."

During his wayward journey home, Odysseus and his men landed on Aeaea, the island of Circe, a goddess of magic and herbs. Angered by their presence, Circe turned some of his crewmembers into pigs. Aided by Hermes, who gave Odysseus a magical herb called moly, he resisted her witchcraft. Circe fell in love with Odysseus' courage and released his men. For a year, the travelers stayed on Aeaea, and at the end of the year, Circe told Odysseus that in order to return home, he had to go to the underworld and hear a prophecy from the Theban seer Teiresias. So Odysseus journeyed to where the silent waters of Acheron join the fire of the Phlegethon and the ice of the Cocytus. On the boundary between the dayworld and the abyss, where light fails and darkness takes over, he dug a pit and summoned the shades of the dead by filling it with blood.

Refusal of the Call

When Circe told Odysseus that to return to Ithaca he first had to go to the underworld and speak with Teiresias, Odysseus said, "I felt a weight like stone within me, and moaning, pressed my length against the bed, with no desire to see the daylight more."[1] Refusing or reluctantly answering the call to the adventure of change is a common reaction to life's summons. When we are asked to begin an inner revolution, it is compelling to refuse the call and forego our destiny.

Odysseus' lamentations are an honest reflection of how many of us react when we face the inner world. Heeding the call to adventure seems insane. Why would we embark on a disruptive journey when we feel perfectly safe at home? We build fortresses to avoid pain and suffering, seeking to make life as comfy as possible. Veering off the well-trodden path, we risk finding ourselves in the dark, where nothing is familiar and we find nothing to hold on to. The unknown harbors much to be afraid of – death, ridicule, failure and, of course, change.

Growth requires leaving behind the safe and sensible option and moving toward uncertainty and discomfort. Fear can hold us prisoner and even prevent us from answering our life's call. We deny destiny and choose predictability, reliability, and safety – the anchoring and grounding experiences we can call "home." The hero aspect of our personality, with its power to choose, has to overcome the allure of stagnation. The energy needed to free ourselves from the tyranny of self-preservation should never be underestimated.

The Greeks tell the story of a many-headed Hydra whose heads grow back twofold when they're cut off. Overcoming the grip of calcified notions is like slaying the Hydra; each time you overcome one, two replace it. Refusing the call is to refuse destiny, denying the inner urge to find the depth of meaning in hardship.

When we avoid what the psyche calls us to do, there's a price. And when we risk all and adventure into the profoundest darkness, stumbling down the long black corridor, we open to becoming completely ourselves.

"There was a time," my brother remembered, "when I was resisting engaging with the world. My analyst told me about a friend of his who was destined to be the medicine man of his native tribe, but he didn't want to, so he avoided it by drinking. One day, he got struck by lightning. He survived and realized that he could no longer avoid his summons. This story put a crack in the door I'd slammed shut."

We avoid destiny's call, seeking alternatives and panaceas, or just digging into our known patterns and behaviors. Avoiding the responsibilities implicit in owning our own power is understandable; doing so will change our known world. But sometimes, answering the call is inescapable. After meeting with Ben Kenobi, Luke Skywalker rushed home to his aunt and uncle's farm, fearing they might be in danger. There he found his old life in ashes, and the choice of leaving was no longer hard

– there was nothing to stay for. Like Luke and Odysseus, some people have an inescapable destiny to fulfill.

If there is a task in you that must be lived out, the only satisfying resolution will be to fulfill your purpose. If you don't answer the call, you won't be happy. It's a catch-22: if you resist the weight of destiny, you'll never become yourself, even if answering the call is a titanic burden. Sometimes it feels impossible. We're too tired, immature, unwell, unsafe, acutely in our trauma, or lacking the financial stability to support the necessary changes. It's important to find a balance and the right timing, not overriding these realities and keeping destiny in mind.

I think it's best to be Odyssean – wallow, moan, and then *get out of bed*. No one wants to fall apart or break down, but the desire to remain intact at all costs stalls growth. Admitting reluctance is a part of moving from evasion to acknowledgment. We feel our woes and then, when we can, move forward. Caretaking the elderly or raising young children can take all our resources. But instead of *ignoring* the part of us that wants to scream out in frustration, can we explore what that part of us has to say? How can we exist *in relationship with* these feelings, letting them have a place in our lives? Being open to our resistance to life's challenges can in itself be healing. This is the Odyssean path.

Intention

The divinities of the deep are important to Odysseus. He doesn't seek to trespass or alter the order of the lower realm. Instead, he sacrifices his best heifer to summon the shades and pledges to perform rites to Hades and Persephone upon returning home to Ithaca.

A symbol of Odysseus' devotion to the gods is blood sacrifice. To summon the dead, he digs a pit and fills it with blood. Jungian analyst Edward Edinger explains that pouring sacrificial blood means that psychic energy must be poured into the unconscious in order to stimulate it.[2] Blood was believed to return consciousness to the dead, awakening their longing for the light of life. As with the shades, unconscious material seeks manifestation, it desires life. We have to engage with the unconscious intentionally, and direct our energy toward it if we want to receive and integrate its messages.

Blood symbolizes life itself, a precious thing to sacrifice. To give of something so vital represents profound commitment. To build a relationship with darkness, we have to see it as a precious part of life.

A schoolteacher I worked with came to therapy because she felt she was being sucked dry by her work. Instead of caring for herself in ways that were nourishing, she gave her all to her students, leaving little for herself. Self-nurturing didn't come easy. As a teenager, she lost two close friends, and in the aftermath of their deaths, she became wary of sharing herself in relationships. She feared that anyone she loved would die, leaving her alone once again. She felt undeserving of the life she had while her friends, whom she perceived as better people, did not. To protect her pain and vulnerability, she distanced herself from others – and from herself – through overwork, a defense against her sense of worthlessness.

A few months into therapy, she had a dream of a grocery store full of people celebrating. Unable to join the festivities, she stole food. Later, an image arose in her of a hollow man, which she interpreted as adulthood. We discussed why she wasn't able to nourish herself, leaving her hollow and unable to participate in life in the ways she desired. She had the following dream:

> I enter a decrepit theater, full of discarded old trash and beverages. I see a powerful and directive man and follow him out of the theater toward a beautiful lake. We paddleboard and I fall in love with him. Soon we return

to the theater, but it's not dilapidated. This time it's
smaller, bright, and clean, and I'm invited to get on stage.

Around the time of this dream, she'd begun to create balance
and meaning in her life – spending time in nature, cooking,
taking alone time, connecting with people, and believing in
herself. Although these new feelings were unfamiliar and even
uncomfortable, she redirected the current of her intention,
pouring new energies into her life. She forced herself to believe
she was deserving of life and its vitality. From the dream's point
of view, she was no longer standing on a worn-out stage full of
useless and spent energy, but on a new platform, glittering with
possibility – the reward of pouring energy into change.

Initiating real change requires committing to the journey
and a willingness to go beyond the comforts of our habits and
give it all we can. We need to remain upright before the rising
storm. True commitment to transformation is an act of dying, of
completely ending one way of being and beginning another. This
is why death is such an important symbol for transformation. It
means allowing something we need to release to venture forth,
to depart from our life.

Preparing the ground for change can begin with small steps
like noticing and naming your feelings. Reflective journaling,
mindfulness, seeking to understand dreams, praying, exercising,
dancing, surrendering, whatever approaches help us live
more intentionally, can be important seeds in the garden of
transformation. If we redirect our energies in these ways, habits
and neural pathways that no longer serve us may change of
their own accord.

Epigenetics explores how psychological, dietary, ancestral,
environmental, and lifestyle conditions influence and modify gene
expression. Our genetic predispositions ("nature") interface
with our inner and outer environment ("nurture") and co-
create our well-being. To influence our predispositions, we have

to commit fully to making conscious the interactions between our life choices. If one of these areas is left untended, it will show up in our health. No matter how many supplements we take to mitigate adrenal fatigue, if we live a stressful lifestyle, we'll be depleted. Our blood work will show our lack of commitment and, over time, not much will change.

When a frightening disease or a mental breakdown looms, it's easy to sacrifice old patterns and make space for new ones. But without such a big scare, it can be difficult to find the motivation to change, and instead we let older, more fortified patterns bulldoze over our emerging selves. It takes caring about ourselves and our life and believing in what we're doing to integrate this kind of inner revolution.

Teiresias

Odysseus journeyed to the underworld to speak with the blind prophet Teiresias, who – alone among the shades – kept the capacity for consciousness: "His eyes were closed to the broken forms of the light-world … he saw in his own interior darkness."[3]

A denizen of the lower world, Teiresias does not offer knowledge from a dayworld source, but from the unconscious. "I am reminded once more," Robert Macfarlane recalled about deep cave systems, "how resistant the underland remains to our usual forms of seeing: how it hides so much from us."[4] Odysseus journeys to the underworld because he needs foresight that only Teiresias can give – knowledge that's inaccessible to sunlight. The powers of the deep have a different wisdom, often portrayed as omniscient; the dead can see the future.

The deep places in the mind both hide *and* reveal. Jungians call this *compensation*, the psyche's capacity to offer corrective and balancing perspectives. By its very nature, the ego remains blind to the unconscious. Its propensity toward selecting what to perceive and what to overlook forces undesired, unintegrated contents, such as repressed memories or associations, into the unconscious, where they form a counterpoint to the conscious "attitude." When ego becomes one-sided, the counterforce in the unconscious will strengthen in the opposite direction.

My husband was plagued for many years by a repetitive dream sequence. As a child he dreamed of being trapped in a pitch-black room with no doors or windows. As he grew up, the dream grew with him. He found himself in the familiar obscure room, then his house, and finally navigating a boat down a river – all in utter darkness. The dreams brought with them feelings of being entombed and helpless, confused and panicked.

"The dark dreams always start off disorienting and end in something terrifying," he recalled. "I grew up in an affluent family. I internalized the importance of being directive and successful. I put a lot of pressure on myself. Finally, I said aloud what I thought the dream was trying to tell me. I acknowledged that I didn't know where I was going in life and affirmed that being afraid of the unknown was okay, it didn't mean I wasn't living a good life. Uncertainty is a part of what life is about. I felt relief, as though an invisible weight had been removed. And I never had that dream again."

These dreams express the compensatory function of the unconscious. An essential part of my husband was out of balance – focused on understanding and controlling his life's direction. The dreams tried to encourage him to accept that some things are unknown. Dreams try to nudge the ego to see something it's missing. As his life evolved, the dream adapted its message to his current situation. By naming the meaning of the dream, that he had received the message, the nightmares disappeared.

It is from the blind seer Teiresias, a figure who blends ego and unconscious, that Odysseus receives the inner sight he needs in order to follow his destiny. To "return home," he must reconnect with his unique path. If we lose contact with the unconscious, particularly the Self, we may begin to feel alienated, bereft of meaning, and depressed. This disconnect can feel like being imprisoned in a dark room, helpless and stuck. Odysseus is a hero lost at sea, adrift on the vast ocean of life. To reclaim the plot of his life, he must open to the guidance of the unconscious.

Teiresias foretells the anguish that awaits Odysseus – the fall of his shipmates and survival of only himself, of the men dishonoring his household whom he must kill, and that he will live his life away from the sea, but in death rejoin it. The seer tells him how to get past the sea monster Scylla, avoid the ship-devouring whirlpool Charybdis, and warns him not to eat the sacred cattle of Helios, the sun god (and when his men disobey, they are killed by Zeus' thunderbolts).

In a poignant reaction to his fate, Odysseus replies, "Teiresias, my life runs on then as the gods have spun it."[5] Sometimes it's best to surrender to the hand we are dealt. Despite his desire to return to his homeland, he is fated to wander and live a restless life for another decade, and again thereafter. Darkness is a part of the life we are fated to lead. Attempting to avoid or deny the truth of who we are and what we're experiencing can inhibit growth and healing. When we allow ourselves to be part of the larger story, acting as though our lives are spun by the gods, we're better able to accept our lives in their entirety, darkness and all.

Asking Questions

Teiresias is not the only shade summoned to Odysseus' pit. In fact, no other hero engages with as many shades. Odysseus talks with the warrior Achilles and his son Neoptolemus, Agamemnon (the king of Mycenae who led the Greek forces in the Trojan War), Hercules' mother, Alkmene, and Antiope, the queen of the Amazons. Lastly, he speaks with his own mother, Anticlea, and until she drifts toward his pool of blood, he doesn't even realize that she's dead.

At a certain point, Odysseus transitions from listening to the shades to asking them questions, and the remainder of his journey involves inquiries. He asks his recently deceased companion Elpenor how he reached Hades so quickly, inquires how death is treating Agamemnon and Achilles, and talks at length with his mother.

Odysseus is a wordsmith. The hero Ajax called him "skilled in wiles" and Homer described him as a "strategist" and "great tactician." His patron, the goddess Athena, once said to him, "Chameleon? Bottomless bags of tricks … give your stratagems a rest or stop spellbinding for an instant."[6] Relying on his innate gifts, Odysseus uses his wit to question the shades. He "thought how best to separate and question them,"[7] displaying his clever mind skilled at prying, seeking, and differentiating among the unconscious's desires, instincts, and fantasies. Doing so, he represents that inquisitive part of us that seeks to learn from darkness. The hero engages in coagulation, emergence, and becoming – fighting against the forces of the unconscious *and* separating from them. At the same time, the hero turns and faces the underworld and *asks what it wants of him or her.*

After being diagnosed with multiple sclerosis, a woman spends six months suffering from pain, fatigue, and the humiliation brought about by her impaired coordination. As the days trickle by, she distances herself from friends and family. In silence and seclusion, she builds a protective wall. A friend gifts her *The Power of Now* by Eckhart Tolle, a modern classic of spiritual practice and personal growth. As she reads, a dormant part of her is stirred, and she begins to miss the sweet fragrance of burning Palo Santo, a mystical tree related to frankincense and myrrh that literally means "holy wood." She remembers her father lighting the holy wood and praying. When did she lose God, she wonders. When did she forget her ancestry? The doors of inquiry open, and she asks herself why she's afraid and embarrassed of her condition. So she joins a healing group and despite the continuation of chronic pain, the darkness begins to lift.

There are moments in life when we transition from learning about ourselves by withdrawing and listening, to proactively asking questions and engaging with our stories. When we ask questions, we seek answers to things we don't know. Questioning means recognizing what we don't understand and becoming curious about exploring our thoughts, feelings, and behaviors. We all face inner conundrums – how to become a better person, to make meaning of our circumstances, to reimagine negative stories, to explain our choices to others, manage stress, or get honest about our struggles and assumptions … Asking helps us evolve.

When it no longer works to patch over our darkness, we know that it's time to journey within and begin the difficult work of inner exploration, to ask ourselves the questions of self-growth: What is it that I don't yet know about myself? What do I need to give up in order to grow into myself? And most Odyssean of all: *What do I need to learn?* The key is to ask the right questions, those that will invite hidden truths to reveal themselves. Instead of acting as though we're victims of a cosmic moral drama – *why me?* – we can ask, "*Why?*" as an invitation to look within.

Clients ask what they should do to overcome a certain problem, putting the responsibility for navigating their inner world in my hands. A conscious therapist will avoid such temptations. Asking is essential, but growth comes not from an authority's answer, but from the client deepening their self-understanding through reflection. We learn a lot by turning toward our wounds and asking what they want of us. Getting curious about what part of us they represent.

Conversing with the dead, Odysseus enters the *tension of opposites*. He symbolizes the ego-mind, while the shades represent the unconscious. When two different energies encounter one another, the tension creates a third perspective, or attitude, which has its own consciousness. This is called the *transcendent function*, the transformative energy that arises from the tension between consciousness and the unconscious.

It's tempting, even relieving, to collapse the tension caused by contrasting inner energies. Often holding a pantheon of different forces within us is overwhelming, even painful. When we select one idea or energy – good or bad, right or wrong, wonderful or terrible – pressure is released. Yet, by collapsing the energy we take the lid off the bottle, freeing the energy that otherwise could transform us.

Inner growth often requires tension between the behaviors, beliefs, and identity of our current sense of self, which is often based on childhood survival needs or societal expectations, and who we actually are – that is, between what we're aware of and our unconscious complexes. Tension stirs the waters, allows us to progress in consciousness, and pushes us toward our true self. In holding inner tension, we are called to understand and accept all sides of ourselves and fulfill a deeper purpose. Comfort can prevent us from experiencing ourselves more deeply. Odyssean questioning shows us how the reason-making faculty of mind can deepen our connection with the unconscious.

"I've always known I was gay," a man shared with me. "In my early twenties, I thought that if I came out, my conservative father would shun me and my mother, who was always on his side, would follow suit. I also knew I had to live my life and show my parents who I am. I began having migraines and panic attacks, and eventually the conflict became unbearable. When I told my mother, she said they'd always known and wanted me to be myself. In hindsight, the panic pushed me forward so in a weird way I'm grateful for it, because now I get to be who I am."

Often the new attitude that emerges is expressed by a dream image or synchronicity, when the inner world is mirrored in the outer world. When my brother was in the hospital, I found strength in imagining myself as a bunny watching over a bear's (Ben's) hibernation. One morning I went to the hospital gardens to cry on a bench, and a few feet away was a cottontail bunny. The rabbit affirmed what was growing inside me – a newfound strength that came not from controlling the situation but accepting that I couldn't. It was a moment of dialogue between my conscious personality and the unconscious that helped me access my true capability, *the importance of feeling small*, of softness, and the value of letting go.

In *Soul in Grief*, psychologist Robert Romanyshyn shares that after the abrupt death of his wife he awoke to a mysterious crashing in his home. Wandering like a ghost through his house, he discovered the bookshelf in his office that held all his publications had collapsed. Painfully, he replaced and repaired this altar to his old life, and three days later the books fell again. "I wondered," he wrote, "if there was some connection between these two collapses: if these things, these books, a record of my life, were mirroring the collapse of my soul."[8] The fallen books reflected the state of his life, a window into understanding and knowing that could not be rationally understood.

In the Western world, we're taught to think in terms of either/or – rational and directive thinking or intuitive and fantastical thinking. Something is either scientifically proven or a contrived fantasy. But rational and imaginal thinking aren't mutually exclusive. Knowledge that comes from conversing with imaginal figures may be a different type of learning, but it is still learning. If we can hold the tension between what in us is known and established and what is new and emergent, a new attitude may emerge.

The Pain of Acceptance

Odysseus' mother, Anticlea, was unable to recognize her son at first. Odysseus bit his "lip, rising perplexed, with longing to embrace her, and tried three times, putting my arms around her, but she went sifting through my hands."[9]

Unlike Orpheus, who refused to accept Eurydice's death, the Odyssean hero understands that some things are beyond his control. Odysseus described his pain as "embittered," saying he "cried in the darkness." He felt and honored his pain but did not allow his grief to rip him apart or remove him from life. Although he wished to be with his mother, Odysseus knew he had a life to live and a family to return to, while she had to remain in the realm of the dead. And so he bowed his head and left the past behind.

Instead of regressing and willfully seeking the ghost of an old life, Odysseus refrained from rashly seeking what was beyond his control. He represents the discipline that comes from love rather than power. It takes a focused love of self to give up what is beyond our control – ideas that no longer serve our well-being or behaviors that have long steered our ships. Power comes from our ability to connect with who we are, deeply, and lead from that place.

Odysseus was not above longing for different circumstances. He begged his mother, crying, "O my mother, will you not stay, be still, here in my arms, may we not, in this place of Death, as well, hold one another."[10] In a gentle way, Odysseus did what Hercules did with brute strength – he resisted the regressive pull of the unconscious. He resisted the temptation to fight for what was beyond his control and to fall back into the comforts of the past. Nearing the end of their conversation, Anticlea told her son, "You must crave sunlight soon."[11] She encouraged him to return to the surface, reminding him that he could not change her fate. Odysseus turned away, mustering the heroism to accept what could not be changed.

After taking a year off from college to recover from the acute stages of his brain injury, Ben went back to school. A part of the hardship was accepting the limitations the injury had set upon his life: "I resigned myself to a solitary, ghostlike experience with academics, no relationships and no sleep. I had to let 'my world' become smaller and smaller as 'the world' continued on without me. The only reason I wasn't defeated by all this was that I still had a pulse and went to class every day. But I was enshrouded in a dark veil."

Like Ben, Odysseus captured the agony of accepting that sometimes our goals, desires, past sense of selves, or what we love lie beyond our control. This is the opposite of popular understanding of heroic action, which dominates reality by subduing it. Control is the way of Herculean strength and Orphic resistance. For Odysseus, *letting things slip through his fingers* was an act of heroism. It can be more painful than holding on and trying to dominate, but it provides us the chance to deepen and grow. These aren't the vertical shoots of springtime blooms. They're not round and uplifting. This is a black, thick, and sad growth that comes from *mourning* the loss of what has been taken, paying it respect, and being present with our pain and lack of control.

"If I had resisted the changes," Ben said, "and tried to be the man I used to be, I would have died of longing. I worked hard and trudged through it, letting myself be the ghost of the person I remembered. I had plenty of self-pity but did my best to surrender instead of idolizing my past."

Faltering Courage

Courage wears many faces — valor, audacity, love, bravery, letting go, vulnerability, admitting faults, and learning from failures. Treating courage as a state in which one's footsteps never falter is unrealistic. It takes courage to cope with anxiety, admit you were wrong, get back up after falling down, face traumas and fears, cope with illness, and try new things. Always being daring and bold is a nice ideal, but in real life our steps are not always unfaltering.

Odysseus, a formidable presence in the Trojan War, represents many aspects of traditional heroic courage — the strength of will to face the unknown and the lionheartedness to fight monsters. Yet in the underworld, that courage faltered. While speaking with the dead, hordes of shades swarmed his pit, and Odysseus fled in fear. Even the greatest among us cannot always face hardship with steadfast and unwavering courage.

Sometimes our inner monsters and living nightmares get the better of us. No matter our fortitude and composure, we can always be threatened by darkness. Those who live with mood disorders such as bipolarity know the waves traversing between inflation and grandiosity on the one hand, to stillness and depression on the other. Those who suffer from chronic trauma like PTSD know the ebbs and flows of unsafety, dissociation, panic, and retreat. Healing includes patience, and sometimes it's most effective to pause, retreat, regroup, and then, when ready, begin again.

After being raped, a young woman struggled to rebuild her sense of safety. She kept lights on at night and feared having sexual partners. Slowly she began to create new connections and empower herself. First, she had to feel safe with others. "Recovery," writes psychiatrist Judith Herman, "can take place only within the context of relationships; it cannot occur in isolation."[12] I would add, in safety. The young woman's goal was to restore power and diminish helplessness by increasing her capacity to connect to others. It took her a long time to ask for help. So, she started small, giving herself permission to be both strong and overwhelmed at the same time, to bravely take a step forward and know when to take a step back.

"As soon as we feel ourselves slipping," wrote Jung, "we begin to combat this tendency and erect barriers against the dark, rising flood of the unconscious and its enticements to regression, which all too easily takes on the deceptive guise of sacrosanct ideals."[13] To integrate the lessons and personal expansion we've reached, we must struggle constantly to consolidate our hard-earned wisdom. Some fights we can't win. The shades gather, and we flee.

Odysseus' encounter with the shades personifies *shadow confrontation*. The shadow is the living part of the personality that's been repressed for the sake of the ego ideal, the unlived and unwanted parts of ourselves containing more of our instinctive and unrefined selves than any other archetype. The shadow is a force of immorality and animalism, comprised of all we may wish we weren't. Yet shadow confrontation is a doorway to ourselves, the first moment we glimpse who we really are.

Sitting in my office, a woman cried for the part of herself that has felt stupid her whole life. For the first time, she reconnected with the young girl who so desperately wanted her father's approval, who lived for even a morsel of recognition. Instead of love and acceptance, she got brutalized, humiliated. "You will never be smart," is the only thing she remembers him telling her.

Jung believed that confrontation with the shadow reveals our helplessness, explaining that "anyone who descends into the unconscious … is exposed to the attack of all the ferocious beasts which the caverns of the psychic underworld are supposed to harbor."[14] No matter how evolved we become or how much analytical work we do, we can be overpowered by life circumstance, shadow material, or complexes.

Sometimes we show up with bravery and sometimes we don't. Inner work includes this ebb and flow. When our nerve falters, there's no need for shame or avoidance. Some things in life are too profound, shattering, or terrible to face all at once. The Greeks believed that most of the gods (Hermes and Eros being the exceptions) came into existence at age nine or above. Gods pop into the world fully formed. The rest of us need to learn about ourselves, endure losses, and struggle to better ourselves. The battle for self-growth is reserved for humans and the heroes who stand between the gods and us.

The Odyssean archetype pertains to the parts of us that answer the call of life, heed the summons of our density. He carries our capacity to devote ourselves to the journey of individuation, pouring our own vitality into our growth. Odysseus is a hero who asks questions and gains knowledge from the unconscious – engaging, untangling, and learning from what he experiences so darkly. He is an image of accepting, despite our longing and desire, what cannot be changed. And when the darkness becomes too much, Odysseus tells us that there is heroism in knowing our limits.

Reflections

Odysseus is about answering the call to life, i.e., heeding the summons of destiny. He embodies our capacity to pour energy into growth through suffering. Odysseus asks question and gains knowledge from the unconscious, using this information to accept what cannot be changed. When we question what is and make great sacrifices to find our way "home," Odysseus is present.

Reflect on how these Odyssean qualities may be present within your experience in:

- Answering the call of your destiny.
- Making sacrifices to grow.
- Pouring psychic energy into making change.
- Asking questions of your suffering.
- Accepting what is beyond your control.
- Knowing when you've met your limits.
- Shadow confrontation – facing the unlived and unwanted parts of yourself.

CHAPTER 7
AENEAS

After the fall of Troy, Aeneas, son of the Trojan prince Anchises and the goddess Aphrodite, gathered a group of fellow survivors and traveled to Italy to find a place where the defeated Trojans could rebuild their lives. After six years, their ship landed on the shores of Cumae. There he went to the temple of Apollo to seek counsel from a prophetess, the Sibyl.[1]

"One thing I must ask," he inquired. "Since here is said to be the gateway of the lower kingdom and here the marsh of overflowing Acheron, may it be granted me to go before the face and presence of my dearest father [Anchises]."[2]

The Sibyl responded, "Have no fear, Trojan, you will obtain your request and, with me as your guide, you will behold the homes of Elysium, the ultimate kingdoms of the universe, and the ghost of your beloved father. There is no path that virtue cannot tread."[3]

Seeking Guidance

Aeneas sought out the Sibyl because he wanted her to join him on his quest. When we reach a roadblock, we can simply wait for assistance or we can actively seek support. An Aenean hero is willing to go after the help he or she needs, reminding us that there's heroism in knowing when we've reached our limit and need guidance.

Some of us find guidance in poems and simplicity. Others in talking to family, friends, therapists, or animals. People rely on art or music, dance or long bike rides. Some people call on their ministers or gurus; others find support in writing, healing others, or teaching. Some take early morning walks to behold the silence of winter trees. Others turn towards tools of divination such as oracles. If we are true to the uniqueness of our experiences, our support systems will be as kaleidoscopic as we are. The type of supportive energy we choose matters less than knowing when we need to ask for help.

Reverence and Talisman

The name Aeneas comes from the Greek Aineías, meaning "praised." Veneration for the divine is his defining characteristic. He doesn't use force, cunning, or song to subdue the powers of the deep. Instead, he is armed with his reverence for the gods. With unparalleled willingness and devotion, Aeneas followed the instructions of the Sibyl.

The Sibyl told Aeneas that to enter the lower world and have any hope of returning, he had to have a sign of his worthiness.

She instructed him to go to a forest where he would find a golden bough. If the bough broke off the tree with ease, he was fated to journey to the underworld. If passage to Hades was not part of his destiny, the bough would not snap off. Gazing into the forest, Aeneas prayed to his mother, Aphrodite, to help him find the bough. Two doves flew by and pointed to the correct branch, which he broke off effortlessly.

While crossing the River Styx, the Sibyl told the ferryman Charon that they brought no "trickery" or "violence" but instead: "'Trojan Aeneas, famed for piety and arms, descends to meet his father, down into the deepest shades of Erebus. If the image of such piety is not enough to move you, then still you must recognize this bough' – and here she shows the branch concealed beneath her robe."[4] Sometimes, when facing the heaviest moments of life, the darkest corners of our souls, all we have to do is believe in a higher energy. Surrendering to a source of guidance beyond ourselves can, in itself, be heroic.

"Believing there is a larger meaning to my accident," Ben said, "helps me convert my pain and create from it. What otherwise could feel meaningless seems like a calling guiding me forward. Roadblocks become passable when I feel there is a deeper purpose at work."

Every aspect of Aeneas' journey was steeped in reverence for the gods. His behavior is a metaphor for following the archetypal energies of life, completely devoting ourselves to listening to the messages of the psyche. In preparing to make his descent, Aeneas sacrificed a "black-fleeced lamb for Night, the Furies' mother, and Terra, her greater sister;" for Persephone he "kills a barren heifer;" and for Hades "he raises nocturnal altars, laying on their fires whole carcasses of bulls; he pours fat oil across the burning entrails."[5] Always, Aeneas fulfilled the Sibyl's behest with unquestioning haste.

Reverence for whatever higher meaning guides – religion, spirituality, tradition, dreams, family, or moral values – can help us make meaning out of the journey. Seeking support from an energy that cannot be seen, measured, or tangibly interacted with often requires admitting our vulnerability and need for help. Aenean energy pertains to moments in life when we bow our heads and ask for strength — praying for safe passage, clarity, release, peace, or acceptance. Doing so, we place our experience on the altar of something beyond ourselves, beyond the whims of the ego-mind. This contrasts with the popular understanding of heroic domination. To let go of the need for control and step into the embrace of whatever mystery guides you takes heroism.

Aenean reverence is different from Orphic prayer, which is focused on petitioning the divine for aid to accomplish the deed oneself. For Aeneas, reverence is about following the guidance of a larger entity. In his own dreams and those of his patients, Jung found himself confronted by what he believed was overwhelming proof of a larger source of wisdom in the psyche which often presented a different story of the patient's true life than the one held by their ego. This source seemed to compensate for the limited purview of the ego's attitude, striving to correct imbalanced perspectives by reaching for a goal of self-development that embraced one's whole identity. Based on this, Jung saw the ego as the center of consciousness but not of the entire psyche, which he called the Self. The Self is the god image within us, a center that directs our highest purpose. To be guided by the Self is to have reverence for the mysterious, unseen, but strangely personal and knowable center of our being.

Jungians call it the Self, others describe it as a lightning bolt of insight, while others believe it to be spirits of the forest or a mysterious natural intelligence. For some people, the archetype of wholeness comes in dream figures such as an old man or a soul-animal. For most, connection with the transpersonal is held by God. "I do not pray to Jesus," a woman told me. "I pray to the universe's life force, God energy, the power to heal, the power to create life when there is darkness."

To be with underworld feelings takes a great deal of trust. We need to trust we'll survive when we let go of our old ways of being and that doing so will bring renewed wellness into our lives. We need to trust in our own strength and purpose, and that we have support and will be able to move through the chaos of the dark night. Aeneas represents the ability to trust something greater than ourselves and follow that presence into darkness.

Aenean reverence is symbolized by his talismanic golden bough. In the hero's journey, the hero is aided by advice or amulets of a supernatural helper. When the road is full of confusing turns and dangerous obstacles, we need protection and guidance. Talismans, objects that have magical powers, offer the hero assurance and assistance. The Greek hero Perseus received a helmet that made him invisible and a reflective shield that protected him from the gaze of the snake-headed Gorgon Medusa. Jason and his famous Argonauts sought a golden fleece to symbolize his right to the throne of Iolcus.

Traditionally earned by overcoming initiatory trials, talismans are markers of an individual's destiny – given to those worthy of the call of life. For Aeneas, his calling is represented by the golden bough. In the deep forest, he reached for his destiny and the bough fell easily into his hands, judging him worthy of passing beneath the world's surface.

A talisman can be a tangible object – a jagged rock found atop a distant mountain, an owl's feather offering wisdom, or an evil eye that guards against misfortune and brings good luck. A Buddhist *mala* (rosary) is a string of 108 beads signifying our spiritual essence, which acts as a medium for the positive energy of the universe. In ancient Rome, amulets were believed to be containers of divine magic: Jupiter (Zeus) was represented by quartz-like chalcedony, Mars (Ares) with fiery jasper, Ceres (Demeter) by green jasper, and Bacchus (Dionysus) with amethyst. In China, Daoist masters called Fulu Pai create calligraphy to protect against evil spirits.

Talismans can also be imaginative and internal — a vision of angels, a dream image, a memory, or a voiceless prayer. I once dreamed of a room with a perfect white bed. In the corner of the room a small orb pulsed with numinous blue light. From the Latin *numen*, "divine will," the numinous refers to a strong spiritual or religious quality. The glittery light was mystical, the closest I've ever felt to the sacred. A personally meaningful and profoundly alive symbol of the divine is a talisman.

Internal and imaginative talismans are like down jackets. It is the warmth of our bodies trapped by the goose down that keeps us warm. If we didn't have a warm core, the down would not keep us warm. A talisman acts in a similar way — an inner presence which, when kept close, protects and warms us as we venture underworld.

I work with a woman whose inner talismans are blue butterflies. As she navigated illness, she imagined the butterflies landing on her head, filling her being. Butterflies are symbols of metamorphosis, of gentle (though sometimes violent) change. With each beat of a tiny wing, she told her body it could heal. The butterflies comforted her, reaching across the divide between mind and matter. After his divorce, a man was only allowed to see his children every other weekend. They were five and seven, and he felt he was missing everything. His parents divorced when he was eight and he had promised himself he'd always be there for his kids, that he would heal his own wounds by being fully present as a parent. He grieved the loss of this dream as he would a death. He carries a photo of his children grinning ear to ear, with faces covered in blueberries. The picture is now the most priceless thing he owns, a talisman that serves as a shield against sadness, reminding him that he's still a good father.

A woman I spoke with wanted to heal her early childhood trauma. The verbal and physical exploitation of her father had left her emotionally paralyzed, diminished, and trapped in negative coping strategies. As she began her healing path, she noticed pink lotus flowers – seeing them in her room, her art choices, in buildings she passed, and in books she glanced at. The lotus symbolizes the spirt of life and beauty rising out of mud and the mire of darkness. She felt the lotus flower was her guardian angel, watching and caring for the neglected and wounded parts of herself and reminding her she too could rise above the shadows of her past.

The lotus is talismanic; it gave her the sense of safety and empowerment needed to believe she could be reborn from a darkness that affected her deeply. When shameful memories engulfed her, old sensations returned, and she once more became the scared and violated child, her lotus flower was there – replacing her body's memory of pain with soft petals, trading her insecurities for gentle blooms. Imagining a lotus unfurling from darkness, she began to heal.

Aeneas' talismanic power came from his relationship to the archetypal realm, symbolized by his guide (the Sibyl) and the golden bough. In the hero's journey, supernatural aid represents *the protective power of destiny*. The myth tells us that when Charon sees the bough, his "swollen heart … stills its anger. He says no more. He wonders at the sacred gift of the destined wand, so long unseen, and turns his blue-black keel toward shore."[6] In Bill Moyers's interview with Joseph Campbell, the mythologist spoke of "invisible hands" that seem to come to our aid when we are aligned with our true calling. It's no mistake that "talisman" comes from *telos*, "fulfillment, completion," bespeaking the energy that drives the manifestation of our ultimate purpose or design.

Jung wrote, "It is not I who create myself, rather, I happen to myself."[7] The telos, or ultimate aim of the psyche, is to live a fulfilled life in accord with our destiny. It suggests there is a hidden operator behind our lives; that we're imprinted with a sense of self which must be actualized in order to live a fulfilled life. For Jungians, this is the core journey of individuation, the lifelong process of waking up to our unique individuality.

Just as an acorn grows into an oak tree, who we are is to a large extent "predestined." At first, there exists an architectural sketch, and only the general blueprint is visible. In time, the building takes form and we begin to see what the final design holds. As construction continues, the building is polished and starts to resemble the original blueprint, but it also has a life of its own. Walls go up, floors are laid, electricity wired, and finally after much hard work, the finishing touches are applied and the larger plan manifests.

Aeneas was not set on accomplishing his agenda by himself. The Aenean hero is not too proud to ask for guidance. Herculean hyper-individualism is the opposite. Today, we believe it's the responsibility of the individual to navigate their journey – to find their path, brave their demons, and face life's misfortunes alone. But instead of moving forward with sheer will like Hercules or a self-serving goal like Orpheus, the Aenean hero acknowledges that his success and his survival depend on divine guidance.

Of all the heroes, Aeneas makes the most comprehensive and immersive tour of the lower realm. He's described as wandering "over all that region, across the wide and misted plains, surveying everything."[8] He saw the spirits of the recently dead line up before King Minos for judgment; he walked through the Fields of Mourning, where those who died for love wander; he crossed the Field of War Heroes, where he saw many casualties of the Trojan War; he passed the fortress where Rhadamanthus doles out judgments for the most evil; and finally he came to Elysium, the Blessed Groves, where the good wander in peace and comfort.

Upon reaching Elysium, Aeneas reverently sprinkled his body with fresh water and, as instructed by the Sibyl, lay the bough across the sacred threshold. Even after accomplishing his task, when he no longer needed the same degree of guidance, he continued to serve the gods, reminding us that faith in the archetypal forces of the psyche, the God force within us, is a lifelong project that continues to create understanding and healing. When the lights go out, it takes heroism to believe that you're supported by something you can't see or touch.

Listening

Upon reaching Elysium, Aeneas approaches his father, Anchises, while his father stands surveying the imprisoned souls as they wait to pass to the land of the living. Seeing Aeneas, Anchises cries out, "You come at last." Standing side by side, Anchises tells his son of the destiny of souls waiting to be reborn, the rise of Rome, a nation Aeneas will father, the war he must wage against the Laurentians, and the tragedies he must avoid and endure throughout his life. "Yours will be the rulership of nations," Anchises proudly exclaims. "Roman, these will be your arts: to teach the ways of peace to those you conquer, to spare defeated peoples, tame the proud."[9]

Standing next to his father, Aeneas hardly asks questions. Unlike Odysseus, who interrogates to gain insight, the Aenean hero *listens*. The Western mind has an appetite for asking questions and seeking understanding. We want the comfort of diagnoses, live within a fantasy of upward growth, seek the clarity of explanations, and mine for the security of facts. We measure greatness through financial success, individual drive, and the capacity to dominate, celebrating those who lead from the front of the pack.

Aeneas offers a different way of studying. Through *listening in a quiet and reflective way*, Aeneas discovers how to fulfill his destiny. Despite his introverted, contemplative stance, his accomplishments are among the most impactful and remembered of all the ancient heroes. He's the savior of the fallen Trojans and believed to be the father of the founders of Rome, Romulus and Remus. His multiplicity of successes remind us that listening to others can be just as powerful and inspiring as controlling the dialogue and seeking well-defined answers.

In her book *Quiet*, Susan Cain argues that modern Western culture undervalues the traits and capabilities of introverts, those who value listening and reflecting before speaking. She explains that the character of the Western personality champions the extraverted ideal and views the qualities of introversion as inferior. The Herculean hero is an alpha male who thrives in the spotlight and prefers action over contemplation. Yet Hercules is also rash, makes uninformed decisions, and chooses to attack before understanding. Aeneas is the opposite. Although he has qualities of might, courage, and drive, he's reflective, unobtrusive, and listens deeply to those around him before reaching conclusions. With this attitude, Aeneas learns more about the hidden secrets of the universe than any other hero.

The Aeneid, the legendary story of Aeneas, tells us that he learns to save his people and that he will found Rome by listening to the phantom image of his father. His knowledge comes from connecting to his father, a figure of the deep psyche. In archetypal psychology, this is called *psychological faith*, the notion of images as guiding entities within the psyche, to which one is connected, similar to Jung's concept of the teleological nature of the Self. This could be attending to a dream image, a synchronicity, living symbolically, or using active imagination to deepen our understanding and exploration. Listening to the images of the unconscious is about attuning oneself to the archetypal realm and discerning as best we can what it wants of us.

My brother dreamed he was in our parents' bathroom. "My mother beckons me to look at a figure laying in the tub," he recalled. "I see that it's my father and I ask, 'Is he dead?' As I ask this question, his revitalized head rises above the water. When I had this dream," he continued, "I was emerging from the brain injury, which had left me feeling deadened. I felt torn between a healing process that was not yet complete and a desire to reenter the world, expand, and become my own person. My analyst suggested that my previously 'deadened' paternal energy was reinvigorated with an injection of life principle. My mother beckons to me, which we understood as a maternal invitation to embrace this new energy. I was ready to begin."

The conscious mind is not the only tool we have to heal and expand our being. If we want to enlist strong, non-Herculean inner allies, we can turn toward images, sensations, spiritual practices, meditation, and dreams as ways of envisioning our healing by listening to the deeper, more whole part of ourselves, the Self. The Aenean hero balances the intellect with unconscious guidance. His underworld escort, the Sibyl, is a prophetess of Apollo, the sun god of rational awareness. Aeneas' reliance on the imaginal *and* his connection to reason symbolize the overlap between the two – a strong rational ego (Apollo) and respect for the unconscious (the shade of his father).

The Gift of the Father

Aeneas adored his father to such a degree that, "moved by such a love, so great a longing," twice he swam "the lake of Styx and twice to see black Tartarus." Upon reaching his father, Anchises asked, "[H]as the pious love that your father waited for defeated the difficulty of the journey?" "My father," Aeneas replied, "it was your sad image, so often come, that urged me to these thresholds." In response, Anchises said, "Son, you will have the answer; I shall not keep you in doubt."[10]

Aeneas journeys to gain wisdom that only his father can give him. The father archetype represents the external and forward energy to manifest in the world, constellating feelings of authority, prowess, know-how, confidence, agency, and the wisdom needed to make one's mark on the world. Fathers also represent boundaries, guidance, and protection.

Today, we're no longer connected to the archetypal father as a soul-figure. Jungian Thomas Moore reasoned that we've replaced the deep wisdom of fatherhood with sterile data.

"Information," he explained, "does not evoke fatherhood, and it does not effect initiation."[11] Moore distinguished between informational learning and soul-learning – the teachings of darkness are different from those of the light. To learn from the depths, we must approach them as Aeneas does – with reverence, presence, listening, and openness. This is how we can be fathered and gain the ability to manifest ourselves in the world. We become the "father" of our own life if we're willing to make the journey inward and seek what the depths imbue our life with. It is not a small task.

Moore argued that without a sense of paternity, we're left with mere reason and ideology as guides. "Then we suffer collective fatherlessness," he explained, "not having a clear national direction; giving the spoils of a wealthy economy to a few; finding only rare examples of deep morality, law, and community; not seeking out odyssey because we prefer the solid ground of opinion and ideology."[12]

The absence of the archetypal father can lead a personality structure toward a harmful lack of self-definition and boundaries. A woman whose father was emotionally distant and uninvolved in her childhood worries she is too porous, getting overly involved with other people's lives. Boundaries are hard because she believes that if she doesn't overextend, people won't love her as (she believes) her father didn't. In therapy, she begins to see that because her father didn't provide "fathering," she continues to struggle to know who she is in the inner and outer worlds. She depends on external circumstances to regulate and define her internal emotions and sense of self. The slightest criticism makes her feel as though her existence is in jeopardy.

Without the constellation of the father archetype, being fathered well enough during the developmental stages of childhood and young adulthood, one has to work much harder to develop a strong sense of personal authority. So men (and women) continue through a lifetime projecting "father" onto persons more or less suited to bring them what they lack. But when we miss that boat in childhood, the substitute has to be internal. No college professor, sports coach, or guru can do what needs to be accomplished interiorly, though an image, a sensation, a talisman can represent a father's support and be called upon when needed – when self-doubts arise.

Hillman believed the need for the father created the *heroic self-creator*. Without the father, we risk staying within the bounds of nurturance and being taken care of, which are the qualities of the archetypal mother. To wean ourselves from the mother, we must also embark on a hero's journey and find our own self-reliance – a personal confidence that who we individually are is lovable and okay, with the feeling of "I belong." By journeying to connect with his father, Aeneas awakened his own inner authority.

Anchises gifted his son the clarity he needed to follow his destiny. The role of the father archetype in initiation is to help us release childish ways and become the author of our own life. By listening deeply to his father, Aeneas eventually became the father of a great nation, adopting the epithet *Pater*, Latin for "father." The hero's quest for the father is about the search for one's origination story and unique purpose and manifestation. In darkness, the doubtful part of Aeneas who worried about where his people would build their home was overcome. To gain the boons of the father, one needs to stretch beyond the confines of the puerile ego – self-importance and personal desires only. By facing the father archetype, we can become the father of our lives, transcending the need to be taken care of and finding the inner authority to bring forth who we really are.

To become the father of a nation and of his own destiny, Aeneas had to follow specific rules and accomplish particular tasks that taught him about his fate and the rules and protocols of the universe. His inner sense of fatherhood wasn't gained by brandishing a sword or flexing his muscles, but by being *initiated* into fatherhood.

In many traditional cultures, a person becomes an adult member of their tribe or community by hearing the secrets and stories of their ancestry. Elders tell youth of the origin of their people, pass down rituals and art, and teach laws and culture. During initiation, the neophyte endures ordeals designed to challenge and push them into adulthood. Their place in and value to their community is earned through overcoming a challenge so great that they experience a transformation of character.

The self-centered and immature part of Aeneas died in the underworld, and in its place stood a hero infused with his own creative life force and thus the ability to serve the collective. To breathe life into our future, we must visit our own depths, wander through the caverns of our soul, and converse with the inner figures populating our unconscious. As dependency dies off, agency is born. By passing into the lower world, Aeneas was initiated into the next phase of his life.

World Builder

When a hero is triumphant in his or her adventure, the gods bestow their blessings, and the hero returns to the surface with a treasure capable of restoring the world. His or her heroic achievement is in service not only to self-growth, but also to civilization and the gods. "The more one forgets himself," Victor Frankl wrote, "by giving himself to a cause to serve or another person to love – the more human he is and the more he actualizes himself." [13]

During a time in life when he was trying to sort out his vocational path, a man read a book by a well-known meditation teacher. "I remember a passage," he told me, "that defined immaturity as an unwillingness to contribute to the collective and an inclination toward one's own pleasure. In contrast, maturity was described as a willingness and a readiness to contribute and uphold what you stand for, to give back."

Nelson Mandela built upon his imprisonment and suffering to lead his people from the chains of apartheid. The colonial oppression of India inspired Mahatma Gandhi to spearhead a movement that liberated his people from British rule. A key part of the hero's path is returning from the underworld and teaching the lessons learned to others – translating the wisdom of the depths into the vernacular of the dayworld.

Diagnosed with terminal brain cancer, a woman built her revolution. She imagined creating a center where she would bring together healers who could help others navigate illnesses like hers. Since childhood, she had a spark that others were drawn to. Her path glittered and beckoned; people from all walks of life reached out to her, fascinated by how she was approaching her healing. With images and faith, positivity and reverence for her body, she healed herself. As her tumor shrank, her arms began to work again and her fingers wiggled. She was determined to use these experiences to help others. "Now," she told me, "I can say things to people that I wasn't able to before."

The most consequential thing Aeneas learned was his role in building the world-shaping city of Rome. A part of heroism is, after exposing yourself to the chaos of the inner world, to work to better those around you. Jung felt that the best way for individuals to affect the collective was through their own inner work. We have to distinguish who we are before we can access our unique gifts and use them for societal betterment. Oprah Winfrey's incredibly successful talk show has impacted the lives of millions. She was born into poverty to a teenage single mother. During her career, she has disclosed sexual abuse, pregnancy, and the death of her child. She's overcome tremendous personal challenges to be a force of influence and philanthropy in the world.

Often my clients tell me they want to live more connected and purposeful lives in their communities and networks. On some level, they know that extending beyond themselves and connecting to others is a source of healing.

The hero's path may ultimately serve the collective, but it starts on a personal level. My father shared with me the following dream:

> I'm standing at the edge of a warm ocean on a sunny day. It's peaceful, the water is softly lapping at my toes. Then, gently, I drown in the incoming tide. I'm not afraid and I don't resist. The only witness is a faceless, gray figure, not at all threatening, just there.

"When I woke up," he recalled, "I knew I had died; I remembered every detail and realized that the shadowy figure was me waiting to take shape after the death of what needed to die within so I could become myself."

The hero's ability to build a new world comes, in part, from a symbolic dying to the world they've known. During the journey, some part of him or her dies. When they return, they're infused with energy and potential. As past behaviors, worn-out or limited, are released, new energy flows in. Aeneas left the undeveloped and insecure parts of himself in the underworld. He entered Hades confused about his role and his path, and he left determined and clear.

The Courage of Peace

Aenean courage isn't violent, forceful, or ego-driven. It's thoughtful and serves the betterment of the collective. The Sibyl, while defending Aeneas from approaching shades, cried, "Now leave the grove; only Aeneas move ahead, unsheathe your sword; you need your courage now; you need your heart."[14] To journey into darkness with your heart open takes a different courage than charging forth with willpower. "Courage" derives from the Latin *cor* meaning "heart." *Cor*-age is bravery that comes from emotion, not from egoic determination or forcefulness.

Facing what frightens us from a place of wholeheartedness takes as much strength, or more, than brandishing a weapon at what we fear or don't understand. Anger can be an easy emotion to feel. More often than not, leading with the heart is more difficult. American Tibetan Buddhist nun Pema Chödrön teaches her students to meet difficulties with confidence and grace. The key, she says, is when things fall apart, having the courage *to rest in the open space of uncertainty* instead of trying to put them back together.

After Aeneas' journey, Apollo told him to "grow in your new courage, child; O son of gods and ancestor of gods, this is the way to scale the stars. All fated, future wars shall end in peace beneath Assaracus' house; for the walls of Troy cannot contain you."[15] The Aenean hero has *the courage to be peaceful* – to build a lasting civilization, stop wars, and end inner conflicts. It's said that in the Trojan War, Aeneas' courage forced all the gods, including the wrathful Hera, to put an end to their longstanding anger. There is colossal power in Aenean courage – a valor so profound that it ended the greatest battle of the gods.

Although his footsteps are said to have been "unfaltering," a picture that brings to mind Herculean fortitude, Aenean courage is soft, serves the well-being of his people, and comes from emotionality and heart, not force. This expression of courage, so different from Hercules', is Aeneas' path to becoming a god. As they do with Hercules, the gods honor Aeneas' achievements with immortality, reminding us that leading with heart is as honorable as moving forward with might and sword.

Aeneas' growth isn't Orphic – resistant and unforeseen, Herculean – forceful and temporary, or Odyssean – questioning and accepting. His is a quality of maturation that comes from a *willingness to trust* and *surrender to* the guiding influence of the unconscious.

Unlike other heroes, Aeneas showed compassion. Virgil described him as wandering through the oppressive gloom of Hades and pitying the fates of the dead. When he met the shade of his past lover Dido, Queen of Carthage, he tried to comfort her by explaining why he left her kingdom. Unable to recognize him, she glided past in silence. "Seldom," wrote Jungian analyst James Hollis, "has silence spoken so thunderously."[16] Aeneas followed Dido in tears, feeling the pain of her death and suffering. When he reached his father, he "sighed heavily with pity and stretched out his right hand; the image of his love for his own father touched his mind."[17] He is frequently said to have concealed his woes from his companions and although "sick with heavy cares ... he counterfeits hope in his face; his pain is held within, hidden."[18] Aeneas put his own woes aside to care for the well-being of others.

It takes courage to feel compassion for ourselves *and* others, particularly when we're lost in the dark caverns of our minds. "We are often more tender to the dead than to the living," writes Robert MacFarlane, "though it is the living who need our tenderness most."[19] Why don't we show the neglected parts of psyches the same tenderness as the ones we wear in plain sight? It's easier to return to an old diary and feel compassion for the version of ourselves immortalized on the pages than for the one tenderly rereading today. Then in five or ten years, we look back on who we are today and find compassion for that struggling, growing, and searching part of us. *It's the living part of ourselves in the present moment that needs our tenderness most.*

Journeying into darkness requires *self*-compassion. In the wake of brutal violence, emotional abuse, illness, and complexes of shame or insecurity, we have no choice but to retreat and survive. The defense mechanisms of the psyche take over and we build psychological systems that distance and remove us from our pain, and at the same time from our true selves. To heal, we have to honor the fragmentation, grieve for what we had to abandon in order to survive, and give the pain we felt a place in our lives. To do this, we turn toward the trauma we continue to inflict on ourselves, re-enacting the survival circuitry that saved us once, in order to heal. By compassionately turning inward, we see how we abandoned ourselves to survive and feel the unhealed wound beneath the defense.

"There's a lot of power and freedom in being vulnerable," my brother said. "To be vulnerable is to express your own truth. If you come to that place, there isn't anything anyone can do to hurt you, because you're speaking and acting from your baseline essence. That's how I free myself from feeling unencumbered by the baggage of defense, protection, and the hindrance of not being able to express myself because I'm afraid what someone might think of me."

"How does that help you navigate your darkness?" I asked.

"It allows me to say and feel okay about where I honestly am, even when I'm unable to step up to external or internal expectations. I don't have to pretend to be someone in their mid-twenties in their prime gallivanting around the world like my friends. I need to be okay that I'm living with my parents and taking care of my health. Being vulnerable taps me back into the opportunity and the redemption that comes from giving the parts of myself that are growing because of the experience their place. It's being compassionate to myself."

Brené Brown is widely known for her research and presentations on vulnerability. Her TEDx talk, "The Power of Vulnerability," is one of the most viewed TED talks in the world. She defines vulnerability as uncertainty, risk, and emotional exposure, and shares that because she grew up in a family and culture that valued sucking it up and containing emotion, she wasn't taught how to deal with uncertainty or manage emotional risk.

"I spent a lot of years trying to outrun or outsmart vulnerability by making things certain and definite, black and white, good and bad," she explained. "My inability to lean into the discomfort of vulnerability limited the fullness of those important experiences that are wrought with uncertainty: love, belonging, trust, joy, and creativity to name a few. Learning how to be vulnerable has been a street fight for me, but it's been worth it."[20] She wisely points out, "We cannot selectively numb emotions, when we numb the painful emotions, we also numb the positive emotions."[21]

So often we avoid the unconscious energies of difficult stories, painful memories, and overwhelming experiences because we want to appear steady and in control. When this intention fails, we're consumed with guilt, shame, regret, and disappointment. Coping with hardship begins with accepting our imperfections. During his journey, Aeneas stopped to feel for the figures he met along the way, watching and grieving for their suffering. Imagine facing hardship with such compassion – accepting your and others' failures, suffering, and weakness – vulnerably *being with* the dark emotions that stir in you. The courage to do compassionate and vulnerable inner work is a part of what makes Aeneas a great hero and leader among his people.

Ascending

Aenean ascent deserves special recognition, because in Greek and Roman mythology, his and Orpheus' are the only heroic returns to the dayworld that are fleshed out. Aeneas and the Sibyl returned through a gate made of polished ivory. As they retraced their steps, Aeneas told the Sibyl that she was equal to a goddess in his eyes and promised to build a temple in her honor: "The Sibyl looked back at him and with a deep sigh replied, 'I am no goddess, and you must not think any human being worthy of the honor of holy incense. Lest you should err in ignorance, I shall tell you my story.'"[22]

Once more Aeneas reveals his unparalleled reverence, promising a temple in return for the Sibyl's guidance. Unlike other hero myths, this shows that characteristics of modesty and gratitude are also heroic. The Sibyl, consistently described as fierce and wild, shared with Aeneas her life story. In this moment there is gentleness, curiosity, and longing for deep connection. Sometimes we return from the journey humbled, grateful, and curious about the forces we encountered and endured. Replacing feelings of disconnection, failure, and worthlessness with gratitude for our struggles, our safe return, lessons learned, and personal growth can help us live more fully.

Aeneas' is one of two heroic ascents that mentions the challenges of the return. The Sibyl warned, "[T]o recall your steps, to rise again into the upper air: that is the labor; that is the task."[23] Integration is the ultimate challenge of the heroic journey – having had the experience of darkness, the real work begins. We fell into the underworld, a shock to the system, and scrambled to survive. But when the storm settles and life resumes, how do we allow this experience and all we've learned to enter and inform our routines, our daily life? Falling is challenging and usually unpleasant. Now, the labor is *rising to the upper air*. How we show up for a lifetime of ascending and returning shapes who we will become. The hardest part of underworld journeying is returning to our lives, forever changed, and having the courage and commitment to weave our newly informed selves back into the world, and not return to the addictions and numbing habits that no longer serve us.

Integration is a lifetime affair. We're always healing from moments of greater and lesser darkness and recalibrating who we are. Through the death of a parent, loss of a spouse, physical injury, or mental collapse, we plummet into the underworld. To heal and integrate what has befallen us, we must eventually ascend from darkness and bring all we've experienced into our new reality. Like the sun, we rise and set each day.

Aeneas is an image of reverence for the powers of the deep psyche. He follows the archetypal energies of life by deeply listening, valuing, and trusting the messages of the inner world. He pertains to the parts of us that ask for guidance and aren't determined to rely on ourselves alone to navigate the journey within. In the underworld, Aeneas listens and because of his vulnerability and self-compassion he comes into a greater sense of his own authentic wholeness and authority. He is an image of the immense challenges of integration and ascending from darkness.

Reflections

Aeneas is about openness to that which is beyond us and a willingness to follow the messages of the larger energies – the unconscious psyche. His character tells us what's required of us to trust a guide to navigate the journey within. He is a figure that honors, listens, and understands the lifelong challenges of ascending from darkness. We evoke Aeneas when we enter the abyss with acceptance and reverence.

Reflect on how these Aenean qualities may be present within your experience in:

- Seeking guidance.
- Reverence – believing a higher purpose or source guides you.
- Using a talisman – an inner image or object – to provide strength and comfort.
- Listening in a quiet and reflective way.
- Psychological faith – letting images, dreams, or fantasies inspire and guide.
- Healing through world-building, i.e., helping the collective and learning to be ourselves in relationship to others.
- The courage to be peaceful and compassionate.
- Honoring the challenges of ascending and integrating what you've encountered.

III.

THE GODS

CHAPTER 8
HERMES

The ancient Greeks told stories of a young and elusive god, lithe-footed, fair, and winged. Hermes, son of Zeus and the nymph Maia, was the god of communication, travel, and trade. He ruled over thresholds and trickery, and guided souls into and from the land of death.

Although we are no longer in the classical era, Hermes – known as Mercury in Rome – continues to pervade our world. His presence is revealed in our messages and interactions, our innovations and upheavals. He was patron to all forms of movement, and thus pertains to the parts of us that are creative and changing, quick and persuasive. Woven together, the characteristics of this nimble and devious god give shape to a particular way of handling darkness.

Guide of Souls

As a psychopomp, a "guide of souls," Hermes escorted all heroes, immortals, and souls as they journeyed into and from the underworld. He was honored as *Psukhais Pompos* ("the souls you bring"), *Kataibates* ("one who descends"), and *Diaktoros* ("guide"). In an Orphic hymn, Hermes was said to:

> Dwell on the road all must take, the road of no return,
> by the Kokytos, you guide the souls of mortals to
> the nether gloom … you haunt the sacred house of
> Persephone as guide throughout the earth of ill-fated
> souls, the souls you bring to their destined harbor
> when their time has come; you charm them with your
> sacred wand, you give them sleep from which you
> rouse them again.[1]

Hermes understands inherently how to find, enter, inhabit, and integrate underworlding. His undertaking was the journey; he was the only Olympian to deal directly with the mysteries of death, a specific and important role. He personifies an innate and familiar connection to the underworld, not needing to learn how to navigate these realms, a quality that earned him the epithet *Ad Utrumque Peritu,* "skilled in both worlds."

When we are in need of guidance and life plummets us into the underworld, when we're face to face with our fears, insecurities, coping strategies, and losses, the *essence of Hermes* manifests as a guide. The path into the deep is full of unknown hurdles and emotions. Darkness is not a place to wander alone.

In the beginning of his journey into hell, Dante says, "Midway in our life's journey, I went astray from the straight road and woke to find myself alone in a dark wood."[2] Underworlding can be terrifying; we fear becoming lost forever and never finding our way back to sunlight. In darkness, the ordinary things of life seem disjointed, as if at unnatural angles, slightly unbalanced and askew. I'm reminded of the Holocaust Memorial museum in Berlin, where thousands of stones are placed on sloping ground in a disorienting, wavelike pattern. The architecture's effect is to make the visitor feel lost and confused. The horror of Nazism is captured in the off-kilter stones that create a feeling of being lost.

A guide can give us the security needed to stand at the edge of the unknown or the edge of new growth and see in the distant horizon the areas of ourselves that need to be explored. Sometimes guidance comes from a tangible source. When helping students handle life's unfamiliarities, a teacher can be "Hermes." When connecting followers to the divine, a religious leader is Hermetic. When navigating illness with a patient, a doctor is Hermes-like. Guidance can come from a friend, mentor, process group, family member, or partner. As a psychotherapist, my work includes helping people find orientation and meaning in the face of challenges, companioning them as they engage with otherworldly energies.

A man who serves as a guide for wilderness therapy programs summarized his job as chaperoning people through their own worst nightmares. "I bring them to hell, keep them safe, and guide them out," he told me. "I'm the container – the ferryman, the boat, and the river." He too experiences growth and self-empowerment in his work. To stand with others in their own darkness, he has to face his own.

Guidance doesn't only come from people. It also comes from intangible sources such as symbols, dreams, images, fantasy, literature, art, and the divine. In *Anxiety and Magic Thinking*, psychoanalyst Charles Odier recounts the story of a patient named Ariane, who was violently criticized by her father and often abandoned as a child. Ariane's childhood trauma strangled her ability to feel safe, strong in herself, and mature. Odier recounts a dream in which Ariane found herself in a strange land. There, a god appeared who showed her an image of her family in deep mourning. The dream connected her to an inner figure that helped her accept her shame, fear of abandonment, and lack of meaning. In the abyss, she discovered an energy that nurtured and guided her on the path to wholeness.

The ancient Greeks called a sanctuary dedicated to the worship of a god a *temenos*, an "enclosed sacred space." The temenos of Hermes is an imaginative inner space we turn to for guidance and containment during underworlding. In this inner sanctuary, images and metaphor can be held and honored. We can't eliminate the unyielding grip of fear, the taunting voice of trauma, the bluntness of death, or the whisper of worry, but it's possible to carve a place of safety within, to rest our weary bones.

I've seen many people rely on a Hermetic temenos when they need guidance and support. During radiation treatments, a woman had a spontaneous image of empty space. At first she thought the space represented all the places in her life cancer had killed – her vitality, sense of confidence, and identity as a fighter. When she explored the void more deeply, she was surprised to feel a presence of fullness that made her feel less alone.

Of the many dreams I've had, a sequence of two lingers in my soul. In the first, which I had as a child, I am sitting in a waterless bathtub looking out a window at a distant castle. I gaze at the castle and see inside its walls. A giant staircase coils upward, the walls lined with books. The space is filled with a golden light – soft, gentle, and magical. The light is a deep breath. Upstairs, I hear a faint rustling and know it's a dragon, playfully rummaging around the bookshelves.

The light in this dream has long been a place of inner safety and beauty for me. I return to it when I feel lost and alone, confused about life steps, in grief, fear and overwhelm. I also return here to release a client's energy I've taken on. In my brother's gray and sterile hospital room, I spent hours envisioning that light filling his room.

I remembered the light from the castle, but I didn't dream of it again for many years. In the beginning of my mother-in-law's cancer journey, I struggled to a find balance between my powerlessness in the face of it and my ability to offer her care options through my professional networks. The ice I stood upon felt thin. I was unsure and helpless, and the light returned, resourcing me again after so many years.

In the other dream, I enter a dusty antique shop in search of an ancient object. The shopkeeper, a disheveled young man, says we can discuss the item in his home office. I follow him to the back of the gloomy shop where he pushes open an old door. We step into a colossal room — marble floors, brick walls, and the same golden, familiar, magical, entirely "other" light. Awestruck, I tell the shopkeeper how beautiful his home is. We make our way to his office, which is lined with white bookshelves full of sacred books, objects, and flowers. I feel at peace.

When the ego runs out of options, something new needs to step in. In my darkness, the light returned, reorienting me to the old things, the ancient realm, and my memory of a world full of magic, beauty, and harmony. The light helps me accept what is happening around me. It reminds me of energies and forces greater and more intelligent than I.

The underworld doesn't always mean terrifying blackness. What is interior and deep within the inner world can offer light and guidance. If we live only externally, there's no way to survive the unbearable. To lose a connection with the inner world is to lose connection with the Self, the source of life and meaning. Without a relationship with the dark places of our minds and souls, we cannot hope to find the chambers that are well lit and full of hope.

The Greeks told the story of the Minotaur, a bull-headed monster imprisoned in the center of a labyrinth beneath the island of Crete. The beast was a flesh-eating horror named Asterion, "star." Our experiences of death, suffering, and depression consume us, as does this mythic beast – devouring our souls and forcing us into dark tunnels without hope of escape. But we must be careful not to overlook the shining star, even within the darkest night. Astronomer Carl Sagan told us that all we are is made in the interior of a dying star; *we are the stuff of stars.*

Legends tell of dragons and monsters that turn into princes and princesses. Many fairytales begin with an old hag who is in fact a beautiful sorceress. Aladdin was called the diamond in the rough, referring to being unpolished but having the potential to become a priceless jewel. Perhaps all monsters are secret treasures – everything terrible, unfathomable, and dark may be in its deepest sense something enriching and meaningful. Sometimes darkness has its own source of light.

Hermes was god of the roundtrip journey. Out of the depths, he pointed the way to the surface, making the return possible. When the air is thick and black, Hermes is the light at the end of the tunnel, the life vest in the storm. Guidance can help us feel witnessed and supported enough to endure the meaning-making process so essential to healing. In an interview about dreams, Jungian analyst Barry Williams said, "When great dreams announce the journey you're undertaking, you need to have a guide, because it's an initiatory journey."[3] The dream is a guide, as is the analyst who helps interpret the unconscious and holds the container for integration. Aeneas journeyed deeper into the underworld and learned more about the order of the cosmos because of his guide, not his muscle or valor. Finding the courage to stride into the dark parts of ourselves and be with the hardest moments of life often requires trusting we're not alone.

Let's return to the woman I mentioned in chapter 5, who shared her journey as a wounded healer. Her trauma forced her to fall headfirst into a darkness so complete she lost her way entirely. As she shared with a therapist willing to go with her into the deep underworld of trauma, her healing journey began. The magic ingredient of change wasn't a seismic intervention or clever theory; it was that she no longer felt alone in her suffering. Her wounds remained, memories continued to torment her; but by meeting someone who wasn't afraid to join her in the darkness, she was able to return to the surface.

We all need guidance when underworlding. The need for support during times of change and suffering has long been the domain of spiritual traditions, myths, legends, and folklore. Elders guide initiates into caves or isolated cabins where they undergo days of fasting and isolation. Fear kills the youthful part of them, darkness transforms them into adults. Religious leaders listen to confessions and dole out reparations. Myths and fairytales relay archetypal wisdom expressed through the images and imagination of their culture of origin.

In a world that has lost much of its spiritual footing, it's common to rely on yourself and not seek guidance. The underworld may be dark and full of terror, but it's our burden and our business. This Herculean ideal teaches us to be strong and independent. But in Greek myth, all mortals and divinities who journey into the lower realm received the favor of guidance – even Hercules, who was aided by Hermes. Odysseus was given directions by the goddess Circe; Aeneas heeded the advice of the Sibyl; Persephone also followed Hermes; and Dionysus learned the way from a herdsman. A part of finding new and healthier ways to enter into relationship with our pain and our limiting behaviors is to ask for help.

The roads of life are rarely straight or unhindered. Branches fall and obstacles present themselves. One moment our way seems unencumbered, only to be disrupted the moment we turn the bend. In cult worship, Hermes' incarnation was the *herm* stone heaps used to mark roads and pathways – the piles of stones where trails meet, to help us find our way. A herm is a symbol of set-in-stone, steadfast guidance. No matter how unfamiliar or frightening life becomes, Hermetic guidance is as constant and durable as stone.

Worshiped as *Akaketa*, the "painless one," Hermes is the helping hand supporting every level of human life. He is the god of shepherds, servants, and everyday duties – lighting fires, chopping wood, preparing meals. He guides perilous journeys, presides over commerce and thoroughfares, conveys prayers and messages to the gods, and conducts souls to the underworld. More than any other god, Hermes is concerned with our well-being. Every unexpected find on the road was believed to be a gift of Hermes, a *hermaion*.

During the Trojan War, King Priam's son Hector was killed by Achilles. After Hector's death, Priam was filled with grief and worry for his people. The goddess Thetis told the sorrowful king not to "let any thought of death trouble your heart, nor fear; for Hermes, Slayer of Argos, will follow you as escort."[4] As his kingdom fell and his heir lay dead, Priam found comfort in the belief that a god was steadying his faltering footsteps.

Hermes may be the god of the day-to-day rhythms of life, but as a god he's also beyond mortal tasks. He aids and assists in our endeavors but does not experience them with us. One of the essential aspects of psychotherapy is processing life with someone removed from our own experiences. For many, the therapeutic alliance is the only relationship in which we can freely share ourselves without the fear of judgment, hurting someone in our lives, or feeling ashamed. To bear our uncertainty and turmoil alone is unrealistic and, in my opinion, not healthy.

Psychotherapist as psychopomp is about guiding another into the depths of their inner world to find unknown parts of themselves and explore the beliefs and behaviors that bring them pain. The therapist must be able to deal with the untouchable things – death, disease, suffering, fear, and mental illness – in ways that allow the client to be in dialogue with these energies. It is about being with people who are at thresholds.

The importance of the task of guiding a soul into darkness cannot be underestimated. It's an extraordinary art to lead someone into the heights or depths of their experiences and a profound gift to have someone who will take you right to the River Styx. At that point therapy becomes shamanic: the therapist accompanies you to the threshold, opening the pathway to soul and image that guide you as you journey beyond. I'm reminded of the dedication at the beginning of Marion Woodman's book, *Bone: Dying into Life*: "To those who have dared the darkness, and those who have walked with them, without pity."[5]

Jungian analyst Marie-Louise von Franz once worked with a client who wasn't able to share much in their sessions. One day, the client said she'd had a dream image of an egg. Excited, von Franz went to work analyzing the image. Years later, the woman told von Franz she never remembered anything she'd said that day. She only remembered the excitement and hope von Franz conveyed, which helped her return hope to her life.

Most often, guidance is positive, preventing us from getting lost and helping us access deeper parts of ourselves. Yet losing our way can also be a step toward finding ourselves. When life is going well, we don't have to make the same kinds of changes as when it's falling apart. But when the stories that define us become irrelevant or even obstructive, we're tasked with trying something new. We lean toward security and familiarity, but getting lost, particularly if we are lucky enough to have a guide, can be the beginning of finding who we really are. In the words of J. R. R. Tolkien: "Not all those who wander are lost."

Familiarity with Death

As guide of souls, Hermes shows us how to have a relationship with death. From life's point of view, death is an ending – the destruction of everything known and treasured. However, psychologically, death is rarely a problem; it's a forerunner to rebirth – the cornerstone upon which the new is born, not failure or finality. The secret to change is to focus energy not on fighting the threats to the old, but on building the new.

I once dreamed Nazi fighters were chasing me through the demolished streets of a war-stricken city. I reached a stream and ran into the water. A gun fired and I saw blood pouring from my chest. Gently, I fell into the stream. Lifeblood drained from my body and I felt comforted. From the dream's point of view, I needed to let go of the world-shaping battles I was fighting – the direction of my career, where to live, whether or not to have children. I needed to let myself be in the current of my life.

A life protected from death and disruption is unrealistic. We all lose friends, family, and jobs, suffer illnesses, and face the demons of the inner world, over and over. A golden life is not promised to us; it's a fantasy that constricts our ability to respond to actual challenges. "To be, and to enjoy your being," reflected Jung, "you need death … limitation enables you to fulfill your being."[6] Impermanence extenuates the preciousness and wonder of being alive.

Death takes hold of us in ways that are difficult to understand and hard to cope with. Death's manifestations, whether tangible, symbolic, or imaginal, want a relationship, an inner dialogue. To avoid or deny death imagery because we're afraid or unfamiliar with the territory is to invite it to pop into our lives in other ways. Marion Woodman said her cancer "was death asking to be accepted into my life."[7] Death does not exist in the absence of life, but in its presence. "Life and death are journeys that must be taken," said Russel Lockhart, "shrinking back from either is fuel for the tragedy of meaninglessness."[8]

Hermes created specific sacrificial rituals. He poured the first wine for the gods and spilled the blood of the first bull. "Sacrifice is not destruction," wrote Jung, "sacrifice is the foundation stone of what is to come."[9] A part of responding to life differently and building a relationship with death is giving up behaviors, beliefs, and ways of living that no longer apply; they have already served their purpose. To be present for adulthood, one must sacrifice youth – freedom and lack of responsibility are put to rest. To join a partnership, one must sacrifice certain aspects of independence – self-centeredness is let go of. To mature, we must sacrifice dependence – assuming authority and taking responsibility replace reliance on others.

For trauma survivors, letting-go processes are particularly hard because shifts in their environment threaten retraumatization. Suffering is linked to change and so change is avoided, and the personality closes itself to new experiences. What is old, even if unhealthy, is at least safe and known. As Marion Woodman puts it:

> Every time I am overcome with the terror of getting
> born into a new reality, in every case I was moving out
> of an area in which I could perform well into a new area,
> and I was sure that some terrible disaster would happen,
> so I wanted to stay put. Being born had taken me into a
> hostile and dangerous environment, and that seeded a
> bone-deep ambivalence about change and growth.[10]

To make the sacrifices needed to integrate darkness, we need to recognize that death in the psyche is not about finality, but beginning. The sacrifices of underworlding are for the sake of renewing life. The concept of "persuasion" is linked to the Greek goddess Peitho, herald of Aphrodite and goddess of charming speech. An underworld perspective requires a *peithos* of death, a way to persuade yourself of the value of death and darkness, be that the many symbolic deaths that presage growth and wholeness, or the death of the body. We have to acquaint ourselves with death's images, messages, and insights, asking what needs to die so we can grow into who we really are.

Sacrifice and death are core to working with the symbolism of cancer. There's a complex biological and genetic aspect to cancer, but there is also a psychological one. The urge in the body to die must be tended symbolically and archetypally. As mentioned, cancer is unchecked cellular growth; symbolically it mirrors the unconstrained growth of harmful behaviors, limiting coping skills, denial of the unconscious and the seat of our being. We need to explore what parts of us need to die for new life to appear. If you don't have growth in one way, you'll have it in another. How can letting go of what needs to be released restore balance and boundaries, and cool the inflammation of the body by calming the mind? If harmful parts of the psyche are allowed to die, death may not have to move in such a literal way, taking the body.

We need to hold the opposites of creation and destruction – life and death – and ask ourselves what needs to die in us to allow for new life. Woodman describes going low to feel the pulse of life in the deep places of the earth. From this place we can see our limited clutch on life and undergo a death experience that is often needed to live differently. Sometimes it takes facing death to live our best life.

Movement

Much of Hermes' character boils down to movement and the capacity to cross thresholds, bridge gaps, and dart between the upper and lower realms. Hermes is ever-moving, ever-changing, going beyond borders of definition and limitation to seek what is emerging and stirring. He is described as moving with haste moments after his birth. He was called "the swift runner," pausing only "long enough to put on his winged sandals, to take in his potent hand the rod which induces slumber, and to set his cap upon his head."[11]

Nothing about Hermes sits still. No label, idea, symptom, or belief system binds the Hermetic (Mercurial) personality. He pertains to parts of us that are constantly shifting, volatizing, changing. Hermes' winged sandals, called *talaria,* allowed him to traverse land and water, sky and earth. The avian god of flight and spirit was never bound to one locale.

Completely absorbed by movement, Hermes personifies the complexity of a constantly shifting world. "Hermes is crucial," writes Keiron Le Grice, "in that he represents the potential to move between different archetypal universes, as it were, and to not become trapped in a singular perspective."[12] The god of ever-shifting perspectives carries our ability to be in-flux, embodying the truism that the only constant is change.

Darkness is constantly in motion. Panic passes, fear softens, confidence replaces insecurity, failure and achievement ebb and flow, solitude changes into connection, and dawn replaces night. Anxiety can be so extreme we have to sit down, but after grounding ourselves, our alarm returns to the depths and the water is once again still. Grief is often described as a tide, a river, waves, or a current, all expressions of water's fluid properties.

Hermes is the nexus of transitions. He is the god of travel – changes in location, shapeshifting – changes in form, communication – exchanges in language and ideas, and business – exchanges of commodities and services. He pertains to evolution, new ideas, and anything that stimulates our psyches, moving us from where we are to places we haven't known before.

The first death I experienced was of a high school friend, and to cope, I wanted to be around friends. I needed to talk about his death. Later, when an old boyfriend died, I was angry at the loss of such a bright light. I wanted to go back in time and correct lingering mistakes I felt I'd made. When my mother-in-law died, I accepted grief as a partner to my life, knowing her loss and all she represented would take many forms throughout the rest of my life. And I wanted to know how best to care for my husband. Each circumstance was different, and so was each response.

Life is full of transitions – birth to maturity, maidenhood to marriage, dependence to independence, healthy to sick, familiar to unfamiliar, life to death. At any moment, we have countless thresholds to choose from; we can step forward into growth or back into familiarity, we can move into the unknown or remain comfy. There's always the option to respond to the call of life and the trials of development or remain on protected, albeit stagnant, ground. Hermes embodies the ability to be in the changing currents of life – to bear the storm for the promise of sunshine, to endure winter to hear the birds of spring.

Fluctuating between realms, Hermes is neither here nor there. When life seems narrow, Hermes kindles the fire of potential. If something is blocked or gated, he slips between the cracks, inviting flexibility and freedom. "The mercurial element within a personality," said Professor Ginette Paris, "brings mobility and unpredictability."[13] He pertains to our ability to adapt, glide over obstacles, and sit amid the unsettling nature of the unfamiliar.

Hermetic journeys don't build with time and intention. They appear in a blaze – as if by magic. They halt us mid-stride, slap us in the face, or hit us like a bus. The underworld has a knack for surprise. Pain flits in and out, grief is a pendulum, and moments of daylight and darkness are quick to appear and disappear. Premeditated underworld descents are the exception. More often than not, we just plummet into the abyss.

We've all experienced or know someone who abruptly found themselves in darkness. When their mother passed away in her sleep, a woman's sister called to tell her the news. She felt the world fall away. In a second, she no longer had a living parent. I mentioned earlier the friend of mine who was killed when an overhanding ledge of snow fell on him while he was skiing. In a moment of shifting of ice and water, a brilliant mind, a wild soul, a goofball loved by many was gone, and a community wandered in the black tunnels of pain and remorse.

Hermes flexes, dissolves, ungrounds, and lifts. Sometimes it's the shifting of the old world, sometimes the opening of the new. Clinical psychology champions therapies that reduce the complexity of human experience to categories and diagnoses. Characteristics of the personality that are enigmatic and unpredictable are labeled unstable, even pathological. Psychological understanding comes from standardization, measurement, and stability, not movement or flexibility. When our psychology has less freedom, we become more rigid.

We all know people with Hermetic qualities – they are curious, seek to understand but don't feel bound to partake or be responsible for an outcome or an idea, and seem to be more at ease while underworlding. Hermetic personalities seek the novel; they're caught up in devising new stories, roads, and options. These people lithely move from one attitude to another – nothing sticks, snags, or binds, embodying what the Greeks called *omnes colores,* "all colors." They are open to the complexity and fluidity of life, absorbed in movement, always seeking new perspectives instead of holding on to the old ways.

Hermes was associated with the metal quicksilver (mercury), a transformative substance capable of incredible malleability. "At a temperature where other metals are hard," writes Ginette Paris, "mercury is liquid and flowing."[14] When other parts of life cool off and solidify, the Hermetic personality is still in flux. He never settles or congeals, always flickering and transforming. Hillman called this *mercurial opportunism,* "having no fixed position, no sense of being at the center, keeps his eye on the door, the thresholds where transiencies pass over from statement to implication, from fact to supposition, from report to fantasy."[15] By inviting us to explore all possibilities, good and bad, light and dark, Hermes prevents us from reducing the complexity of life to a single story or suite of beliefs. Even the most calcified and ingrained parts of ourselves can shift – anything solid can be made liquid once again.

Puer and Puella

Constant fluctuation and movement can create a personality that's always filled with *potential*, never congealing to mature. The mercurial nature produces people who can be hard to get a hold of, transforming endlessly, and impossible to restrain. If the capacity to select and manifest is lost, the wheel turns endlessly. Hermes, wrote Hillman, has "no footnotes and you can't get a handle on its idea … [He is the] breeze through the window, freshening but ungraspable."[16]

A personality under this archetypal influence is called a *puer* or *puella*. The archetype of the *puer* (masculine) or *puella* (feminine) are expressions of eternal youth. *Puer aeternus*, Latin for "eternal boy," relates to qualities of freshness, spirit, freedom, and opportunity. It's a sensibility enchanted by the desire to rise above the ordinary, seeking height rather than depth, speed rather than gravitas. The *puer* is absorbed with soaring, rising, and of course, inflating. This personality is driven to remain unchained, ungrounded, and uninhibited.

The Greeks told the story of Icarus, the son of Daedalus. Seeking to escape King Minos of Crete, Daedalus crafted two sets of waxen wings, and together father and son escaped across the sea. As they flew, Icarus soared higher and higher. Ignoring his father's warnings, he flew so close to the sun that his waxen wings melted and he fell into the sea.

The shadow quality of the *puer* is ego inflation. Hypnotized by his own ability, ideas, and freedom, Icarus flies ever closer to peril. Inflation is an energy of height, spirit, and godliness. It bespeaks a lack of roots and reality. We can't be grounded while soaring above the tedium of reality. If someone with unbalanced *puer* energy is forced downward too quickly, their life force fades. They become depressed, plummeting to earth with melted wings.

Puer energy is inspiring, alluring, quick, and inventive. The danger is preferring potential over choice and maturation.

Peter Pan is the quintessential *puer* figure; everything remains in the hypothetical. "I could have been …" becomes the anthem of one's life. There is a reason Peter Pan lives in Neverland: nothing happens there. *Puer* personalities could have had the kingdom, but they *imagined* life instead of living it. An unbalanced preference for possibilities leads to a pathological lack of actualization. Part here, part there, but nowhere at all.

In my mid-twenties I had a dream sequence in which I was repeatedly kicked out of fancy resorts. Dream figures refused to serve me at the pool, my hotel room flooded, and my credit card stopped working. At the time, freedom and lack of responsibility were my main food groups. The parts of me that didn't want to grow up coveted the comforts of resort life, where everything is easy and taken care of. Over and over, the dreams told me I don't belong in a resort.

The archetype that brings balance to the *puer* is the *senex*, meaning "old man." The *senex* represents wisdom earned through repetition, tradition, age, order, time, suffering, and coagulation. The capacity to harvest the fields. Life happens through making choices, not by keeping all the doors ajar. The paradox of the *puer/senex* dynamic is that if we give up everything, we gain everything. If the *senex* aspect of personality development is denied, individuals limit themselves by an inapt clinging to youth and possibility.

The *senex* was associated with the Titan Cronus, later adopted by the Romans as the god Saturn. Cronus was the grandfather of the gods, embodying the wisdom of time, experience, and suffering. Saturnian energy weathers and ages, like the wind slowly reshaping the desert. Cronus had the attribute of a harvester's sickle, signifying the reaping of a season's toil. Associated with the metal lead, Saturn is about form, weight, and substance. A life too enchanted by promise leads to an inability to take life seriously, a hollow sense of identity, being nebulous and insubstantial.

It's difficult to let go of youth and its promise of freedom. Maturation requires an acknowledgment of the *senex's* influence – death, repetition, depression, solidification, and the heaviness of tradition and responsibility. Those that choose eternal youth invite the *senex* into their lives in shadow form. Cronus heard a prophecy warning that his children would overthrow him. In fear, he devoured his children – Demeter, Hestia, Hera, Hades, and Poseidon. His sixth child, Zeus, was spared and eventually rose up to battle his father, claiming the title of ruler of the gods for himself. In shadow form, life energy can be devoured by the *senex*, preventing us from emerging into the world. Instead of prudence and the gifts of manifestation, we become overly disciplined and controlled, forgetting to shift, change, or be lighthearted. *Puer* and *senex* need each other; together they create balance.

Messenger

Hermes was the herald (messenger) of the immortals, eternally responsible for enforcing the will of the gods. He carried a caduceus or herald's staff. "I shall give you a beautiful staff of wealth and prosperity," said Apollo, "a golden one with three branches, to protect you against harm and to accomplish all the laws of noble words and deeds."[17] The caduceus allowed Hermes to travel between Olympus, the mortal realm, and Hades, passing messages between gods and mortals.

After Zeus agreed to permit Persephone's return to her mother, he dispatched "Argeiphontes with his golden wand to Erebus, to exhort Hades with soft words and to bring back the gentle Persephone from the dark mist." Many gods clashed over Persephone's abduction – Aphrodite caused Hades to fall in love with the maiden Kore, Zeus gave his brother permission to steal her, Hades abducted his bride, and Demeter starved the world due to her grief. All the while, Hermes passed their messages.

Hermes was the divine middleman, what Karl Kerényi called "a linguistic mediator" that comes from "the deep primordial darkness where one expects only animal muteness, wordless silence, or cries of pleasure and pain."[18] Hermes could listen to and relay messages in whatever form of communication they were said. His fluency with the underworld and ability to pass messages meant he translated the raw archetypal energy of underworlding into something we mortals could understand, talk about, and make meaning of. Donald Kalsched explains that "archetypal energy is high-voltage stuff – let us say 440 volts – and in order to be integrated into conscious human ego it needs to be transformed into a more manageable 220 volts."[19] Without modification, archetypal energy is too powerful to be integrated. Whether it's an active complex that "has us" or we are triggered by someone, integrating so much raw and painful energy requires repackaging and repurposing in ways we can tolerate and digest.

A supervisor once told me that being a therapist is like being a mother bird. The bird digs in the dirt for the entire worm. She then chews up the worm, breaks it into smaller pieces, and gives it bit by bit to her hatchling. The therapist has to be aware of what their client is taking in and how much they can digest. It isn't wise to force an entire meal down someone's throat. Dynamite is ineffective and unskillful as a therapeutic tool.

Dreams, images, and metaphors are ways of translating the messages of the unconscious into conscious awareness. I worked with a man who was ashamed of feeling second-best to his brother. His father was overtly disappointed in him, which inspired him to be competitive and driven, always seeking to do more and be better. He had a hard time relaxing and just "being." When he described this energy that wouldn't let up, he said it was the little boy in him that never felt he was enough. "But I don't remember that little boy," he added. Go find him, I suggested, listen to his voice, hear his message. The little boy communicates with images and sensations, emotions and memories. To reconnect with that part of himself, he had to "listen" differently.

Understanding abstract psychological terms such as dissociation, attachment disorder, or diagnoses of emotional neglect, mania, or generalized anxiety can be evasive. But we can *visualize* dissociation as a circuit breaker, attachment as glue, emotional neglect as a desert, or we can *personify* emotions as a young child. Doing so can help us feel into the messages and archetypal energies coming to us from the soul through these images.

The origin and imagery of cancer bespeaks a Hermetic quality. Over and over, clients tell me their cancer first revealed itself through images. A client recalled having an image in October of fire moving through her veins. The flames made her think of cancer, but she discounted the possibility. In January, she was diagnosed with glioblastoma. Another woman saw a cloaked figure, the Grim Reaper, on her shoulder. She lost ten pounds but still didn't worry. Looking back, she realized her cancer started the day she saw the Reaper: "My body was trying to tell me; it knew. I was just too busy to listen." In my practice, cancer dreams show images of tornadoes, mandalas, burning buildings, dark figures, wars (often World War II), threats, dinosaurs, and nemeses, to name a few. The warning images seem to come with numinous and vivid imagery, energy that feels overwhelming to be in the presence of.

In *Words as Eggs*, Russel Lockhart tells of an elderly man who came to see him after his wife died of cancer. Prior to her diagnosis, she had horrific nightmares in which she was preyed upon by animals. She would wake in the night screaming, dogs tearing at her stomach, fires burning her flesh. She was diagnosed with cancer several months after the dreams, and died three months later. The man said to Lockhart, "You know, those dreams were the beginning of it. The cancer was announcing itself. I feel the truth of this in my bones. But people won't listen to an old man."[20]

Origin images are often ignored until they become symptoms. Medicine chases symptoms while depth psychotherapy tries to get at the archetypal core of illness. To do so, we must listen to the messages of the deep that come to us translated into symbols, metaphors, and images, so we can act on their warnings.

Many people use poetic and metaphorical language to express their suffering. A woman called the death of her husband "a black hole" – everything in her life moves toward his absence. A young man described a friend on whom he projects his shadow as his very own time machine – reverting him back to the little boy everyone avoided. I've heard heartbreak described as an anvil, the voice of a spouse as a gunshot, grief as sand, and various emotions as heat, wind, ice, or peaches. After the death of his wife, Robert Romanyshyn said his grief was "the slow heartbeat of stones."[21] I asked my five-year-old niece what it feels like when someone doesn't share. She said it feels like a monster.

None of these descriptions are measurable or even rational, but they capture a layer of expression that cannot be held in literalized form. Instead of fact-finding and observation, Hermes uses image-making, flashes of insight, metaphor, intuition, and imagination to grapple with the intricacies of life. We notice the Hermetic presence when we're comfortable somewhere between explicit and implicit, precise and unspoken, obvious and invisible, never tiring of exploring different forms of communication to have our message heard and placed in context.

There's immense complexity in holding and deciphering the gray areas of life. Underworlding is rarely black and white, fitting into orderly boxes or tucked behind trim hedges. Intricacy and confusion are not the same thing. Hermes may be complex, but he isn't befuddling. He's the god of articulation. He conveys too many messages to be incoherent, his fluid and imaginal ways of expression effectively communicate important layers of experience.

Healing Fiction

Stories shape our lives. We tell narratives that are inspiring, curative, restrictive, and even violent. The scripts we write cast ourselves as leaders, victims, mothers, warriors, and failures. Stories are *expressions of meaning*; the plots we imagine matter.

With the right story (or image), perspective can be reshaped. Hillman called this *healing fiction*, the belief that our stories are flexible and, with the right inventive outlook, can be rewritten. Every day, no matter how consuming our pain, how heart-breaking our loss, how weighty our complex, or how devastating our illness, we decide anew what will become of us. We may tell ourselves we're too afraid, dependent, worthless, or ill-equipped to handle what's happening, or we can tell ourselves that we're capable, compassionate, strong, and supported.

"At the beginning of my recovery," my brother said, "I had a romanticized notion of my ability to overcome obstacles. I felt that to do it well, meaning bravely and heroically, there needed to be grace and dignity." I asked him what had changed. "I learned that the only thing I could control was my perspective – how I show up, that we have the opportunity to create our story. To survive, I had to reimagine my *challenges* as *opportunity*." By treating stories as healing opportunities, we bring imagination and choice to the unforeseen and unpredictable movements of life.

Many of us hold ourselves hostage with painful, shaming, or regressive stories. After her mother died, a woman felt guilty for not giving her mom as much as she could. She had young children to care for and her partner traveled for work. Her pain was penance, but it prevented her from moving through acute grief. Her therapist mirrored back the story she had around her mother's passing, asking if there was anything she missed. The woman was annoyed; of course there were things she missed. She hadn't told her therapist about the many letters she read to her mother that were from her father, how much time she spent going back and forth between home and her mom's residential facility, or the many sweet moments they had when her mother was still lucid. The therapist reminded her that she needed to include these parts of the story in her inner narrative, not just what she hadn't done. It's easy to limit our healing and growth by remembering select pieces of reality. The woman suffered because she was overlooking important details of how she actually showed up for her mother's passing.

"In my experience," writes Donald Kalsched, "change only becomes possible once we are able to take responsibility and grieve for the life-denying and self-traumatizing system that we ourselves have constructed."[22] We cannot change the circumstances that put us in the underworld; however we can change the story, the system we've constructed. How we *tell* stories and what we *feel* as we remember are often more important than the facts of the narrative. Fiction, from Latin *fictionem* "a fashioning or feigning" and *fingere* "to shape," bespeaks craftsmanship and creation. The fictions of our lives fashion and shape our worlds, our responses, roles, and identities.

Fictions are paths in the woods. The more we walk along one path, the easier, wider, and more familiar it becomes. Wandering off a well-trodden path can be frightening; the old markers are lost and the new path is unfamiliar. We have to step carefully, our destination is unknown. Yet no matter how seemingly safe the path most traveled is, we have the capacity to create a new one, especially when there's a need for fresh perspectives.

The words we use to describe ourselves can be seen as creation myths, or origin stories. In the biblical book of Genesis, God speaks the world into being. At the core of the primary Western creation story, words give birth to all living things. The Gospel of John (1: 1–2) echoes, "In the beginning was the Word, and the Word was with God, and the Word was God." The word is the living expression of the archetypal, of the spirit of creation that is within everything. Through our words we render psyche into reality, we can build or destroy our personalities, ideas, and even worlds.

Grief therapist David Kessler draws a distinction between pain and suffering. He says pain is the inevitable feeling of loss, while suffering is how our mind digests pain. Pain is a part of loss, suffering is a choice that comes from the stories we tell ourselves and others. The words we choose to describe darkness are powerful. They can keep us imprisoned or help us live with meaning. As Kessler explains, if our old story is "this death happened to me," a new story could be "death happens." Or "this death was a punishment" to "death is usually random."[23]

Changing the story expands possibility. If we believe our lives are forged by one story, we'll always see proof of that story. If we feel unlovable, we'll find proof of our worthlessness everywhere, and we're trapped in cycles of self-hatred. We can't even see our bondage unless we imagine freedom. We can't feel valued unless we envision worth. We can't expect agency unless we recognize our strengths.

We're drawn to what comes into consciousness without expending effort. We want quick results, measurable outcomes, and diagnoses to explain why we feel and act a certain way. Instant anything appeals to the ego, not to the depths. The deep places in our being, our soul, are not drawn to quick fixes. It prefers the eternal, sacred, image, myth, the greatness of life as told for millennia. It prefers poetics and storytelling, narratives of dreams and images woven for generations. As Jung wrote:

> Our actual mind is the result of the work of thousands
> or perhaps a million years. There is a long history in
> every sentence, every word we speak has a tremendous
> history, every metaphor is full of historical symbolism;
> they would not carry at all if that were not true. Our
> words carry the totality of that history which was once
> so alive and still exists in every human being.[24]

"Through words we can alter reality," Hillman said. "We can bring into being and remove from being; we can shape and change the very structure and essence of what is real."[25] By being conscious of our fictions, we bring imagination to underworld experiences, freeing ourselves from interpreting the journey from only one perspective. If we convince ourselves we're defective, we will suffer shame. If we tell ourselves we're failures, success will be unattainable. If we live in fear of death, we'll fail to live fully.

We human beings are wired for storytelling. First we expressed ourselves on stone using paint, then in spoken word, papyrus, parchment, and paper. We have a rich history of sharing myths, fables, folklores, and fairytales to explain ourselves and our world. We tell stories that point to fertile hunting grounds, heroes who save the world, myths that describe the seasons and stars, princesses who kiss frogs, gods who destroy the faithless, and witches who see into past, present, and future. A part of us needs to tell stories of our life, and we feel supported when we do so.

When grief envelops us, we tell stories about those we've lost. We continue their lives through shared memories, keeping them alive with words. We find strength in the gifts they left behind – the times they made us French toast, walks on sunrise beaches – and our memories become lifelines. These can't be taken from us.

Storytelling is a profound platform for sharing. My parents founded Deer Hill Expeditions in Colorado to lead young adults on wilderness and service adventures. Of all the experiences participants have, we hear over and over of the value and impact of the Circle. Every night, the group gathers in a circle to speak on a set topic. A treasure of that day – a stone, a stick, or a branch – is passed around, and when someone is holding this power object, they're tasked with two simple things: speak from the heart and listen with respect.

I've seen people who barely know each other tell stories they've never given voice to before, bare parts of their souls they didn't know existed, empower themselves, and integrate change and self-discovery under the protection and support of their newfound community.

The gift and power of the Circle is an archetypal experience that runs through our veins. For centuries we've gathered to tell stories, make meaning, experience initiation, and collectively usher in powers beyond our tender lives. To the modern mind, it feels new to be exposed, supported, and ritualized simultaneously, and to find ourselves *that* connected. We're starving for validation, meaning, and images to explain the currents that shape our lives. We thirst for archetypal connection, hunger for deeper, more authentic, more nuanced stories to help us integrate the challenges of life. We need rituals of storytelling. Certainly, psychotherapy is such a ritual, but we need more as well; we need ways of living, connecting to each other, and expressing the soul. For centuries the Greek imagination sought the secrets of rhetoric, song, and prose that would speak to the soul – healing through talking.

Maya Angelou said that there's no greater agony than bearing an untold story inside you. Folk traditions are filled with ghosts who refuse to rest in their graves until their stories are heard. There is great power in speaking the unspeakable. "In many cases in psychiatry," Jung reflected, "the patient who comes to us has a story that is not told, and which as a rule no one knows of. To my mind, therapy only really begins after the investigation of that wholly personal story. It is the patient's secret, the rock against which he is shattered."[26]

Just as our behaviors, ideas, histories, and wounds have stories, so do our symptoms. Anxiety, depression, and panic each has its own character, origin, and wisdom. A self-worth complex tells the story of weakness and insecurity, panic is a narrative of overwhelm.

We manufacture leviathans to overcome, beat down, and escape our suffering, destroying our ability to hear and heed its message. Hillman coined the term *pathologizing* to shine light on its opposite – suffering, disorder, chaos, and imbalance have important stories to tell. Symptoms signify something is wrong in our relation to life. If we're lucky, these warnings will be whispers, giving us time and the opportunity to seek out paths to reclaim our unlived life.

"The gods," Jung said, "have become diseases."[27] Today the gods are manifest in our fears, obsessions, complexes, and what Jung summarized as *neurotic symptoms*. Gods become angered and vengeful when they're denied and devalued. "What is needed," writes Russel Lockhart, "is to go *into* the symptom, into the sickness, and connect again with the God hidden there."[28] Suffering, sickness, and even the process of dying can be roads to individuation – albeit painful ones. We need only turn toward their messages and heed their wisdom. "Man needs difficulties," Jung said, "they are necessary for health."[29]

I worked with a young woman who suffered from crippling anxiety, which she experienced as tightening in her chest and a sense of hypervigilance. I asked her to try to be open-minded and explore how these qualities of tightening and vigilance might actually be serving her. Immediately, she told me she needed to create a tight protective shield around herself by standing up for her values and not caring for others at the expense of her well-being. She betrayed herself when she sacrificed her voice for the sake of others. And as she created healthy boundaries, her anxiety diminished considerably.

Simply fearing or overcoming darkness cuts us off from the tragic realities of life and the curative messaging the soul is sending to help us regain balance. Depression seems an enemy, sickness seems unfair, and death seems impossible to include as part of wholeness and life. But at some point, we're challenged to deal with it, and we have to abandon our ideal of a bright and privileged life and accept the disorganizing presence of darkness. We're trapped in the age-old pattern of imagining afflictions as happenstance, rather than a part of the fabric of our life, and a response to our one-sided lives. When we give our symptoms a seat at the table, they become not just less threatening and destructive, but allies.

The blind effort to keep our life on the surface can be exhausting. Hermes represents our ability to dive deep and explore the darkness. We can't change the existence of a symptom or circumstance with the snap of a finger, but we can cultivate a conscious response to it. We can face darkness as pathology or imaginatively. When we try imagination, *everything* seems relevant. Imagination bridges, binds, and connects. Hermes is a connection-maker – a psychopomp, messenger, and storyteller. He is concerned with making the invisible visible, translating the impossible into images and language. Discerning the messages embedded in our symptoms helps us get to the source of suffering.

Research shows that listening to stories releases cortisol and oxytocin, neurochemicals that help us connect, empathize, make meaning, and fall in love. Stories help us learn from others, express ourselves, build tradition and culture, and connect with our ancestral lineage. The primary function of myth is to explain what it means to be human in relationship to the universe. Our capacity to story-tell gives us the power to reimagine and reinvent our lives, and connect with the deep vein of truth flowing through us.

Paradox

Hermes is a god of contradiction, cleverness, and beguilement, constantly changing, and at the same time the ruler of boundaries, roads, and communication. He's the "winged and wingless ... the dry and earthly, the moist and viscous," Jung tells us.[30] He appears as success *and* failure, kindness *and* misfortune, bribery *and* honesty, and he lives in the heaviness of grief *and* the lightness of spirit. A symbol of "all conceivable opposites,"[31] Hermes grapples with life's impossibilities.

Darkness is paradoxical, showing us how that which breaks creates expansion, what ruins recreates, what kills gives life. Underworlding is often painful yet beautiful, debilitating yet empowering, lonely yet connecting. All the deaths, hospital rooms, therapy sessions, and trauma I've witnessed or experienced have been terrible, yet they've given me a depth of presence and understanding that have made me a better therapist, wife, friend, daughter, aunt, and sister. I'm grateful for the underworld, despite wishing I never had to go there.

One who desires the favor of Hermes must at the same time accept loss and destruction; for there cannot be one without the other. Hermes personifies the winding road, the twists and turns of life. "We turn to him," writes Christine Downing, "when we want to learn from and make use of underworld experience, to turn it to advantage, to find the luck hidden in it."[32] We never know what life has in store for us – we may be cheated or misled, destroyed or remodeled, betrayed or rewarded. Trying to be a conscious and whole individual is a path as slippery as Hermes is himself.

Estranged for many years, a brother and sister reconnected during their father's dying. The wounds of the past were less important than their shared pain. In their dad's final moments, they locked eyes over his hospital bed and understanding replaced years of isolation, and each remembered the preciousness of the bond of blood. Although they grieved the death of their father, they also felt grateful for reconnecting.

It is to Hermes that we owe experiences of betrayal, theft, misfortune, rule-breaking, as well as luck. He guides us and he leads us astray, representing energy that's benign, channeled, and safe, but which can turn harsh, painful, and pointlessly cruel. He's both threat and protector, guide and destabilizer, representing the obscuration of night and the clarity of dawn. Hermes is "the sudden giving and taking away," wrote Walter Otto, "the wisdom and cunning, the spirit of propitious love, the witchery of twilight, the weirdness of night and death – this diverse whole, which is inexhaustible and yet nowhere denies the unity of its being."[33] He's lifeless and living, alert and asleep, quick and steady, sparkling and dull.

Hermes is an archetypal trickster, a symbol of the unpredictability of life. Trickster energy disrupts and derails, embodying mischievous ways of being, sharp and sweet-talking that move through life inspiring deceit, manipulation, and upheaval. When life flips this way, new energy can pour in. Disruption seeds growth by forcing us into new territory, stirring the waters quickly, beckoning us toward new perspectives.

By undermining our life structures, the trickster reveals the workings of a greater force in life. If we chose to look, we may find hidden purpose behind the pandemonium of life. Loss makes us more empathetic, trauma motivates us to help others, abandonment helps us reclaim ourselves, death teaches us how to live. Like the trickster, underworlding's perils often destroy deeply grooved patterns, forcing us onto the fine line between who we have been and what we can become. This is where growth happens. Putting stability and comfort in jeopardy challenges us to step into the unknown and face the call of life.

Our world is always in flux and constantly being reshaped by countless conditions. My brother's accident inspired my interest in underworld journeying, which guided me toward becoming a psychotherapist. Helen Keller's condition led to her life as a groundbreaking author and activist, the assassination of Archduke Franz Ferdinand led to the outbreak of World War I, and the terrorist attacks on the World Trade Center motivated the War on Terror and subsequent invasion of Iraq. Unforeseen events shape the world as we know it.

When Hermes is involved, we can't foresee the outcome or lasting effects of an underworld journey. Unpredictability is what is predictable about this mischievous god. Without clear footing, we must face the present and adapt and seek new meaning and perspectives. The underworld journey can be the end of one way of living, and also an initiation into the great energies of life and the next phase of our journey. Through connections that Hermes shows us, we can transform our lives and the lives of others.

Hermes is more about opposites that reflect a whole than sharp distinctions. His reality exists on a spectrum where even contradictory thoughts, behaviors, and actions are in relationship. We can be slightly or destructively jealous, marginally or debilitatingly insecure, nervous or terrified, lonely and content, heartbroken and relieved, inspired and ground down by tedium. It's not either/or; it's often both—and.

A woman shared with me that the physical abuse she suffered from her husband gave her the strength to leave the toxic relationship and pursue a life she called "worth living." For another person, a cancer diagnosis forced him to slow down and notice how fast he'd been running. He ran from his father's death and from how much he loved and wanted his father's respect and also how much he hated him. He ran from memories of his dad coming home drunk and hitting him, the shame of his childhood, and the self-disappointment that became a partner to his life – a dark hunger that devoured him. Cancer told him to stop, and he listened.

The underworld is complex and layered. We can't afford to look at our experiences of darkness in isolation. "Matrix," a word associated with interconnection, comes from the Latin *matris*, "womb." The matrix of shame, grief, insecurity, distress, doubt, and other emotions of underworlding reveal themselves in intertwining and contradiction. These experiences are the womb of suffering and growth, clarity and decision.

I see Hermes as the god of chaos theory – the hypothesis that within the apparent randomness of complex systems, there are underlying patterns, connections, feedback loops, repetition, and self-organization. Even the most random and painful moments have purpose and order. If we hold things in their innate complexity and paradox while being with the matrix of darkness, we move toward wholeness.

Chaos is hard to swallow. When darkness seizes us, we look for the reason behind the tragedy, believing our suffering must have had an external cause. And we posit a favorable or unfavorable outcome based on conditions that have nothing to do with the facts on the ground or simply staying present with what is. At the beginning of my brother's journey, people said he would survive because he's a good person. I found strength and hope in this validation until I realized that his "goodness" would have nothing do with his survival. His accident had much more to do the unpredictable currents of life than his moral worth. We believe goodness should be rewarded and living a principled life can prevent mischance. Moral judgments have little correlation with the ebbs and flows of life. Good people die, loving people break hearts, honest people make mistakes, and terrible things happen to innocents.

Whether it's illness, out-of-control family dynamics, job loss, or terrible violations, we limit our chance of find meaning if we think we *deserve* the torments of chance. Some terrors just happen. Or they are the outcome of deeper, more complex streams than blame, guilt, or a wrathful deity.

Finding the Sacred

Hermes was patron of the spiritual dimensions of life. He's associated with flight, illumination, mountain peaks, sudden inspiration, birds, and divine revelation. As messenger of the gods, he connects us to the sacred dimensions of life. Jung wrote, Hermes will make "you a witness of the mysteries of God."[34]

Today, many people want to live a spiritually meaningful life without embracing any religious tradition. Theology tells us specific ways the divine manifests and gives us set places to worship and dogma to follow. For many, that path is no longer compelling. Instead, they seek a sense of the sacred that is not beholden to the teachings, doctrines, or stories of the religion of their childhood.

Tales of desire for connection to the divine are as old as literature itself. Everywhere in myth and theology we find the imagery of a magical link between the profane world and the divine. Something of the eternal enters the world and forever changes it. Water flows in the desert, the divine child of light is born in the night, a bush burns without being destroyed. These symbols all have to do with the divine entering our world, forging a link between the spiritual life force of individuals with the everyday world.

Numinous, from the Latin *numen*, "divine will," bespeaks an encounter with the sacred dimension of life, the archetypal realm. Numinous experiences have a quality of the transpersonal, powerful effect, unearthliness. A glimpse of the numinous can transform our sense of meaning and shift the direction of our life. Many who experience a powerful darkness have mystical, even lifesaving experiences of the numinous.

A few months after his mother passed away, my husband was lying down outside. He felt overwhelmed by the weight of his grief and anger. As he lay there a little bird landed on his chest. He closed his eyes and felt the tiny feet hop around – a nimble spirit gently resting on top of a heart heavy with loss and pain. The bird reminded him of his mother – her lightness of spirit, tenderness, busy nature, quick mind, and immense wingspan for love and appreciating life. Lying there, he felt the awe of the world, the numinosity of it all, and, despite the ponderance of his grief, he felt lighter.

The presence of the divine provides many of us with explanation, connection, and support in times of suffering. Without connection to these transpersonal powers, we may be left with a painful yearning that impels us to search for substitutes in unfulfilling places. Jung was concerned that without a connection to the sacred, many people would be unable to find meaning and understanding in their lives. He saw a fine line between spirituality and psychology, and felt that the psychological dimension of spiritual experience is essential to appreciate. Jung argued that we each need a personally significant relationship to the sacred, which he believed could be found in contact with the Self – an image of psychic totality equivalent to the divine.

"I used to pray offhandedly, little bits here and there," a woman told me, "but now, I get on my knees and am doing it formally." Her life has been dark and complex – childhood trauma, changes in life stage – there's a lot to resist. Prayer helps her surrender to something beyond herself. "I don't feel so alone. Praying gives me an outlet to give up the weight of personal responsibility. I've been working so hard to be seen, heard, and make the right choices. God helps me breathe into my helplessness." It doesn't matter what our relationship with the sacred looks like – it can be through dreams, scriptures, mindfulness, nature, art, or any other resource. What matters is that we have access to guidance greater than our own lives.

Psychotamias (Keeper of Souls)

Hermes faced darkness with a less directive, goal-oriented attitude than the heroes. Qualities of strength, willpower, direct confrontation, and hyper-individuality have no place in his world. His character thrives in mystery, cunning, and inventiveness rather than might, lucidity, or valor. His realm isn't about progress, achievement, or the temptation to divide the world into two. To move with such dayworld intentions runs counter to Hermes' intimacy with the underworld. He's the god of complexity, limbo, and trickery. He isn't practiced in combat, but stays present as life randomly pivots – whether furtherances or failures.

When we face darkness with flexibility and imagination, the essence of Hermes manifests. His style of journeying evokes guidance and paradox, messages and communication, connection and liminality, creativity and dexterity. He holds the space for a lengthier and indirect process of inner discovery, one that recognizes that there's always another layer, an additional challenge, dimension, or unforeseen consequence to be untangled. For the god of movement and depth, there's no ideal, established, or correct path into the underworld. Underworlding that's open to meeting whatever arises, adapting and changing course as needed, these are Hermetic journeys.

Reflections

God of the crossroads, messages, and happenstance, Hermes pertains to the ever-changing, nebulous, and paradoxical. He guides within, gifting us a deep connection with the imaginal and the realm of death. He is the mysterious substance within the bottle that stirs up transformation. With Hermes involved you never know what you'll get – the impossibilities of life are endless. We become complex and clear, clever and thieving, charming and persuasive, never settling on one thing but stirring like a whirlwind. He is the trickster at the doorway, the prowler on the street corner. Hermes is nowhere and everywhere, capturing possibilities like a restless breeze by demanding of us a lithe and fluid nature.

Reflect on how these Hermetic qualities may be present within your experience in:

- The guide of souls – the archetype of the guide.
- Feeling you belong in both the realm of light and dark.
- Building a relationship with death, literally and symbolically.
- Moments when you feel in motion, where nothing sticks and all is in flux.

- Being caught in the gray areas of life, the place where anything can happen – good or bad.
- Finding your way to communicate about what's happening so darkly.
- Healing fictions – retelling your story.
- Inventive knowledge – creation as a means of healing and change.
- Facing darkness with charm and humor.
- Feeling life's paradoxical moments.
- Trickster energy, i.e., the curve balls of life.
- The impulse to move on.
- Your shapeshifting ability to see many different possibilities in the world. Honoring of multiplicity over singularity.
- Finding your sense of the sacred.

CHAPTER 9
PERSEPHONE

Kore was picking narcissus flowers when the earth opened up and out came Hades "with his immortal horses, that son of Cronus with so many names … [and] grabbed her, resisting, and he took her in his gold chariot, weeping."[1] Hades bore Kore into the underworld to be his queen. There she adopted the name Persephone.[2]

The goddess Demeter, feverishly searched for her lost daughter. Overwhelmed by grief, Demeter refused to allow the crops to grow, so the land lay barren and the world began to starve. When she learned of Kore's fate, Demeter beseeched Zeus to help her get Persephone back, promising she would continue to prevent the crops from growing until he met her demand.

Zeus agreed under the condition that no food passed Persephone's lips while in the underworld. But in her gloom, Persephone had eaten six pomegranate seeds, so she was forced to spend six months each year – the winter months – with Hades. Every spring, she ascends to the dayworld and Demeter's joy is reflected in the fertilization of crops and the growth of new vegetation. In autumn when Persephone returns to the underworld, her mother's sorrow is echoed in the coldness of decay and emptiness of winter.

The Loss of Innocence

Kore, Persephone's identity before she was abducted into the underworld, is a symbol of maidenhood – pure and innocent. In art and sculpture, she was depicted as a robed girl standing next to her mother, hidden and protected from the world. Being abducted shattered this budlike idyll. She was pulled away from all she knew and dragged into the realm of the dead. No longer an untouched, naïve maiden, Kore became Persephone, the dreaded queen of the lower realm.

Innocence is inevitably lost, and it's a brutal stage in the expansion of consciousness. As we grow and mature, the original wholeness of our world is destroyed, ego is separated from fantasy, consciousness from the unconscious, and to a greater and lesser extent, the Koric parts of us are pulled into darkness.

Even the purest personality is subject to the reach of darkness. Our most protected fantasies, those that whisper of a sun-kissed and safe life, will be taken. At any moment darkness can tear itself from the ground and seize us. Complexes grip, traumatic memories surface, accidents ensue, loved ones die. Hades and his immortal horses are right below the surface. This is a dramatic truth of life.

A man suffered a long, contentious, even abusive divorce process. As his marriage was falling apart, he began a tailspin that included a cocktail of overly prescribed psychiatric drugs, gaslighting, expensive alimony, and a crippling loss of identity – all of which led to his attempted suicide. The experience ruptured his belief that people are inherently good, trustworthy, and authentic. He no longer trusted the integrity of family, believed love was possible for him, or thought people even care about each other. The world no longer felt safe, people weren't to be trusted. His innocence was forced into the lower world and devoured.

To live without an understanding of the underworld can make us dangerously unprepared to deal with hardship when it comes. To stay Koric, avoiding darkness, is to ignore life as it is. As Ovid told the story, Kore was abducted in a glade where it was always spring, and with "childlike eagerness, she gathered the flowers into baskets and into the folds of her gown."[3] Spring evokes beginnings and seedlings – everything is young, fresh, fragile, and innocent.

When we are unaware of the dark underbelly of the world, Kore manifests. We all enact Kore in soul, argued Hillman, when we are "lulled drowsy with innocence and pretty comforts until we are dragged off and pulled down by Hades, our intact natural consciousness violated and opened to the perspective of death."[4] Innocence lives in an enchanted glade, where we foolishly believe we are protected from the darkening of life.

Right before Hades hurtled from the deep, Kore was dazzled, unknowingly reaching for the heavily scented narcissi. It was said that the delicate white flowers had a stupefying effect – it's easy to be lulled by the comforts of innocence. The desire to stay ignorant of the dark side is tempting, even soothing, but it comes at a cost. If we cling to a surface-oriented mindsight, we'll be caught off guard when life inevitably darkens.

Innocence must be sacrificed in order to handle life's realities as they arise. The unthinkable can happen – parents, friends, lovers, and children die; traumas occur, disasters strike. Kore represents the desire to turn a blind eye to darkness, but the goldenness of innocence will recede when we're tempered by severe challenges.

We in the West tend to worship perfection and promote only the bright side of life. We share what's beautiful, polished, organized, and successful. Mainstream psychologies are interventional, offering tools and methods to maintain our well-being on the surface, keeping Hades from stealing us into the darkness. We prefer sweet meadows and springtime, and work hard to keep a lid on the portal to the underworld. Yet the soul is forged in darkness; the rawness of life can be a source of deepening.

It's natural, even healthy, to seek relief from darkness. Underworlding obscures daylight and holding on to the belief that life can be bright, joyful, and filled with hope and potential is important. There's a difference between positivity and naïve innocence. Ignoring the potential of Hades does not prevent him from coming into our life.

Persephone's annual cycle allows death its rightful place, while choosing life and abundance as well. Demeter, the mother of Kore/Persephone, was a goddess of earthly riches while Hades, also called Aïdoneus, "hidden" or "unseen," was the invisible yet unavoidable presence of darkness. Persephone is a daughter of the wonders of the dayworld and wife to the hidden riches of darkness, personifying a balance between daylight and darkness.

When darkness kidnaps us, we must keep Demeter's gifts in mind – fruitfulness, harvest, sunshine, and grain. In the ancient Eleusinian mysteries, worshipers held stalks of grain to symbolize that even in a world affected by death, life continues. The cult reenacted the abduction of Persephone and reunion with Demeter. When neophytes performed the rituals properly, said the right words, and made the correct offerings, they would be assured the protection of the great goddess and the certainty of a blessed afterlife.

After World War II, psychiatrist Elisabeth Kübler-Ross visited Nazi concentration camps and saw butterflies etched into the walls. Many years later, she noticed in her work with dying children that they too drew butterflies. She realized that butterflies, symbols of transformation, helped the dying feel the continuation of life instead of just death. There is always life in darkness, transformation in death.

Narcissi are associated with the myth of Narcissus. Consumed by his unrequited love for Narcissus, Ameinias prayed to the goddess Nemesis for revenge. His prayer was granted, and Narcissus fell in love with his own reflection. He became so infatuated with his own beauty that he forsook all others, withered, and transformed into a tantalizing white flower. Narcissism has come to mean the vain and egotistic admiration of one's idealized self-image and attributes.

"Narcissus" comes from the Greek *narkao*, "to be stiff" or "dead." In Greek religion, narcissi were the sacred flowers of Hades and associated with opening the doors to his realm. It was Kore's self-absorbed innocence that called Hades from his domain. By denying his reality, she, paradoxically, summoned him.

We can neither remain innocent nor give up a hopeful and bright life. If we're vainly engrossed with innocence and purity, though, we risk ignoring the enriching potential of darkness. When the natural missteps, losses, and imperfections of life find our unsuspecting souls, it may well feel like an abduction.

Abduction

Sometimes a powerful and destructive force springs from the earth and pulls us into the underworld. Describing Kore's abduction, Ovid wrote:

> Pluto [Hades] saw her, and loved her, and bore her
> off – so swift is love. With wailing cries the terrified

goddess called to her mother, and to her comrades, but more often to her mother. She rent and tore the upper edge of her garment, till the flowers she had gathered fell from its loosened folds: and she was so young and innocent that even this loss [of the flowers] caused her fresh distress.[5]

The "Persephone experience" happens when we feel caught and drawn downward, pulled from our lives by an invisible, dark energy. The sudden death of a loved one, the triggering of a negative mother complex, violent acts of cruelty, mental illness, emotional attachment wounds, disease, natural disasters, and financial misfortune are all abductions. They rip apart the fabric of reality, halt life, change who we are, and plummet us into uncertainty and grief. We are unconsciously dragged into places of turmoil and trial. Abduction is neither desirable nor foreseen, but it can be a summoning to consciousness.

Hades threatens our ingrained ways of being, acting, and understanding the world. He represents the invasion that pulls us downward from stability and security, demanding we relate to deeper and darker parts of ourselves. To be alive is to risk abduction. The loss of perfection, inexperience, safety, stability, and innocence is inevitable. No one is sculpted from flawless marble.

When we're snatched into the lower realm, the world continues around us. People buy apples, play games, and go to work, while we exist in another realm – unable to reach across to the light. We're enveloped by dark matter, powerless to interact with the everyday world.

My mother-in-law's death appeared like Hades' chariot – unforeseen and abrupt. The fantasy of control was replaced by abject helplessness, certainty by confusion, presence by absence. The family constellation altered; there was a hole. My husband lost his mother, my relationship with my own mother changed, my marriage stretched, deepened, and met painful hurdles.

Just as we're seized by inner forces – unhappiness, complexes, psychoses, fears, anxiety, disappointment, and addictions – so too are we kidnapped by external forces: mass shootings, propaganda, social media, news, politics, accidents, pandemics, climate change. In our globalized, media-driven world, collective abduction is a part of life.

Truman Capote depicted one of America's most unforgettable murders in his book *In Cold Blood*. Describing the town of Holcomb as the peaceful poster child of rural America, he explained how it was effectively abducted by Richard Hickock and Perry Smith's failed robbery, turned horrific murder. The community network of trust and closeness was shattered, plummeting the town and country into darkness – the underworld made visible to all.

The Kore personality believes innocence and ease will prevail against shadow and depth. To get caught in that fantasy is to be abducted into reality. Hades doesn't snatch the living with arrows like Artemis or Apollo do, nor does he guide souls like Hermes. He *receives* souls into the afterlife. He's not a god of retribution or judgment, he's the open door, a force that comes for us all, the great equalizer.

How we describe and know ourselves before and after an abduction is important. Hades takes something from us all; sometimes the darkness is so complete that we forget who we were before the theft.

In my first session with a woman who had stage-four breast cancer, she told me exactly why she had the disease. It began when her youngest child was horrifically burned as an infant. The family moved to access better long-term medical care. What was intended to be a temporary stay turned into eight years.

The day of the accident, Hades tore himself from the depths and stole her life. She left behind community, abandoned the lush mountains that fed her soul, moved to the desert, and gave up a meaningful vocation. Over the years, her family moved frequently, struggled financially, her marriage turned into a kind of business arrangement, she was increasingly isolated from nature, and beneath all this, her unprocessed trauma was simmering until it boiled. It isn't hard to see disease in her story.

For eight years she'd been trapped on a fast-moving train, unable to get off. On the train was grief for her old life, mourning for her abandoned community, self-reliance patterns to compensate for feeling helpless, strategies to undo or override her guilt, the desire to rewind time, and fear born from knowing Hades. She entombed herself in a loop of self-blame, disappointment, and victimization.

Her face lit up when she talked about moving to the mountains and returning to nature. She had been imprisoned by suburban life, her soul in protest at this sterile environment. She sought the juiciness of life – imagination, images, and feeling. Her mind filled with fantasies of living in a forest cabin and rewilding her children, taking them into the forest to eat berries, drink clear water, and run on the land. She craved the waters of life, the longing to hydrate a desiccated soul.

She had gone to bed in the pines and awakened in Mordor, the realm of the evil Sauron. All choice had been stolen from her; she was torn from the life she loved and dragged into Hades. This fall from grace, loss of innocence, forfeiture of control, and seeing her child suffer was a constant underworld. Cancer wove itself into this entrapment, loss of life, suffering, and tragedy. Disease doesn't happen, it's made. The illness grew over time, but the abrupt and life-halting realization of its presence is an abduction. She had been abducted by Hades, forced into darkness, and trapped, while her inner world stayed stuck in the horror of the accident, unable to move on or feel again.

All illnesses can be a summons to transformation through abduction. Illness can be an initiation – a destruction of the old ways of being and a forceful snatching into the underworld of loss and death. The journey of illness is never chosen but it can be a pathway to individuation. We are forced away from the ego and our persona and made to relate to something deeper, more complete – our authentic Self.

"No one," wrote Hesiod, "either of the deathless gods or of mortal men, heard her voice, nor yet the olive-trees bearing rich fruit."[6] There are no forces – not even the mighty gods – that can protect us from abduction. Kore is the fantasy that the dark claws of life can't touch us; Persephone is the reality that they can.

The journey is certain, the outcome is not. When Hades seizes us, the Persephonic question is: How do we show up? All descent and ascent mythologies deal with this question – Orpheus laments his grief, Aeneas prays and accepts, Hermes moves continuously, and Persephone becomes queen of the underworld. We can't prevent abduction, we can only choose how to respond.

Persephone's myth introduces death into life and life into death. Knowing that Hades awaits us makes our dayworlding more meaningful. Life and death are partners; an awareness of death helps us live more fully and intentionally. "I behold death," wrote Jung, "since it teaches me how to live."[7] Life and death must strike a balance for the fragility and wonder of life to be seen clearly. I am reminded of these words by Rumi: "When was I less by dying?"[8] Darkness is always close at hand, a hidden presence ready to abduct us. To know this blunt truth is to have the potential to live fully.

Our focus on positivity and happiness makes us surprised by the inevitable darkness of life. We set ourselves up to be abducted. The brightness of the daylight is one of many moments in life, but the truth is that we have a range of emotions and experiences. When we have immense pressure to always be happy, we have immense pressure not to suffer. "Trauma" has become our way of giving ourselves permission to be abducted. We say: "I can suffer because I have trauma," and everyone nods. In a world that demands happiness, suffering doesn't evaporate;

it sinks below the surface, brews, and eventually erupts to snatch us. Persephone's story reminds us of this hard reality.

The people I love who have passed away help me see the tenuous miracle of life. Their lives and their deaths motivate me to show up for my friends with presence and love, let go of what I can't control, be grateful for what I have, bring empathy and depth to my work, and live my life as a way to honor theirs.

To be taken into darkness allows us to become familiar with the underworld and its threshold. It's painful to be torn from our safe and comfortable existence. An underworld summons is not something anyone desires. But it is one of life's many thresholds that will drag us toward new perspectives, habits, ways of being, and above all, growth and transformation. We may become wise, empathetic, open, and learn how to be with others when darkness takes over, when we are pulled toward a personal expansion that includes deathly, terrifying, and painful darkness. In other words, we become Persephone.

The Telos of the Gods

Hades asked Zeus for Kore's hand in marriage. Zeus approved the match, but correctly guessed that Demeter would refuse, so advised Hades to carry Kore off by force. "No other immortal," revealed the goddess Hecate, "is to be blamed save cloud-gathering Zeus who gave her to Hades, his own brother, to become his buxom bride."[9]

The extent of Zeus' meddling implies there's a larger design to Persephone's fate. As king of the gods, Zeus personifies the *teleology of the Self* – the idea that the inner world is directed by a larger, more complete source of wholeness. The meddling of the gods reveals the larger significance of forced underworlding. Their intervention creates the conditions for change that can only be born by being exposed to something deep and troublesome. For the sake of wholeness, the unconscious works its will in our minds and bodies, pushing our ego-minds toward a *coniunctio* of the upper and lower realms.

Kore's abduction was necessary – psychologically. Persephone "needed to become herself," reasons Christine Downing. "She reached for that beautiful dark narcissus; she ate the pomegranate seeds."[10] By eating the seeds, Persephone opened to a deeper side of herself. Darkness forced her to become who she truly is, no longer a maiden but the queen of Hades. "Knowledge of the unconscious," argued Marie Louise von Franz, "is indispensable to a thorough investigation of the transformation of the personality ... plunging into the unconscious depths of one's being, is the essential condition for taking on a higher responsibility for one's life."[11]

Zeus and Hades were not the only gods that interfered. As Ovid described it, the goddess Aphrodite was the source of Hades' love. The goddess of love asked her son Eros, "Why is Tartarus left alone from the powers of love?"[12] Aphrodite feared that love was dwindling in the world, leaving the underworld seemingly untouched by the power of love, and worried that if she allowed this to continue, Kore would remain a virgin. In response to his mother's woes, Eros opened his quiver of enchanted arrows, bent his bow against his knee, and struck Hades in the heart with the barbed shaft.

My brother didn't want his brain injury. We don't want our neuroses, our traumas, or our abandonments. When bombs drop on cities, tanks roll into villages, and soldiers knock down doors, civilians are forced into wars they don't want, and certainly don't have power over. Energies beyond our control, sometimes unconsciously driven and seemingly circumstantial, can force us into situations we would not have chosen and over which we have little authority. Yet they can be the most important moments of our life, breaking old patterns (and breaking us, hopefully temporarily) and opening the space for something new, something more true to take their place.

The Queen of Darkness

When she enters the underworld, Kore transforms into the queen of darkness. "While you are here," Hades tells her, "you shall rule all that lives and moves and shall have the greatest rights among the deathless gods: those who defraud you and do not appease your power with offerings, reverently preforming rites and paying fit gifts, shall be punished for evermore."[13] All who desire safe passage into the lower world seek Persephone's aid and permission. Odysseus made sacrifices to her while pursuing Teiresias. When the gathering shades frightened him, he confessed, "The horror took me that Persephone had brought from darker hell some saurian death's head. I whirled then, made for ship, shouted to crewmen to get aboard and cast off the stern thwarts."[14]

The nymph Cyane told Demeter that when she saw Persephone, "She was sad, certainly, and her face still showed signs of fear: none the less, she was queen, the greatest in the world of shadows, the powerful consort of the tyrant of the underworld."[15] Abducted, forced to eat pomegranate seeds, and destined to remain in the underworld for half of each year, Persephone did something powerful with her lot – she *embraced* her transformation from Kore to queen of the underworld.

How any process of abduction and recrystallization unfolds depends on our reactions and attitudes. If we deny and ignore the reality before us, we risk the loneliness and despair of Orpheus. If we are rash and overconfident, we may suffer Theseus' bondage. If we don't integrate the lessons we learn, we may not learn anything, as Hercules didn't. Persephone symbolizes yet another way of making the journey – amid her horror and helplessness *she became a ruler.*

Abduction into the depths of depression, loss, violence, and trauma creates a choice: Will you spend the rest of your life grieving for what has passed, dwelling in your pain and suffering? Or you will weave the darkness thrown at you into a new sense of self? There's no denying the difference between innocent Kore and ruler of the lower realm. No matter the circumstance, we each have an opportunity to become rulers of our fate. When we confront the darkest moments of our lives as integral occasions for finding parts of ourselves that can only be found in darkness, Persephone is there.

Post-Traumatic Growth

In 1995, psychologists Richard Tedeschi and Lawrence Calhoun described psychological growth caused by underworlding "post-traumatic growth." It's what happens when trauma changes us and deepens life's meaning. Although the pain may never vanish, something powerful is likely to come from underworlding. Author David Kushner discussed post-traumatic growth in relationship to the kidnapping and murder of his younger brother, Jon. At first, he said the possibility of growth was impossible: his family's focus was surviving what happened. Like Jon, their lives and souls had been abducted. In an article for *The New Yorker*, Kushner shared a journal entry by his father:

> There's something built-in that enables most human
> beings, not all, to be sure, but most, to get thru this …
> It is built-in to enable us to get thru, *force* us, to survive,
> to stay alive. After you've understood that it WILL be
> different, less raw, that the death can not be undone,
> that you will continue to live, the question becomes …
> "What shall I do with the rest of my life?"[16]

Those who have come through the underworld display empathy, passion, and openness, and are often less defensive, kinder, more curious, and more optimistic. Despite their pain and suffering, many people experience immense growth, which, notwithstanding bereavement, wounds, and stress, deepens their lives. But the underworld alone doesn't make for wisdom; it's what we do with our suffering, how we let darkness move us, that expands our horizons.

My mother had an isolating, unloved childhood. Her first memory was of feeling shame. "I didn't want that life," she explained to me. "So I chose to live in a very different way. I got a degree in early childhood education, became a schoolteacher, had our family, and many years later started a preschool for my granddaughter. I'd always wanted to give children a space of imagination, love, and support – the space I never had. I know the importance of those feelings because I know their absence."

We always have the choice to engage consciously and intentionally, becoming stronger than we thought possible, kinder than we imagined, and more compassionate than we've been before. Whether or not we come face to face with darkness is often not our choice, but we definitely get a vote in *who we become* as a result of the experience.

As the queen of darkness, Persephone symbolizes the earth's fertility. In Greek religion, chthonic deities were associated with fertility. The deep earth is the womb from which life grows – the body of Mother Earth where the seeds of life are planted and nurtured. Pagan religions worship earth goddesses and spirits such as Gaia. In the Judeo-Christian mythos, the earth and feminine are associated with life, fertility, and sin.

Persephone is the seed that grows in darkness – the parts of ourselves that sink deep into the ground, germinate, and bloom again. She's new life stored in the underworld throughout the cold winter that bursts forth in spring, transforming the land into a cornucopia. When we're in a dark place, we may think we've been buried alive, lost in a loveless gloom, but perhaps we've been *planted*.

"The accident destroyed a part of me," my brother reflected, "but it also gave me my life. Now I want to be a healer. I understand pain better; I have real empathy for people's struggles. Of course, I wish the accident hadn't happened, but I can see how it affects me positively, too." With a meaningful mindset, even the darkest moments of life can be incubators. They can be hidden beginnings that challenge us, stretch us, and expand our lives.

"There are tears in the fabric of life," psychologist Tanya Wilkinson wrote, "that can never be completely repaired, directions taken that, even if unchosen and unfair, can never be fully reversed because the self is changed by them."[17] Even when she returned to the dayworld, Persephone was bound to the underworld as well. Darkness was now woven into her being. She frolicked with the nymphs in sweet meadows, but inside she was different. In her depths, she was no longer Kore. She had become the dreaded goddess of death. No one who experiences the underworld forgets it; there's no return to who we were.

To become the rulers of darkness, we must be blindsided by Hades' black chariot. We find ourselves in darkness – afraid, alone, and longing for the comforts of the innocent world left behind. After a period of acclimation and tending, we have to decide if we want to stay under the formidable weight of our pain or if step by step, we can become familiar with parts of ourselves not seen before, and learn to rule this new kingdom.

Victim

When the underworld befalls us, the healing journey is set in motion when we begin to integrate the darkening. If we remain a "victim," blaming others for what was done to us, it's difficult to initiate lasting change.

Many survivors of early childhood trauma identify as the victim of another's aggression. Of course, the story behind their suffering begins with this truth. Donald Kalsched calls this identity *identification with the aggressor*, reasoning that over time the survivor takes the outward aggression they experienced during the traumata into their inner world and begins to hate themselves and in many cases lash out at others. "Obviously at some time or other," explained Jung, "the idea of being a persecuted victim gained the upper hand, became autonomous, and formed a second subject which at times completely replaces the healthy ego."[18] In this state, the ego dwells in constant fear that the trauma might recur. The wounded and regressed portion of the personality fails to participate in the development of other parts of the self. Eventually, the survivor becomes the victim of both the original external trauma and the violence that fills their inner world.

A man was heavily criticized by his father as a child. His father yelled at him and punished him for anything less than perfect grades. He hit him in the kitchen, the yard, and in his room. The sounds of his past haunt this man. He hears his father's belt being pulled out, his vicious voice yelling his name. Today, whenever he is in conflict – at work, in relationships, with his teenage daughters – he's transported back to his father's presence. He becomes a scared and unworthy boy. He seeks therapy because he no longer wants to be the victim of his father's wrath, now internalized.

Trauma-informed therapy relinks fragmented pieces of the personality. The process is not about removing pain, but reimagining and repairing our relationship to reality. To heal the inner splits caused by traumata, careful steps are taken to help the patient tolerate the fear and anxiety of holding contradictory ideas and images. The therapist uses techniques like grounding – connecting to the senses, breathing – and mindfulness, focusing the patient's awareness on the present moment to help transform their victimized parts into a personality system that has a sense of independence, creates realistic expectations, connects to the body, and can self-regulate. This process is complex, repetitive, and slow. Over time, the work reconfigures the inner world from a state of flight or fight, survival, and victimization to self-agency, integration, and freedom.

Many regard having journeyed to the underworld as indicating a failure, and they feel ashamed. Instead of endeavoring to integrate the complexity of their humanness, they believe they've been wronged, attacked, or misunderstood, giving rise to scapegoating, blaming, and seeking to be rescued.

Remember that Jungians call taking unwanted emotions or traits about yourself and assigning them to someone else, *projection*. Projection is how we deal with what is painful to our egos. By putting our fear, anxiety, anger, desire, and prejudice onto another, it appears to be outside of us, creating a sense of clarity and relief that we've removed the intolerable feelings. A pressure release happens because ideas incompatible with our sense of self are now not ours.

In our global world, we're besieged with how the ideas and actions of others affect us. In such an interconnected matrix, it's alluring to blame others for the conflicts and tensions of the world. We don't have to look far to witness cultural conflict and division; evidence of climate change, for example, increases visibly while the facts on the ground and in the air and water continue to be debated. Some Americans respond to a pandemic virus by battling against masks, the UK withdraws from the European Union, politics are more partisan than ever, while movements like Black Lives Matter and Me Too seek to bring awareness to the struggles of their populations. In anger, frustration, and overwhelm, it's easy to judge others wrong, excusing ourselves of co-responsibility. The more we point fingers, the more we're protected from our role and accountability.

To take responsibility for our healing journeys, we have to forego the temptation to blame others for our suffering. When someone is emotionally neglected, abused, shamed, or humiliated, they are often the victims of a power outside themselves. But if we continue to imagine ourselves as victims, we remain oblivious to our role, responsibility, and agency, and risk staying stuck in loops of blaming others for our distress. We become a victim of anything outside our control. We suffer in relationship to outside danger we can't control, an attitude that makes us feel alone and helpless. Nothing changes until we take responsibility for ourselves. "Compassion" comes from the Latin *compati*, to "suffer with." To heal, we have to suffer *with* our pain instead of putting it on others.

Persephone switched from helpless victim to owning her plight. Instead of projecting her suffering onto Hades, remaining victim of his abduction, she became sovereign. Wondering why something happened to us or what we did to deserve it is a natural pastime. Many tragedies never make sense – losing your job when the economy crashes, a narcissistic mother, or childhood sexual abuse.

Believing darkness can't happen is Kore energy, the innocence of the ego seeking the impossible return to a pristine world. Processing our pain through a "why me?" lens is enticing, but not helpful. There will never be a satisfying "why" for the tragedies of life: Why did my sister die? Why did my fiancé leave before our wedding? Why did my child drown? Why do I have bipolar disorder? Why him? Why me?

Persephone invites us to ponder a philosophical, even theological, question: Why do bad things happen to good people? This is one of the tasks of underworlding – how do we make peace with the shadow world? How do we surrender to the reality of where we are, even if it's harsh, dissociated, and cold? Sometimes we have to face what cannot be changed. Our unlived life is a beach ball we may try to keep submerged. But it keeps popping back up.

Many people spend years looking for answers that never come. The question is, do we remain Kore, stunted and longing for the past, projecting our difficulties onto others, imploring them to protect us, letting trauma slowly consume our life and our freedom, or do we take the dark underbelly of fate and become its ruler, turning darkness into destiny?

"Victim" comes from the Latin *victima,* "sacrificial animal; person or animal killed as a sacrifice." A sacrifice is a sacred offering, giving up something treasured. We look at ourselves as the sacrificial lamb offered *in toto* to darkness, or we can look at darkness as inviting us to give something up in service of the divine, to bring forth our life's fullness. Kore, the naïve, virginal aspects of our *puer* or *puella* complex, is sacrificed in order to become Persephone, the ruler of dormancy and fecundity. Darkness is painful and dreaded, but it's also a part of deepening and stepping into our power.

Imagining ourselves as victim of an unjust horror, on the one hand, or as an active participant in life, on the other, dramatically alters perception and consequence. When the body goes into fight or flight, it releases adrenaline and cortisol, hormones that cause rapid heart rate, heightened senses, increased strength and performance. It takes the body about 90 seconds to metabolize these hormones. After a minute and half, our autonomic response is no longer the source of our rushing heartbeats, shaking hands, and shortness of breath. After that, remaining stressed is a choice. That may be hard to believe, as our nervous system (which does not know past from present) continues the same symptoms, but they are controllable in time.

In 1959, following the brutal suppression of the Tibetan people and culture by Chinese troops, His Holiness the 14th Dalai Lama, Tenzin Gyatso, was forced to flee his homeland on foot and horseback to India. Since then, he has worked tirelessly to promote peace and freedom, for which he was awarded the Nobel Peace Prize and more than 150 other awards, authored and coauthored more than 100 books, and he continues to advocate for his people. It would have been "natural" for him to remain stuck in victimhood, telling the world a story of the oppression and injustices done to his people. But he hasn't. Instead, he's led his people with compassion and peace, becoming the ruler of a fate unjustly thrown upon him and a figure of moral authority admired around the world.

Living in relationship with trauma, grief, complexes, and mental illness is an ongoing journey. Pain doesn't have to be our sole destiny. It doesn't mean we "move on," overcome, or even lessen our suffering. What is possible is that we get bigger. We learn to be *with* the seasons of darkness, working mindfully with our worst moments to help them be impetuses for insight, integration, and transformation. Healing doesn't mean the abduction didn't happen. It means it doesn't rule us.

Persephone's mythology gives shape to a core human lesson: when you're pulled into the darkness, how you respond makes all the difference. To be a ruler or to be a victim are two very different paths to facing hardship. The first helps us accept difficult situations and be transformed by them. On the second path, we flee, ignore, and resist shadows and pain, and remain a victim.

I am not saying this is easy. Some of our core woundedness is huge, and it takes a very long time to be able to tolerate being in its presence long enough for choice to even feel like an option. And some are not called to take the path of presence, and there's no judgment if you must retreat, pause, or withdraw. But the rewards of presence and integration are manifold, no less than the fullness of the life that awaits you.

Cyclical Rhythms

Each spring Persephone ascends the underworld to be with her mother, and the world rejoices with new life – buds and blooms, springtime air and babbling brooks. Each fall she journeys back to the embrace of Hades, and death steals across the wheat fields, birds fly south, the sun sets earlier. Underworlding often happens in cycles. We plunge into darkness, return to the surface, and stumble back downward again. The underworld can't simply be erased, it continues to influence the present – spinning like a wheel, a circle, the seasons.

The periodic undertow of darkness exerts a powerful pull on life. Traumatic darkness creates an inner world that traps us in loops of self-perpetuating defense. When learned fear responses take over, we go on autopilot, behaving in ways that recreate the traumatic feelings as though they are in the outer world, trapping us in cycle of our own making. We shame and berate ourselves, sabotaging the very things we care about, convincing ourselves we're victims and descending into despair. Cycles of self-hatred turn, and turn again.

A woman has always dated men who are incapable of an intimate connection. Emotionally neglected as a child, she believes everyone is untrustworthy. It's safer to have shallow relationships than feel the pain of another disappointment. She's "safe" (armored, really) but lonely – never risking real connection. The movie she plays in her head continually reminds her that something's wrong with her, and she's convinced that others see her this way. "I pretend this feeling of not being enough isn't there," she told me, "and at the same time I want someone to rescue me. This cycle leads me into demeaning relationships, and I feel even more hopeless." She wants to be saved, loved, and needed, but unconsciously she recreates patterns, actions, and behaviors that turn her partners off. And the cycle repeats itself.

We repeat what we don't repair. It's familiar to reenact patterns of shame, pain, and trauma. That feels safe and expected, even if limited and dysfunctional. Survivors of attachment or relationship trauma recreate similar relationships, searching for a different outcome while reinforcing self-hatred and the belief that they deserve to suffer.

The solution appears to be a one-way ascent. They long to be *finished* with hardship, *overcome* illness, *defeat* depression, and *move beyond* their haunting past. We all want freedom from pain and negative cycles, but to do so we have to give underworlding a place in life. If we don't, the suffering doesn't go away. It just sinks back beneath the surface.

Nothing about Persephone's relationship with the underworld is final or one-way. She descends and ascends, year after year. Healing is a lifelong process that starts with accepting what happened in the past, honoring what's happening in the present, and committing ourselves to the path ahead, wherever it takes us. Persephone, remarkably, isn't consumed by the eternity of her trials. Instead, she brings resilience to the repetitive nature of underworlding.

A friend told me about the underworld journey she experienced in the wake of her father's stroke. Although her father survived, his cognition, physical capacity, language, and independence declined sharply. She described a cycle between the acute and small moments of gratitude and discovery for what her father can do, the ebb and flow between loss, grief, and joy. "I'm consistently grieving what *was*," she said, "while stuck in the interminable present. It's difficult to move on when the darkness is there every day. Dad needs support getting into the shower. He needs intensive speech therapy to form the simplest of sounds, and assistance getting up after falling, yet again."

The omnipresence of caring for her father rises and sets like the sun. Every day she descends into darkness and surfaces once more, only to repeat her journey the next day. "I've been unable to integrate back into 'normal,'" she told me. "What happened prevents the return to my own life."

Repeating the journey brings its own terrors – constancy, grief for the life lost, the responsibility and exhaustion of caretaking, stress, hopelessness, overwhelm, and the gloom that sets in when you realize sunlight will never return in the same way.

When we embark upon a healing and meaning-making journey to the underworld, we may strive to reach a place that is free from suffering. But that's not what happens. Some experiences endure no matter how much inner work we do, no matter how many years pass. We can't remove the pain, but we can change our relationship with it.

Persephone did not fester in longing for the past. She accepted darkness as a partner to life. Her journey was cyclic, not linear. She didn't rise above her suffering or remove it. She wove darkness and light into a balanced whole, symbolized by the changing seasons. By spending six months in the lower world and six months in the dayworld, she became the ligament between light and dark. The separation between the two worlds was healed, and balance was restored.

When we experience the underworld through Persephone's lens, we recognize and accept that we'll never rid ourselves of darkness. When abducted by addiction, the death of a loved one, violence, complexes, depression, or other shadow material, we have the option of coming to terms with this essential fact – we'll never be able to "wash" our souls of the underworld. It doesn't work that way. Even in the dayworld, where woes pass and life continues, darkness remains our partner.

Everyone I've spoken to about their underworld journeys lives in constant relationship with their experiences. Years after her daughter died, a woman told me she still feels her daughter's presence. She finds her in the trees she passes while out on a walk, in faces she sees on the streets, and in the tightness in her chest. A friend who struggles with self-doubt told me that every day she convinces herself that her partner loves her, lest she sabotage yet another relationship. When a death surprises us, an accident happens, or a wrong is done to us it's tempting to tantrum against the unjustness of it all. The "why" questions return. No understanding or compartmentalization, removing or overcoming can provide solace. We have to find a way to be *with* the never-ending presence of what's happened so darkly.

Growing up, a little girl was expected to act in ways beyond her capacities. She had to sit still like an adult and keep up with her older sister mentally and physically, and as she failed at each task, she felt inadequate. As an adult, therapy helped her see that her parents had been projecting *their* emotional trauma – their own feelings of inadequacy and the need to try ever harder to accomplish the impossible – onto her. Seeing, though, is not resolution or completion; it's the beginning of the journey. The scar tissue left behind is hard to break down. She feels fundamentally flawed and tries to bully herself into perfection, just as her parents did to her. She reaches for the skies and fails, reinforcing her sense of being flawed. Self-abuse returns amid cycles of alienation and belittlement, like a broken record. As she begins to see and value herself for who she is, trying to discern past from present, she is able to carry on, companioned by her feelings of inadequacy but not defined only by them.

The results of war, neglect, starvation, and racial abuse imprint themselves psychologically and biologically on individuals and entire groups, carrying forward the wounds of the past within new generations. The transgenerational trauma of the Holocaust, slavery, and ethnic cleansing continues to affect Jews, African Americans, Bosnians, and many others into the foreseeable future. Just as a recovering addict is always in relationship with their addiction and a parent who loses a child constantly lives with grief, the touch of the underworld intertwines itself within our beings. Wounds do not disappear, even over time. They may soften and slowly recede into the background, but our relationship with darkness is cyclical. It comes and it goes. It ebbs and flows. We can repress or dissociate from them, but they just go underground until the fault lines slip open and they grab hold of us again.

Weathering the discomfort of psychological development engenders insight and stability. Persephone personifies a wisdom that comes from understanding darkness and its cyclical rhythm. The first time we experience a big loss, it may trigger a feeling of abandonment and utter aloneness. We do not yet have a context in which to place the experience. Our first heartbreak can be devastating, but is it really the worst breakup ever with the only person we will ever love? The first time we interview for a job and are not selected, it has a different tone from later rejections, because we are not yet familiar with the terrain. These first abductions teach us about who we are – our values and preferences, the places we feel inadequate, and our surprising resilience. Life never offers just one underworld journey. Over time, greater and lesser underworld journeys help us become familiar with the rhythm of underworlding, and the descents and ascents may feel less steep as we cultivate a relationship with darkness.

Queen Elizabeth II, the current monarch of the United Kingdom, has lived her life with Persephonic cyclicality. As an 18-year-old princess, she joined the Auxiliary Territorial Service during World War II, wore coveralls, and trained to be a mechanic and military truck driver. She was in London during the bombings. When her father died in 1952, she became Queen of the Commonwealth at age 25. When she acceded to the throne, the British Empire had more than 50 colonies, territories, and nations, and today there are fewer than 15. She's the longest-reigning British monarch and female head of state. Her life is a pillar of self-sacrifice, commitment, and resiliency. For decades, she's met with prime ministers, upheld the constitutional laws of the monarchy, and represented the traditions, values, and interests of the royal family. Her accession was a result of her uncle, Edward VIII, abdicating the throne to her father, King George VI. The abdication was for her an abduction – unexpectedly forcing her from third in line to the throne, to first. Elizabeth didn't reject her destiny. With resilience and acceptance, she has devoted her life to serving her country.

Persephone's cyclical journey gave her wisdom – prudence that comes from knowing we can endure something because we've done it before and will do it again. There's a Saturnian element to Persephone: the wisdom of recurrence, time, endurance, and the ebb and flow of the seasons. The Greeks called this *palingeneisa,* "survival of continuous rebirth." Darkness can strip us to the bone, change everything about our lives, create terrible cycles of pain, criticism, and doubt, and leave us heartbroken and uncertain. Our attempts to understand and integrate its lessons are never a sunny day. Learning to live with and be affected by the challenges of the journey is the work of a lifetime.

Persephonic

"Persephonic" means "great beauty born out of utter chaos and pain, the point where the depth of darkness meets the crest of light, the by-product of two opposing extremes."[19] Persephone is deep, dark, and powerful. She isn't colorful flowers, warm sunlight, or tall grasses. Her beauty is interior, carved from hardship. She personifies the empowerment that comes from being forced into a relationship with Hades, and thus with herself.

From the Greek *pertho,* "to destroy" or "slay," the name Persephone has been translated as "she who destroys the light." Even her name is associated with destruction and rebirth, darkness and dawn. She pertains to underworlding that abducts life, destroys innocence, and in so doing, teaches us to come to grips with and ultimately to rule what has befallen us. Once you've gone through the unthinkable, you become familiar with that threshold, and become, in a manner of speaking, a sovereign of the underworld, a person unafraid of challenge and inquiry.

Reflections

Kore represents the loss of innocence and purity, the experience of darkness stealing us away. Yet in darkness, Kore becomes Persephone – queen of the underworld. Persephone personifies being pulled into darkness and how that abduction can lead to purpose and power. Part of each of us desires to deepen and, given the right attitude, can rule our pain instead of becoming a victim to it. The queen of darkness is an image of resilience that comes from the repetition of suffering.

Reflect on how these Persephonic qualities may be present within your experience in:

- Experiencing the loss of innocence.
- Being abducted into the underworld.
- When you chose to become the ruler of your fate.
- Wisdom that comes from repetitive exposure to darkness.
- The parts of you that were forever changed by suffering.
- Your capacity for integration and acceptance.
- A sense of the preciousness of life that can come from living in relationship with darkness.

CHAPTER 10
DIONYSUS

Dionysus was the god of revelry, wine, release, and insanity. He pertains to nature and community, chaos and regeneration, freedom and destruction, instinct and the body. More than other gods, Dionysus sits uneasily in the Western mind. We have mostly forgotten the god of madness, pleasure, and wildness at its most untamed.

Personalities that are volcanic, unrestrained, and untamed are labeled pathological, unbalanced, neurotic, or manic. Instead of honor and recognition, we treat, filter, shame, and mitigate Dionysian energy. But subjugation has a price – what is repressed is internalized, and it grows and distorts our lenses.

Myth tells us that Zeus fell in love with and impregnated the Theban princess Semele. When Hera, his jealous wife, discovered the affair, she tricked Semele into beseeching Zeus to reveal his divine radiance. Knowing that such exposure would kill her, Zeus implored Semele to give up her plea. Unsuccessful, he revealed himself in his divine form, arriving in a chariot of lightning bolts, and Semele was scorched.

As the flames consumed her, Hermes snatched the infant Dionysus from her womb and gave him to Zeus to place in his thigh until he came to term. After Dionysus was born, Zeus entrusted his son to his aunts Ino, Agaue, and Autonoe. Learning of Dionysus' survival, Hera drove his protectors mad, causing them to kill themselves and their children. In order to save Dionysus, Zeus changed him into a ram and carried him to the elderly satyr Seilenos and the nymphs of Mount Nysa, where he was brought up in a cave. The young god then wandered the world, eventually earning his place as an Olympian.

Anointed as a god, Dionysus decided to journey to the underworld to return his mother, Semele, to life, installing her as the goddess Thyone. His journey is a metaphor for going into darkness to retrieve neglected and forgotten parts of ourselves. To face Dionysus is to turn toward repressed parts of the psyche.

Nature

The name "Semele" comes from the Greek *zemyna,* "new earth." As Semele's son, Dionysus is a child of the earth. In all traditions, Dionysus appears as the representative of nature's wildness. Invoked as *Endendros,* "he in the tree", and depicted as a wild youth, he roamed the glens crowned in ivy and grape clusters carrying a pinecone-tipped staff called a *thyrsus.* Dionysus personifies the soul of nature – a god of wildness and animals, instinct and ivy.

In 2005, Richard Louv published *Last Child in the Woods*, the first book to address a growing body of research indicating that exposure to nature is essential to a child's healthy development.

Louv explored the growing division between children and the outdoors, coining the term "nature-deficit disorder" as a factor in rising childhood obesity, attention disorders, and depression. He warned that our society inadvertently discourages playing outdoors, prioritizing indoor activities. Study after study documents the psychological and physical benefits of connecting with the natural world. Bringing flowers to hospital rooms decreases the need for painkillers and looking at photos of lakes and rivers speeds up mental restoration.

Our connection with the natural world is more tenuous than ever, and over the next 30 years, it's predicted that 60 percent of the world's population will live in cities. As a species, we are moving farther and farther away from the natural world. Playing the videogame *The Oregon Trail* isn't camping. Scrolling through nature photos isn't listening to or entering babbling creeks, feeling the texture of moss, or seeing a wild animal. A British study revealed that kids today know more Pokémon characters than tree names.[1]

Protecting an environment we aren't really connected with presents a challenge. How can we know the value of preserving the wildness of wilderness if we've never felt breathless by its beauty? How can we recognize an ecosystem if we've never been in it? How can we sacrifice some of the conveniences of daily life without understanding how our actions adversely affect animal habitats? Separated from our planet and its fragile ecosystems, we are destroying our very home.

Jung believed that the loss of emotional participation in nature creates isolation and a feeling of disconnection. Not long ago, most humans felt the spirits within nature were alive and actively influencing our world. Industrialization, Judeo-Christian scriptures about man's dominion over nature (and over women), and the creation of non-natural materials have come at a high price – the de-animation of our world. A*nima*, from the Latin "soul," or "air, breathe," means "bring to life."

Our exploitation of the natural world follows from treating the natural world as soulless. We don't feel the weight and grief of destroying what is alive and ensouled. It's easier to foul animals' habitats if we think they don't have souls, feelings, or minds.

Whenever he feels the old pull of chaos and unhappiness, a man finds support by living the simple life – being outside and working with his hands. From memory, the man recites a passage from *Leaf and Tendril* by the naturalist John Burroughs:

> To see the fire that warms you, or better yet, to cut the
> wood that feeds the fire … to be in direct and personal
> contact with the sources of your material life; to want
> no extras, no shields … to find the air and the water
> exhilarating; to be refreshed by a morning walk or an
> evening saunter … to be thrilled by the stars at night,
> to be elated over a bird's nest – these are some of the
> rewards of the simple life.[2]

To stop and listen to the call of the wild and notice the natural perfume in the air that foretells the coming of rain; to pad through the forest and know which plants will sustain you and which to leave in peace; to rely on this harvest to satiate you; to see the deer and squirrels, birds and foxes as sisters and brothers; to use the rhythms of the seasons to track the passage of time – these are ways of immersing ourselves in the natural world that were a given for our ancestors, yet utterly unfamiliar to many today.

We in the modern West tend to live in a myth of discon-nection – God is separate from humans; we are separate from animals; animals are separate from the earth; mind is separate from matter; the dayworld is separate from the underworld. We think of the body as a machine, dreams as epiphenomena of the brain, and nature as without soul. We divide, simplify, and compartmentalize, disconnecting us from the vibrancy and complexity of life.

The Dionysian is a response to this disconnection. As the spirit of nature, Dionysus is about the life force in all things – a natural world filled with charge and spirit, soul and body. To see the shared life between yourself, another person, the bear that sleeps in her cave, the bark of a tree, a wild fern, and a songbird. As environmental activist Steve Van Matre writes:

> Yes, the earth speaks, but only to those who can hear with their hearts. It speaks in a thousand, thousand small ways but like our loves and families and friends, it often sends its messages without words … its voice is the shape of a new leaf, the feel of a water-worn stone, the color of evening sky, the smell of summer rain, the sound of the night wind. The earth's whispers are everywhere, but only those who have slept with it can respond readily to its call.[3]

As long as we leave Dionysus out of our lives, we risk living in a controlled, deadened, and unrelated world, enduring a divided existence that threatens nature and brings us further and further away from the parts of us that are wild, organic, alive, and ensouled.

Cancer is often called a "disease of civilization," the malady of modernity. The name of the patron saint of cancer, St. Peregrine, means "to cross the fields." There is a connection between cancer and earth. In a cancer journey, something of the substance of life is undernourished. As Russel Lockhart puts it, "something of one's psychic and bodily earth is not allowed to live, not allowed to grow."[4] One way to imagine into the underworlding of cancer is to see the disease as an expression of our separation from nature. To what extent is there a connection between how we toxify, destroy, and pillage our earth and inspire disease processes that mimic such destruction in the body? "Cancer is not just an illness of our time," said Russel Lockhart, "but is a symptom of our spirit."[5]

Polluted air is a leading cause of premature death worldwide. Microplastics are in the air and the oceans. The air above the Pyrenees and the Rockies is polluted with microplastics, and nearly one-third of fibers in indoor air are microplastics. We humans eat an average of five grams of plastic a week, the equivalent in weight of a credit card. And microplastics have been found in 97 percent of tumors dissected. They are biologically persistent, which means the body cannot dissolve the toxins they carry. When released in our bodies, they are neurotoxic, injurious to nerve impulse transmission. They lodge in lung tissue, resulting in lesions that can cause breathlessness, persistent inflammation, lung disease, and cancer. I am not a biologist or medical doctor, so I will not enumerate all the ways our disrespect for and disenchantment of the natural world affects us as a species; these are just a few examples of the price we pay for not heeding the call of Dionysus and Mother Nature, who personify the life-giving, nurturing qualities of wildness and wilderness.[6]

There's a parallel between the myth of Erysichthon and the unchecked and disconnected avarice of modern society. As Ovid told the story, Erysichthon took a group of axemen into the sacred grove of Demeter looking for timber. Female spirits of the trees warned him against his hubris and the consequences of denuding the forest. Intent on his aim, he chopped down the sacred oak of Demeter, enraging the goddess. She inflicted an insatiable hunger upon him. After ingesting the entire food supply, he devoured himself.

Without soul nourishment and deep connection to the ground of our being, we devour ourselves – seeking more and more to fill an insatiable emptiness. There's balance and interconnection in nature, yet we perturb it – pouring glyphosate and other toxins on our land, burning forests, destroying habitations for materials we shape into products designed to fill the empty and increasing void within, extracting and burning fossil fuels. Disconnected from source, the machine consumes itself.

Life Force

Dionysus is elemental and instinctive – life force at its most uncontained. We don't find him in cultivated gardens, prim hedges, and bouquets of sweet-smelling flowers. He's *Argios,* the "wild," a personification of undomesticated wilderness, unyielding and indestructible, the vine that grows without cultivation or care – a relentless, vibrant, arcane, and harsh reality. Jung called Dionysus "unbridled and unbroken Nature."[7] In an Orphic hymn, he was described as "loud-roaring reveling Dionysus, primeval, two-natured, thrice-born, Bacchic lord, savage, ineffable, secretive, two-horned and two-shaped, ivy-covered, bull-faced, warlike, howling, pure."[8]

Dionysus pertains to the uncultivated layers of the psyche. The poetics of tragedy and grief, darkness and death that lie beyond words and reason but are elemental in the sense of being deeply ensouled – the natural forces of the psyche. He is a breaking of bonds and the emergence of emotions over reason. There's nothing enclosed or idyllic about Dionysian underworlding. When we're thrust into anything explosive, unrelenting, and vital, his presence is there. He bursts into awareness with thunder, violence, and rawness. He's the vine that appears dead but is alive and re-growing, an embodiment of the incessant growth of nature that connects us to aspects of life we can't trim, forecast, or structure. Underworlding is a wilderness where we encounter the raw forces of the psyche – nature hell-bent on undoing all we have built and polished, protected and refined. To be Dionysian is to feel the feral and instinctive, darkness made carnal, visible, and immediate.

The emotions of the lower realm are ceaseless and consuming whirlpools for broken souls. Depression, grief, self-doubt, and anxiety swell, break, and recede like waves. "Violence" comes from the Latin *vis*, "life force." Life makes itself *vis*-ible through thrusts of dynamism and energy. If we seek to calm and sterilize all that is forceful, we cut ourselves off from the powers that sustain creative life. Dionysus is the life force of the deep, the growing and coiling roots that support life, endless torrents of water that erode foundations. He pertains to the *moisture* of life — feeling, expression, images, instinct. If we try to tame or constrict his energy, perhaps by avoiding emotions, we risk this energy finding its way into our lives violently.

In the underworld, our connection to the dayworld disappears. Yet in the midst of the unraveling, small shoots break through. A descent into the elemental emotions can instill a hunger for raw life. The insatiable power of life force has its ways of climbing up from the darkness toward the sun's warmth. As Robert Romanyshyn writes, "it was this elemental force, this throbbing river of life, which dissolved the icy numbness of my grief." "The green force of life," he added, "had taken hold of me, *had shaken me to life*."[9]

Many of my clients seek therapy because their lives feel heavy, cumbersome, or dried up. They want more passion, creativity, and energy. They want more moisture in their lives. Too much responsibility, repetition, and indifference has damned the flow of life energy. Their souls are dehydrated. Some blame their jobs, partners, or finances, while repressing or ignoring messages from the inner world. As repression festers, warnings morph into illness and meaninglessness. To restore balance, the currents of the unconscious need rehydration.

A woman came to see me with haunting memories of incest during her childhood. As a young girl, she tried to drown her pain in drugs, sex addiction, and self-harm. As she matured, her outer life stabilized, but the inner world still raged with darkness. She was drawn to my work because of my Jungian background and a recent dream image. In the dream, she walked through a deep cave where the ground was sandy and hot. She encountered a natural spring and drank, the cool waters refreshing her. We talked about how dry and dead her life was, how much energy she put toward safety, controlling fear, remaining unemotional, and self-hatred. She cried during many sessions, the waters of life pouring through her, slowly healing the parched earth of her soul.

Worshipers of Dionysus left their homes, responsibilities, and ordered lives to revel in the wild. In the forest, they let down their hair, clothed themselves with the skin of beasts, and crowned their heads with ivy and wild briony. Fires burned and they twirled, stomped their feet, and let go – embracing pure life energy. We recognize Dionysus in moments when we feel wildly alive, in touch with the greening of things – the pulsing, animate vibration of nature forced into the human mind.

Dionysus, writes Ginette Paris, is the "revenge of the forces of instinct over the forces of order … the Roarer, the Loud-Shouter, the Loosener, the Beast, the Mountain Bull."[10] Dionysus happens when we scream, cry, break down, and fall apart. When we allow the raw energy of what we're feeling into our being. In the presence of Dionysus, chaos, suffering, and immediacy are accepted, even encouraged. Instead of containing underworlding through filters of normalcy and control, we express our whole selves.

Animalism

Dionysus is often depicted riding on the back of a leopard or driving a chariot drawn by sacred animals. He was worshiped as *Bromios*, "the roarer," and associated with the panther, leopard, tiger, bull, snake, and goat. Sacrifices in his honor were called *axios tauros*, "worthy bull."

Dionysus is human expression made animalistic. The imagery of animals can be harnessed to help us capture and feel the wildness of underworlding. Sometimes our anger is a roaring bear or lion; other times our transformation is as complex as a butterfly's metamorphosis. Grief can be a weighty beached whale, doubt a clawing falcon, failure a stalking panther.

I worked with a woman who struggled to assert herself. When she felt helpless and vulnerable she visualized a small animal trapped in a tiny cage, malnourished and afraid. The little creature carried her uncertainty and overwhelm. Over time, she started visualizing a white wolf standing next to the cage. The wolf was there to protect the little animal as it left the cage and ventured into the unknown. These animals represented her vulnerability and power, allowing her to hold them both at the same time.

Instincts such as fear, preservation, sexuality, and connection are the polar opposite of learned human behavior. They are hardwired and deeply intuitive, less organized than socially taught and maintained behaviors. Dionysus connects us to our animalism, but he's not mindless, primitive, or inhuman. Those energies are the domain of the Titans, the primitive gods who preceded the Olympians. The Titans dismembered Dionysus as a child. They were his enemy. Dionysus was the only god of the 12-part Greek pantheon who had a mortal mother. He was the only god with mortal blood, infusing human control and civility into his primal nature.

Today, we have few containers to experience the animalism of Dionysus. "Instead of being exposed to wild beasts, tumbling rocks, and inundating waters," wrote Robert A. Johnson, "man is exposed today to the elemental forces of his own psyche."[11] The repression of Dionysian instincts internalizes this energy, where it becomes complexes, neurosis, and shadow figures – sleeping giants waiting to be roused from their slumber.

Writing at the end of World War I, Jung observed that "the animal in us only becomes more beastlike when it is repressed."[12] To ignore our shadowed and instinctive side is to permit its dark energy to strengthen, eventually threatening the ego. Repression never accomplishes what we want. The repressed always returns in demonic form.

A woman's father died of a heart attack when she was a child, too young to process her loss. Her mother internalized her own grief and became distant and unable to comfort her daughter. The woman didn't have a safe emotional environment to feel and grieve her loss, so she buried it. But the pain didn't go away, and instead sadness turned to rage, then shame. Eventually her unattended loss took on a psychic life of its own. She felt ashamed of her need for connection and hated her emotions, all the while drawing sad and lonely people to her to (unconsciously) care for her repressed grief.

Repression is a seductive defense. At a crucial moment, it serves a purpose. Profound darkness such as trauma and death is often impossible to digest without overwhelming suffering, so the mind splits itself to protect what is wounded and overwhelmed. After the death of a parent, horrific sexual violence, or a war, we cannot dive headfirst into the rawness of these wounds – we might drown. Defenses such as repression contain us when we need them to. But there comes a time when coping is no longer needed, facing our demons is possible, and continuing to repress them keeps us stuck, not safe, creating a lifetime of numbness and disconnection, shame and self-hatred, anger, constricting complexes, or addiction.

There is a savage and nocturnal side of Dionysus. In Greece, a hunter who captured living animals was called Zagreus, from the Ionian *zagre*, "a pit for the capture of live animals." Zagreus was another form of Dionysus that pertained to his barbarity – the eating of flesh, blazing bonfires, and howling at night. In some mythic accounts, Zagreus was described as the son of Lethe, "forgetfulness." He's an image of the titanic and horrific. To feel Zagreus is to forget our civilized conditioning, to be free from human influence – violent and otherworldly.

When we think of Dionysus, we also think of Zagreus — revelry and bestiality, insanity and savagery. We have demonized these unrefined parts of ourselves — the windows into souls that are not polished, ordered, or controlled. By not allowing instinct and animalism a place in our personalities, we neglect an important layer of human expression.

It isn't fair to expect to face the unbearable nightmares of living with composure and civility. Sometimes we need to scream, cry, or fall on our knees. There are shadows in life that devour, darkness so penetrating that we lose ourselves entirely. Some moments in life need to be roared at, felt in the body, shouted about, and expressed with raw emotions, not stable, boundaried composure. Sometimes we have to rage and release, destroy and regenerate, fall apart in order to rebuild.

Dionysian instinct mustn't be taken lightly. There are not many people who can ride this energy and keep their balance. The unconscious in its most unfiltered can possess the ego-mind. Lack of containment has serious risks — suicide, accidents, addictions, mania, violence, and deep depression. Our task is to find balance — to feel and even express the power of instinct without being consumed by it.

Intensity

Everything to do with Dionysus is in our face. There's nothing silent or distant about it. He's the blasting cacophony of emotional experience writ large. Jung called him the flood "of overpowering universal feeling, which bursts forth irresistibly, intoxicating the senses like the strongest wine."[13] Dionysus is all-roaring, frenzied, and howling. He's immediate and visceral — aching, rapturous, shooting, gnawing, devouring, fierce, blissful, and shocking. Ovid described his coming: "The crash of unseen drums ... and jingling brass resounded, suddenly the whole house began to shake, the lamps flared up, and all the rooms were bright with flashing crimson fires, and phantom forms of savage beasts of prey howled all around."[14] He is pure affect: instinctive, carnal, compelling, and blinding. Dionysus pertains to forceful, even overwhelming responses to darkness. Instead of bottling up, controlling, and minimizing the intensity of underworlding, the god of wild release offers us liberation through catharsis.

There's an honesty and a release in letting yourself feel in a Dionysian way. When the unthinkable happens our souls need an outlet. We need to cry out in pain, shake our bodies to release our stress, move in a way that embodies our fear, or even howl in despair. Dionysus allows us to *feel* underworlding. It's easier to blame ourselves, make excuses, or play the "what if" or "why" games than be acutely present for the felt experience of suffering. The affective encounter with the archetypal realm is overwhelming, to say the least. Repression is often easier than feeling the intensity of what's happening so darkly. The secret of being Dionysian is to leave the structured, ordered, and Newtonian world and immerse yourself in a place of sensation, intensity, and intuitive rawness.

We label the barbaric, visceral, and ecstatic parts of ourselves as profane, unbalanced, and even sinful. We're unable to experience the intensity of Dionysus in a contained and communal way, and so beneath the surface the unexpressed transforms into rage, mania, compulsion, and addictive behavior. When the immediate and instinctive parts of ourselves do not have an appropriate outlet, in place of release we get uncontained excess.

Zeus impregnated Semele through a lightning bolt – a symbol of the penetrating force of psychic life energy. Likewise, Semele died when exposed to Zeus' divinity. Dionysus was born from a union so overwhelming it was annihilating. Dionysian intensity pertains to interactions, transitions, complexes, illnesses, relationships, or other psychological energies that give us more than we can handle.

The intensity of darkness can be impossible to bear. I spoke with a woman who was raped. Years later she's still unable to live in the present or imagine a future, because she's trapped in the immediacy of her fear. Too many things in life remind her of lying frozen in her room. Even being with the smallest of feelings for 10 or 20 seconds at a time causes dissociation and severs her link to reality. In the beginning, her therapy was slow, careful, and gentle. Healing can't happen by throwing the door open. The intensity of trauma must be approached bit by bit, so she can learn to be with her pain in a new way.

Ginette Paris warned that living too closely to the intensity of Dionysus, what she called the "insatiable hunger for emotion and intense experiences," can eventually "bring the opposite of what they want; nothing much is felt in their presence."[15] With high intensity comes the risk of overexposure. The consequence of Semele's request is to become a lifeless shade in Hades. Too much intensity can lead to burnout, exhaustion, and loss of self.

In the documentary *Meru*, mountaineer Jimmy Chin confesses he's addicted to the dramatic heights of the mountains he climbs. Once you've touched the realm of the gods, he warns, nothing else brings feeling. There is a reason the gods live on the high mountaintops and we mortals far below. To live in a state of extremes is to risk numbness to anything less. Intensity and pain can be hard to distinguish. When we live in chronic imbalance, stability and normalcy can make us feel like a shade. It's important not to match Dionysus' intensity. We humans couldn't sustain life if we dwelled only in such extremes.

In her biographical book, *An Unquiet Mind*, psychiatrist Kay Redfield Jamison captures the terror and allure of living with manic-depressive illness. She vividly describes an inner world furiously alive with madness and pain. Her story darts back and forth between states of heighted manic highs followed by consuming and heavy lows. She wages a personal war between the release, freedom, and grandeur of mania and the need for medication and psychotherapy. Mood disorders such as bipolarity create cycles of inflation and deflation which, for many, make living a consistently stable life challenging.

Darkness is terrifying – the loss of what is known and stable in our personalities is something we in the West avoid. The terrifying shadows of life – what feels "other" and inhuman – can devour. Exposure to raw and terrifying instinct is no light matter. Without a stable ego to patrol the boundaries of identity and a safe container to hold us, the hounds of the deep may howl.

Lysios

Dionysus was called *Lysios*, "the loosener" and pertains to release – shattering composure, abolishing old ways, loosening ties. "Analysis" comes from the Greek *analyein*, meaning "unloose, release, set free," or, as Aristotle reasoned, from *ana* ("up, back, throughout"), *lysis* ("a loosening") and *lyein* ("to unfasten"). Ana-*lysis* is thus a loosening, a setting free. Analysis can be a cutting apart, an untangling to reveal who we really are. If we struggle with inadequacy, self-doubt needs to loosen to make space for self-worth. If we are wounded, our pain must loosen to make space for well-being. If we are stuck, rigidity must loosen for something new to emerge. The solidity of the dam blocks the water from flowing.

We all have confirmation biases that make us search for, interpret, and favor information that confirms our prior assumptions, beliefs, or ideas. These assumptions distort reality and block change. I had a few sessions with a married couple that had each made up their mind about the other. They saw the world differently and were so caught up in their own lives that they'd moved far away from each other, no longer able to connect. They both longed for love, witnessing, and respect, but this need had been so suppressed that it manifested in a state of constant bickering – chronic low-level warfare. Our work together was brief, they weren't willing to see each other in new ways. They'd already bound themselves to a fate of shared disappointment and couldn't see the other, even when they were both trying.

It's easy to get stuck in patterns. The viscosity of complexes, shame, and grief is thick, and we are held down in darkness, unable to recognize the choices that are available. When we stay in a single collection of emotions we become bitter, angry, depressed, stagnant, and fearful.

How do we move beyond the pull of darkness? Part of the answer lies in loosening – making space for fragmentation, change, and emergence. I don't mean a pathological loss of identity but *letting go* so something new can come in.

Not everyone has unbearable underworld moments, but we're all injured to some extent. We all have histories that allow only certain parts of us to thrive. To move beyond these limitations, great or small, and access our wholeness and potential, some of the old ways must be let go of. Death and birth, destruction and renewal – you can't have one without the other.

A woman dreamed that the back of her house was burning. She wasn't home at the time, and upon return she called the fire department. When the fire was put out, the house was severely damaged; all she could see was the exposed rock and brick of the chimney. From the dream's point of view, her life is on fire. With work, children, and marriage, she hadn't saved anything for herself, and she burnt herself out. The hearth, a symbol of the center of life, was burning out of control; she hadn't been at "home" in a balanced way. Yet remnants of the hearth remained, a hopeful augur. Fire is a symbol of destruction and violence, but also purification and renewal – destruction that makes space for new growth. The fire is burning away old edifices, forcing her family to address ghosts that have been hidden for too long. In the flames, the old ways of relating to the world are loosened. "It took all that," she said, "to become aware. Cancer is the second chance I didn't know I needed." The fire revealed the brick and stone, the basic and elemental structures. Now she can see what's important.

When change seems frightening or impossible, we might turn to Dionysus, calling on his unbridled energy. Dionysian loosening is cathartic, releasing anything calcified or repeated. It's a powerful energy of liberation. The Dionysian experience is about freedom from physical, social, emotional, or spiritual constraint. It's the revolution that replenishes old attitudes with fresh ones. Under his influence chains are broken, fabrics unwoven, containers shattered.

Breaking down, loosening, and dissolving all create the possibility of undoing oneself – going mad. Dionysus was the god of the mask, embodying any experience of being removed from our normal and stable sense of self.

Any transformation of character entails a breaking up of the established personality structures. Madness, in this sense, can be a release from bondage. If we want to grow, we have to accept that the mentality that got us where we are must be given up.

It takes courage, bordering on insanity, to surrender to underworlding – to face the terror of darkness and expose yourself to the devouring maw of the unknown. To begin the healing journey is to know you're not whole. What is bound loosens, what is still moves, and what is hidden is revealed. If you can hold the tension between loosening and reforming, you'll discover new ways of being. The word "apocalypse" comes from the Greek apokalyptein, "to reveal." The end of one chapter reveals the beginning of the next.

Striking the balance between madness and being untethered is an achievement of commitment and willpower. It's essential that we don't descend past the point where we can hold on to reality. Our aim should be to engage with Dionysian intensity and loosening without being devoured. "One must still have chaos in oneself," wrote Friedrich Nietzsche, "to give birth to a dancing star."[16]

Many great thinkers, writers, and artists were consumed by the Dionysian flame. Van Gogh suffered from psychosis, spent time in psychiatric hospitals, and eventually shot himself. Edvard Munch, painter of *The Scream*, suffered from depression, agoraphobia, nervous breakdowns, and hallucinations.

It is vitally important to recognize when we are in the territory of psychic energy that could break us. The psychological states of Van Gogh and Munch, although artistic masters, are not ideals to strive for. For most of us, pursuing inner wholeness without loosening to the point of madness is preferred. Growth that sticks only takes place when we feel safe, not when we push limits that we have no business pushing, especially on our own.

If we can hold on to him, Dionysus creates the urge to leave the suffocating patterns of a tired life. He was called *Eleutherios*, "the liberator," representing the parts of us that are free, unformed, and full of life. "The greatest gift of Dionysos," wrote classicist William Guthrie, "was the sense of utter freedom, in Greece it was the women, with their normally confined and straitened lives, to whom the temptation of release made the strongest appeal."[17] One of the hardest things in life is letting go, whether it's of guilt, shame, love, loss, anger, or betrayal. Change is never easy. We struggle to hold on, even as we struggle to let go.

There are few venues where purgative exaltation – shaking and dancing away the ideas and behaviors that cleave to us like dried mud – is encouraged. The festival Burning Man is an exception. It began as a bonfire ritual on the summer solstice as a cathartic venue honoring the need to be released from the confinements of everyday society. Burning Man is a Dionysian event. It replaces the cadence of society with the rhythms of masks, costumes, collective celebration, creativity, dancing, nighttime, and remoteness – a celebration of wildness, instinct, fire, and emotional release.

The cultural decade known as the Sixties captured Dionysus at work in culture, society, and politics. This epoch is defined by counterculture, a revolution in social norms, and the decay of the social confinement and lifelessness of the previous decade. Clothing, music, drugs, and sex all relaxed. Norms of all kinds were shattered – artists such as Bob Dylan, the Grateful Dead, and the Beatles revolutionized music, bringing freedom and self-expression to a generation. Suffocating from a rigid culture unable to allow individual expression, the cultural psyche of America loosened.

Much of Paris was built from its own underground. Beneath the Parisian bustle, a shadow city exists in an altogether different world. Beginning in the 13th century, Parisians quarried the limestone bedrock beneath them and, block by block, constructed iconic buildings such as Notre Dame Cathedral and the Louvre. Parisians first mined the passageways, then abandoned them, eventually returned to entomb centuries of dead that were spilling into the city, and now the remaining chambers and tunnels are the *vides de carriers* – the catacombs.

Today, the Paris catacomb network is a place where people dip into darkness to lose themselves, find different identities, assume new ways of acting, thinking, and moving. Underground, those that wander the tunnels, the *cataphiles*, map the underworld, archive its stories, build sanctuaries, party, explore history, graffiti, and create carvings and statues. The labyrinth offers a place of celebration and exploration – a realm where subcultures flourish and the wild ways are less constrained. A mirror city, underground and uncontained, the catacombs are a dark echo of their dayworld sister, following different laws than its surface counterpart. Yet these tunnels and arteries of darkness, despite their lack of sunlight, are very much alive.

As the god of wine, Dionysus symbolizes revelry and catharsis, awakening the spirit of release, bringing the free and instinctive to life. It's due to the feeling of release that Dionysus is associated with different states of consciousness – psychotropic, trance, alcoholic, and sexual alterations, to name a few. He is the inventor and teacher of wine's cultivation, the giver of its joy and freedom, but also its excess, lack of control, and capacity to connect us to our sorrow.

My mother grew up in a strait-laced family. Everything was always "okay" and "good enough." And there was real darkness – her father was a veteran who suffered violent episodes of PTSD and her mother was emotionally distant. As a young girl, she wanted to do anything that might awaken *something* within her sterile and contained environment. She remembers dancing in front of the TV trying to express herself and being told to leave the room. Freedom of self-expression, loosening and liberation, became longings in her which, over time, internalized into shame.

Catharsis of the ego isn't enough, the unconscious must weigh in. Life that is too self-contained and too closed leaves no room for the overwhelming intensity of feeling something larger. Dionysus is a metaphor for facing the unconscious and allowing ourselves to be impacted and moved by the encounter.

The most important ritual in Dionysus' honor was the Anestheria, a celebration of new wine and an all-souls festival where the dead emerged from the underworld to spend a day among the living. Worshipers used wine to return consciousness to the shades. It was believed that wine reawakened *zoe*, "the energy of the divine in human nature." *Zoe* is the flow of primordial energy, the force that pulses through all of life. In the presence of *zoe*, what is manicured is rewilded, crystallizations dissolve, and the civilized made feral.

In alchemy, the stage of *solutio* occurs when solids are dissolved in water, revitalizing rigid substances. Ancient alchemists told the story of a brittle king whose realm starved because the fields lay dry and barren. One day, the king left his castle and wandered into a field, and it began to flood. The king drowned, dissolved into the water, and was reborn as a young man. The fields turned green and the crops began to grow. By refreshing his soul, the king returned life to the kingdom.

Most people think of Dionysus as merely the god of wine, sexual excitement, and revelry. There's merit to this association, and after returning from the underworld with Semele he renamed her Thyone, "the ecstatically raging." Today, ecstasy has been watered down to mean an emotional, religious, or even sexual, trance-like experience of self-transcendence. Ecstasy is also about feeling rapture – pure joy and bliss. In our constrained and morally refined world, there's often little room for experiences of such tremendous release and reverie.

"The transformative fire of ecstasy," wrote Robert A. Johnson, burns "away the barriers between ourselves and our souls, bestowing on us a greater understanding of our relation to ourselves and to the universe."[18] Dionysian ecstasy is *ex stasis*, "to stand outside oneself." Much of the Dionysian experience pulls us away from patterns of stability and organization. Once removed from what we know, we can stand outside ourselves and see our unconscious patterning in a new way.

Underworlding pulls us away from the familiarity of daily life. In darkness, we're removed from the jurisdiction, responsibilities, and agendas of everyday life. The rhythms of daily life are suspended as the ego loses its bearings.

The capacity to break open and destroy is vital for psychological growth. To awaken Dionysus is not a call to anarchy and bestial regression; it is the recognition that loosening is an essential ingredient in re-formation. The turmoil and chaos of uncertainty, exploration, late nights, and wild behavior are not evil; they're acts of loosening and awakening.

As life unfolds, we become increasingly bound to set responsibilities, expectations, and dependence – all things that diminish experimentation, freedom, and spontaneity. Maturation and development require us to select, repeat, and stay within the lines. To worship Dionysus is to re-evaluate destroying and exploring, honor the undomesticated and instinctive, take anything contained and pry it open. When we reinvigorate passion and zest, infusing pattern and prediction with creativity and possibility, we invoke Dionysus.

Tearing apart the old ways – dissolving the time-honored order – will always be painful. "To know Dionysus," writes Ginette Paris, "one must open up to emotion, to the senses, to the tragic or comic aspects of life. Dionysos is an opening, a happening, not an organizing."[19] We may prefer to be in control, safe, and ordered rather than unleashed, frenzied, unformed, and uncomfortable. Much of daily life necessitates this preference – we pay bills, brush our teeth, drive to work, care for our children, and strive for stable relationships.

Be careful not to confuse the need for stability with the lack of change. We can alter our worlds and still maintain a grip. The very moment we're taken away from ourselves, at least as we customarily know ourselves, we may in some mysterious way be brought closer in touch with who we really are. In moments of darkness, when we feel untethered from all previous sources of knowing, we connect to new and profound parts of ourselves. Persephone was abducted into her independence and rulership, Orpheus became a prophet, and Aeneas suffered the loss of his father in order to end his people's wandering.

Dionysian loosening must not be placed solely within the category of chaos. He has just as much to do with containment as destruction, the roar of release and the silence that follows. His is a realm in which loosening and breaking exist in relationship with containing and binding. On an archetypal level, destruction brings creation, death heralds birth. To re-form we have to let go, to coagulate we need to dissolve.

Dismemberment

Dionysus was *Dithyrambos*: the "killed and resurrected," "the double door," the god who survived the miracle of a second birth. Dionysian dismemberment is about enduring life no matter how scattered or filled with destruction it may be. Dionysus expresses the unrelenting will to live – the sapling that bursts through cement.

"When our day is come for the victory of death," writes Campbell, "there is nothing we can do, except be crucified – and resurrected; dismembered totally, and then reborn."[20] When old bonds fall apart we invite the possibility of experiencing something new. To suffer the movement of death in the psyche, yet not die, to return from the dark is a powerful and transformative experience.

The week my mother-in-law died, I had two dreams. In the first, I'm running through a dark city. I crouch on a rooftop, stare at a window across the way, and am consumed by fear of what might reveal itself. An unnatural, inhuman, and formless darkness moves into the window. In the second dream I'm pregnant. I don't want to be and list all the ways in which I'm ill-prepared. I give birth to emerald green fishes made of glass. They fall into my hands, spilling onto the floor.

In the dreams, the overwhelming presence of darkness is met with the greening of new life – life force, birth, pregnancy. The dreams suggest that the void will someday fill with something new and vibrantly alive. Fish are symbols of the life beneath the surface, the contents of the unconscious. Emerald is a color of rich life, what is unique, precious, and beautiful. The Amazon rainforest is called the Emerald Green Forest. The dreams suggests that whatever will come of the family tragedy will be from the depths, unusual, and, at some point and in some form, full of life.

From the dream's point of view, there's grief and death but also birth. Something new is coming. To tap into new life amid death, to access the relentless call to life even when the unthinkable has happened is to behold Dionysus. Death comes with birth; they're two sides of the same coin. Anything that is separated can be put back together – in new ways. The pain of division can be a harbinger of re-formation.

History is filled with stories of people pushed to the brink, amid terrible horrors, who choose life over annihilation. Victims of the Holocaust, refugee crises, wars, and sexual violence demonstrate humanity's indelible capacity to survive unimaginable suffering. To grow, thrive, and evolve *under any circumstance* is Dionysian.

Dismemberment is a violent tearing apart of what has been. Division can be devastating, a painful fragmentation of self, a psyche in pieces. "One must not underestimate the devastating effect of getting lost in Chaos," wrote Jung, "even if we know that it is the *sine qua non* [essential condition] of any regeneration of spirit and personality."[21] Coping with emergency and crisis is not a time for dismemberment. When we are already being destroyed, we don't need further unraveling; we need the time and space for reflection, expression, and letting ourselves wail and be witnessed. The time will come when we need to untangle our darkness; to do this work, we need to have a level of ego-stability.

We are in a time of Dionysus, when much is in pieces, when disorder, chaos, and dismemberment fill the air. The fragmentation caused by pathological states destroys old ways of relating to ourselves and the world. It is natural to dread destabilization, but destruction is necessary for restoration. To let the old fall apart, we have to sacrifice control, perfection, betterment, and stability. Sacrifice (literally, to make sacred) is about forfeiting something for the sake of renewed life. "No one can or should halt sacrifice," wrote Jung. "Sacrifice is not destruction; sacrifice is the foundation stone of what is to come."[22] We cannot progress and mature without relinquishing worn-out behaviors, identities, and phases of life.

There are seasons of life where sacrificing the old ways is essential for growth. If the sacrifice is not made consciously — grieved and suffered — it will occur unconsciously. What we repress returns in demonic form.

Many of my clients with cancer believe their illness is a sacrifice for the growth of themselves or family constellations. For one woman, her diagnosis motivated her father to stop drinking and her husband from repeating similar patterns. "Now I get what I need," she told me, "my kids get their grandpa, and my husband won't perpetuate the cycle." Part of her healing and meaning-making was believing her illness opened a pathway for her family's healing. From the unwanted cancerous growth in her body came growth of her soul and life.

Every step toward knowing ourselves, the relentless search for self-awareness and wholeness, requires sacrifice and struggle. All who seek change and depth give up ignorance, comfort, and stability. With the pain and turmoil of sacrifice can come the gifts of expansion and emergence.

Community

To hold the intensity of a Dionysian journey safely, we need collective structures of integration — community, rituals, group therapy, religion. Community is essential to help us avoid negative outcomes. Facing the chaos of the inner world and risking deconstruction, we need to know and feel that we are held and supported. When breaking open ingrained and painful defenses, wounds, and traumas, we benefit exponentially by the presence of a kindred mentor, therapist, counselor, friend, or spiritual leader.

In ancient Greece, Dionysus' invocation was always a witnessed communal celebration. People danced, released, sang, and drank, reminding us that the Dionysian experience is too feral, raw, and consuming to contain on our own.

Today, many of us lack a fulfilling sense of community. Suffering and illnesses are rarely collectively attended. We bemoan the loss of intimate neighborhoods and the dearth of churches we find meaningful. We blame social media for increasing isolation, while more and more people work online at home instead of in offices. Our ancestors derived understanding from elders, legends, myths, gods, and traditions, handling the hardship of life as an intergenerational community. Now we rely on ourselves and the internet to answer our questions and even to navigate our inner landscape.

Underworlding inspires community, which tempers grief, loneliness, uncertainty, lack of accountability, and pain. During the initial throes of Ben's accident, the network of support ranged from friends bringing food to prayer circles from San Diego to Florence, Italy. The stories of love and shared experiences filled the dark spaces that might otherwise have been unbearable. We are drawn together in moments of underworlding. We learn something vital about what it means to be human when we explore ourselves in relation to community.

Group therapy or process groups have Dionysian energy, whether this is therapeutically tailored or groups like Alcoholics Anonymous. These containers offer a supportive milieu where participants can speak about their lives while being witnessed. Hearing others share what they're going through helps us feel less alone in our own trials. Group members provide fresh perspectives, validation, mirroring, and accountability. Unlike individual therapy, group work exposes us to how other people tackle problems, face concerns, and make positive change. This encourages empowerment, agency, and meaning, all qualities that inspire motivation, responsibility, resiliency, connection, and commitment. It's the celebration of our shared humanness that heals.

In *Tribe*, Sebastian Junger weaves a story of humanity's shared instinct to belong to small groups organized around shared purpose and understanding. Pulling on his experience as a war journalist, Junger explores the depth of meaning, loyalty, and belonging present in war, and the absence of such unity felt by many veterans. The horror and injustices of war remain, but the cohesion and shared meaning reduce many of the psychological symptoms of war. Adversity becomes a blessing, disaster a bond. "Tribe" comes from the Greek *phyle*, meaning "united by ties of blood and descent, a clan."

My father described the period when he fought forest fires in Southern California as underworld. A member of a crew of firefighters who drop from helicopters into remote locations, his job brought him close to the blazes of hell. He felt trapped, scared of changing winds and unpredictable flames. Yet his team always looked out for each other in ways that made the burning forest bearable and strangely safe.

The Dionysian experience is about drawing people together to build relationships, give back, and cultivate compassion, empathy, and humility. To challenge and push our limits, we must be supported and contained by those around us. Dionysus is about both the intensity of the flood and the energy that can contain the waters.

In 1893, French sociologist Émile Durkheim introduced the concept of *anomie* to define a quality of derangement or insatiable will that leaves a culture without moral standards or guidance. He described it as a "malady of the infinite,"[23] because without boundaries, desire is never fulfilled: it only grows in intensity. Without containment, limits, and balance, the mind, like the body, loses its capacity for restraint and death. Negative habits, ideals, and emotions run wild, growing in intensity and eventually taking over the psyche. What needs to go is, instead, preserved. Anomie is a condition with only the excess of Dionysus, not the communal responsibility and containment.

During underworlding, many of us need to feel that our suffering is acknowledged and reflected by others. A friend told me that after her mother died, the first thing she wanted to do was tell everyone she knew. It felt important that the entire world know that her mother was gone. After Diana, the Princess of Wales died, an estimated 2.5 *billion* people worldwide watched the broadcast of her funeral.

Too often the underworld is minimized and sanitized. After a tragedy, many are given a week off work before being expected to return to life as though nothing happened. In our fast-paced world, we have fewer and fewer rituals to bear witness to and validate our pain and our loss. Take, for example, the decline of traditional Irish wakes, when neighborhood women would come to the house and wash the body of the deceased. The body would then be covered in white linen and wrapped in black or white ribbons and attended throughout the wake. Expressing their depth of sorrow, mourners would *keen*, a vocal lament. The community flowed through the deceased's home, witnessing each other's pain, drinking, eating, and sharing stories of the life lost. Outside of remote Irish villages, traditional wakes are rare now.

Communal mourning is important – funerals and memorials provide a sorrowful structure for the expressions of pain and loss. Together we share our grief, find meaning in our loved one's life, and have our pain mirrored. If darkness remains unwitnessed, it can slip back into the unconscious where it will fester, transforming into chronic grief, disease, complexes, or even fear of life. David Kessler recounts a lecture in which he asked a crowd, "How many of you have issues, wounds, or trauma because you weren't allowed to go to the funeral?" About 15 percent of the people raised their hands. Suppressing pain is not healing. We have to dive down into the stricken places and feel our pain if we want to find meaning in loss.

Something essential is lost when we navigate tragedy without community. Through Dionysus, we see the value of holding darkness in a collective, abundant, and witnessed way. We dance pain, share grief, drink spirits in honor of the deceased, wail, and release. Sharing suffering is medicine for the soul.

Today, our rituals are often shallow and rushed. To feel is to open the doors of release. To suppress is to close those very doors. Group therapy, funerals, lectures, and religious gatherings allow us to share our suffering on the stage of life. To mourn together is to honor our shared humanity.

Theater

In the play *The Frogs*, performed at the Lenaia, one of the festivals of Dionysus in Athens, Aristophanes portrays the city of Athens suffering from a dearth of poetry. Dionysus responds by journeying into the underworld to resurrect one of the great poets. There, he judges a competition between Aeschylus and Euripides, deciding to return with Aeschylus. Once more, he goes into the lower world to reclaim something lost. By returning with Aeschylus, he revitalizes poetic sensibility – viewing life in theatrical, emotional, imaginative, and expressive ways. Prose and poetry, the imaginal expressions of our existence, can take us into other ways of knowing. The language of soul is brought to life by poetics and metaphor, image and inwardness. A dearth of poetry is a problem of imagination, and poetry places us in a soulful of relationship with life.

We turn to Dionysus to express underworlding with poetics, enactment, and metaphor. Victor Frankl said that prisoners and guards in Auschwitz both constructed a rudimentary cabaret where prisoners would gather to laugh, cry, tell poems, and sing. Some even forfeited waiting in the bread line to attend, sacrificing material nutrition to *forget* their reality for a time.[24] In a place of unimaginable horror, theater offered healing, release, and connection.

Dionysian theater is not just about processing or understanding what is happening darkly, but *feeling and enacting* it.

The difference between the intellect's way of knowing and the psyche's seems crucial, a question of how we look and imagine. To invoke his presence, we make a theater of suffering – living out darkness so we can witness its nature, learn its secrets, and discern its messages.

In Shakespeare's *As You Like It*, the melancholy Jacques says, "All the world's a stage,/ And all the men and women merely players;/ They have their exits and their entrances;/ And one man in his time plays many parts." Treating our lives as enactments of myths, plots, characters, or tragedies brings flexibility, choice, and new perspectives. We're less stuck. Instead, as Hillman writes, "[We are all] characters in a fiction, and as the drama intensifies, the catharsis occurs; we are purged from attachments to literal destinies, find freedom in playing parts, partial, dismembered."[25]

Dionysian presence occurs wherever there is drama, role-playing, and fantasy. Our lives are shaped by the stages we choose to stand on, the roles we take, and the plotlines we enact. We don't want to get stuck in one plotline, living the same drama over and over.

The psyche has an amazing capacity to invent fantastical worlds to give the threatened parts of ourselves a safe and engaging place to hide – but it may come at a high price – the ability to connect with reality. When the world of fantasy becomes a permanent state of being, it is like a Siren's call, a spell pulling us away from what's actually going on. We can lose the ability to see ourselves objectively, recognize what stage we're on, or know what actors are at play.

Masks

As the god of masks, Dionysus was associated with masquerades, false identities, the freedom to respond however one chooses, and the choice to hide or to reveal oneself. Understanding darkness "theatrically" includes exploring the psychology of masks.

We respond to life's challenges uniquely. The underworld has countless masks. Even an emotion like grief can wear a multitude of faces; some of us become isolated and disconnected, some keep busy, while others cry and release. Everyone in my family reacted to my brother's accident in a different way. Some were stoic, emotional, or creative; others fearful or depressed. Sorrow can masquerade as anger, isolation, numbness, or distraction. Loneliness can masquerade as desperation, caretaking, or neediness. It's a mistake to expect the faces of darkness to look the same.

A part of inner work is recognizing the masks we wear, what Jungians call the *persona* – the face we present to the world. Persona is "a kind of mask," explained Jung, "designed on the one hand to make a definite impression upon others, and on the other to conceal the true nature of the individual."[26] Our cultures and traditions force us to show specific faces to the world. If our culture values bravery and masculinity, or containment and perfection, those values will be incorporated into the persona so we fit into society. Blending in has its place; the risk is becoming so fused with the façade that our true self remains hidden.

I work with a woman who is bright, energetic, and magnetic – everyone likes her. She calls this part of herself a "song and dance" and identifies it as her mask, an act that keeps people entertained without becoming invested or intimate. For her, wearing this mask is exhausting and shallow. She feels the burden of not allowing her true self to shine.

Life is full of masked moments. Some are deceitful while others are protective, even compassionate. Depression forces some people to wear a cheerful mask, even when they're in pain. Parents mask their exhaustion from their children. Insecurity is often masked by inflation. People mask fear, sadness, or inadequacy with anger or caretaking. As the saying counsels, "Fake it till you make it." A woman told me that after her cancer diagnosis, she "put on a mask." Part of her went to work, talked to her friends about their lives, worked out, and fed the dog. Another part was heavy with fear and exhaustion, worrying about treatment schedules, diet changes, blood work, and how to organize her finances to prepare for her possible death. "I had to wear the mask," she said, "because people couldn't handle talking about cancer."

Masks are also tools of expression, transformation, and healing. In BodySoul Rhythms, a workshop created by Marion Woodman and Ann Skinner, masks give form to shadow energies. Participants decorate plaster molds of their face. Participants are invited to act out and embody the energy behind the mask – becoming powerful or small, angry or sad, lighthearted or childish. For some, the mask is an animal – a bear for motherhood, a fish for fluidity, an eagle of farsightedness. The aim is to give a face to hitherto unconscious parts of ourselves – the voice of our forgotten symptom, the desire of our neglected wound, the visage of our deepest fear. What bubbles up is then processed so each participant can become aware of the unconscious energies revealed.

Masks symbolize freedom from roles and identities, behaviors and beliefs. By noticing the masks we wear, we may become curious why we wear them, where they come from, and how to take them off if we so wish. When we become aware of our masks, we can play with taking them on and off, and change becomes that simple.

The same life story can be told from many different points of view. We can tell ourselves we're victims or rulers, lost in the wilderness or finding a new path, quick and lithe like Hermes or longing for the past like Orpheus. When facing the darkest moments of life, there isn't a correct character, mask, or response.

From day one of my brother's recovery process, I wore the mask of caretaker. I cared for him, my parents, sister, partner, and myself. I'd never been a caretaker in that way before. I'd never worn that mask. The situation called for that role, I felt, and so by "leaning into it," I tapped into a new part of my personality. Over time, the role of caretaker became a burden. I found myself trying to control too much, take too much responsibility, and not allow my family the space to lead their own lives. A mask that had served me began to distort my reality and limit my ability to respond to needs as they changed.

There's a thin veil between roles that serve our daily functioning and masks that confine us. The horrors and drama of underworld experiences can transform us to such a degree that we may not retain certain qualities (masks) of our former personality. And while we're without our familiar masks that protect us from our woundedness, until we find a new stand to take, dissociation might be our response. When pain is unbearable and we simply need a break from standing in its presence, we can cut off our connection to ourselves, and it's felt as a kind of numbness in mind and body. Parts of ourselves are split off from one another. The everyday personality may avoid the shut-down (dissociated) personality. To heal these dissociated traits, we have to become conscious of them, giving the repressed identity ways to feel and express itself. Until we do, we may not even realize that dissociation is also a mask, not one adaptive to the needs of society but one we unconsciously "craft" to prevent sinking in the underworld without a lifeline.

We wear masks and get caught in the character and fantasy of a given role, confusing our image of self with reality. In Greek religion, Dionysus was also associated with possession, worshiped as *Enthousiasmos*, "the god inside." When we wear a mask for too long, our image begins to possess us, we lose sight of our "true self," and over time, the mask becomes our identity.

After a lifetime of abandonment wounds, a woman begins to rest and feel her authenticity. Her drive has historically been incessant: be strong, never take too much, make people like you. She donned a mask to consolidate a strength she didn't really have, a brightness she didn't actually feel. The Hercules in her galvanized the strength to brave the fear of not being enough. Now the energy behind the mask has served its purpose, and instead of warfare and protection, she needs connection, peace, and reconnecting with the parts of herself that were discarded. The mask comes on and off. It's not as simple as putting a book back on the shelf: the attitudes and behaviors within the mask protected her for many years.

We've distanced ourselves from the revelries and guises of the masked god. "A society that no longer puts on carnivals and costumed events," explains Ginette Paris, "loses an important psychological resource and impoverishes the collective imagination."[27] The notion of wearing a mask is negative today; it means being inauthentic. There's truth in this bias; masks do hide our true selves, and at the same time they allow us to embody characteristics we may need temporarily and otherwise neglect. In a masquerade, inhibitions loosen because identities are fluid. For a time, we're free to be someone else. The Dionysian urge awakens in us a celebration of play-acting, freedom, and exploration. Masks also allow unconscious energy to rise, revealing hidden parts of ourselves and freeing us from tired identities, even ones we didn't realize were a provisional cover-up.

The god with many faces shapes our capacity to move beyond a single suite of traits, ideas, or behaviors. Dionysus is the ever-changing, dynamic, unchecked growth of instinct and identity that loosens bondage, form, and boxes. He's defined and undefined, smoke and fire. Swinging between the extremes of joy and suffering, Olympus and Hades, ecstasy and absence, Dionysus invites us to notice the masks we wear and be less rigid in how we appear to ourselves and others.

The Body

Dionysus is also the god of the body. Everything about his presence is phenomenological – lived experience made tangible, immediate, and carnal. Nowadays, people prefer the ego-mind and its capacity for measurement, prediction, and order over somatic intelligence. Gut reactions, intuitions, embodied images, somatic dreams, and emotional sensations are regarded as less credible than reason and logic. But despite these predilections, the body is an immense source of wisdom and healing, oftentimes revealing more than the rational mind.

A woman was emotionally abused as a child. As an adult, she went to a treatment center where she was asked to draw the terrifying figure that stalked her dreams. Every time she tried to capture the figure, her body would refuse to draw it. She'd dissociate and go numb, forgetting the image. Her therapist asked her to draw the figure with her left hand. Immediately, the figure poured out of her, perfectly captured on the page. When she explored this sudden change, she realized that the left hemisphere of her brain – logic, reason, math, language – was still shaming her. Anything left-brained was associated with her father, who told her that she was stupid and worthless. By turning toward her inferior function – the right, intuitive brain that she had overlooked for so many years – she was able to reconnect with parts of herself she'd abandoned.

The connection between our state of mind and the health of our body is undeniable. Researcher and physician Gabor Maté writes and speaks extensively on the relationship between the mind–body connection and disease. He asks an important question: What creates the civil war inside the body? Standard medical practices take a biological view – toxins and genetics swirl together to cause predispositions that are treated as symptoms. This medical dualism, dividing in two that which is one, shapes all Western beliefs on health and illness. We seek to understand the body separate from the psyche – believing our bodies are somehow distinct from the milieu in which we've developed, lived, and will die in. We ignore the personal, not to mention the archetypal, background of illness.

Dr Maté shares the story of a client named Mary who suffered a host of illnesses that eventually accumulated in an auto-immune condition called scleroderma. As her condition worsened, he asked her to share the story of her life. Mary was abused as a child, fell into violent foster care, and at the same time, devoted herself to protecting her sisters. No one protected her, listened to her, or thought she was worthy of attention. As an adult, Mary felt trapped in cycles of taking responsibility for others. Maté wondered if the auto-immune disease that eventually killed her was her body's way of rejecting her tendency of placing others above herself.

"Unconscious contents," wrote Jung, "lurk somewhere in the body like so many demons of sickness, impossible to get hold of, especially when they give rise to physical symptoms the organic causes of which cannot be demonstrated."[28] Our shadows permeate our cells, infecting our tissue and surfacing as illness. We cannot heal the wounds carried by our bodies by residing in spirit and mind. We have to journey within, reclaiming the connection between body and psyche. We have to listen to the wisdom and messages of our bodies, rather than ignoring them and thinking of the body as a machine. In the words of Rumi, "There is a voice that doesn't use words. Listen." We benefit greatly when we respect and love our bodies, listen to their needs, feed them quality nourishment, and give them rest, time in nature, and the freedom to move, stretch, and experience joy.

"In trying to protect ourselves from the thought that there is something fundamentally unlovable about us," wrote Marion Woodman, "women, and increasingly men, blame their bodies." Our unconscious desire for control and perfection leaves many of us critical of the shape of our bodies and ashamed of the need for food, sex, and movement. "It was my self-generated fear," continued Woodman, "that stressed my body and created hell."[29] It wasn't until her second encounter with cancer that she realized that deep in her cells she harbored the belief that she was unwanted and an unconscious part of her felt she deserved to die. Eventually, she was ready to face this reality by developing compassion for herself and her parents. Illness was her body's wake-up call: "My body's agony was a manifestation of my terror and an attempt to keep me in the old, but paradoxically, it gave me no choice except to change, expand my life and live more authentically."[30]

We must also explore the imagistic and symbolic terrain of soma. The soul's language is image, which can be used to bridge body and psyche. Some dreams have vivid sensations, for example, haunting us long after we wake up. In somatic dreams, the unconscious has us in its grip and wants dialogue, using the body as the language of discourse. These dreams may draw attention to a symptom, revelation, or issue we're not aware of. Such embodied images can be terrifying or pleasurable, as they blur the boundary between ego and the unconscious. Learning to tend to the "voices" of the body, we can cultivate a sensate wisdom.

Many who suffer trauma develop embodied symptoms – numbness, migraines, eating disorders, insomnia, allergies, panic attacks, muscle patterning instability, developmental delays, flashbacks, or disease. I spoke with a woman who, as a little girl, was belittled by her father for expressions of joy and laughter, silliness and rambunctiousness, and who told her to grow up, calm down, or stop acting stupid. Now when she feels delight, she represses the emotion and manufactures shame to take its place. At night she clenches her jaw and grinds her teeth. Her body remembers holding back, her voice silenced and her exuberance suppressed.

Many who suffer from emotional trauma live in a state of fear. Their bodies are unable to relax, their cortisol spikes, their breath is constricted, and the part of the orbitofrontal cortex responsible for reflective processing is restricted. Over time, the emotional limbic brain responsible for fight-or-flight responses dominates, and a destructive neurological feedback loop is grooved in place.

In our first session, a woman sat with her legs crossed and her arms wound tightly around her torso. When I asked about her body position, she named it "shield." We got curious about the posture, exploring how she guards herself from her painful past. Her body carries her wounds, and she is trying to shield herself from further wounding. Our work focused on supporting her ability to release, rebuild, and move in ways she hitherto deemed unsafe.

The body keeps score, as psychiatrist Bessel van der Kolk writes. It's a harbor for rejected, forgotten, despised, and unknown aspects of ourselves. Sometimes unconscious energies express in our posture, speech, gestures, or symptoms; other times they seemingly happen outside of ourselves – a car crash on the way to a job interview that we don't really want, or tripping while leaving the house for a date we feel insecure about.

Modern medicine and science are hell-bent on cures, seeking to destroy all symptoms and discomforts before they have a chance to reveal their meaning. They are disciplines of abstraction and reason, turning symptoms into statistics and averages. The literalization of the poetics of the body blocks our ability to imagine into the story underlying a disease, symptom, or inflamed organ. Sickness is a set of symptoms, and it is also a message from the depths of our being.

I often search for the symbol within the disease – how the illness might be inviting someone to reconsider their attitudes, perspectives, and way of life. We've touched upon how Jung believed the "gods" (archetypal energies) have, in modern times, become diseases. Along the lifelong journey of becoming oneself, the "gods" of psyche may push themselves into our awareness through illness. Russell Lockhart suggests we must seek out the god within the illness and tend the part of ourselves the god symbolizes that may have been forgotten. To connect to the god within the disease is to turn toward denied possibilities within ourselves.

This approach to the journey of illness is not focused on curing the disease, although it is always the hope that tending the psyche will have a healing effect on the illness and the soul. The metaphorical, spiritual, and symbolic exploration of illness is about finding depth and meaning through connecting mind and body. It is about growing into oneself.

In addition to measuring and testing our bodies, we need to explore the metaphors. What is the message and symbolism of inflammation? Is the rise of inflammatory diseases such as cancer, autoimmunity, and Alzheimer's merely physical? Or does it mirror a culture of inflammation – cortisol spikes because we overwork, adrenal failure because we can't adapt to the ungodly speed demanded by the modern world, liver toxicity because of poisonous relationships, news, environments, or social media, illness because we aren't connected to the source of our being?

"I've always been intellectual," Ben explained, "and that's been validated and cultivated by our family. But in the process, I've disconnected from my instinctual bodily knowledge. Over and over, my healing journey has brought me back into my body, trying to teach me how to listen to the value of each story, including my brain injury."

"What is the value of that story?" I asked.

"Reconnecting me to the deeper seat of my being. The source that we so often overlook because the mind is powerful, beautiful, and holds so much potential. But it is also subject to the ego, the body less so."

We in the modern West are largely disconnected from Dionysian sensations. Rarely do we embrace them. More often we flee, struggling to free ourselves from the god's demanding presence. Few healers promote Dionysian somatic release – shaking, screaming, crying, undoing. It's overwhelming and scary to be with volcanic, felt, and open emotions. We prefer sensations that are confined, soft, and distant. We've become too measured to embrace the intensity of Dionysian soma.

We rely on information *about* our bodies, but largely ignore its wisdom. We look at lab results, read scientific studies, and analyze our genomes. The Western mind believes truth is what can be tested and measured. Gut reactions, feelings, dreams, and intuition are, by and large, not regarded as valid ways of understanding. Dionysian knowledge is gained through senses and feelings rather than rational thought. Repressing this way of knowing disconnects us from wholeness. *Body and psyche belong together.*

The Forbidden God

By 30 CE, Abrahamic religions had displaced the Greco-Roman gods. The Western world adopted Judeo-Christian monotheism and morality, and by the 18th century, the Western mind had turned away from nature, instinct, and the worship of pagan gods toward reason, individualism, and observation, leaving little room for the overflowing, proximate, intoxicating, and crazed energy of Dionysus. In place of the squall of the wind, torrential flooding, and molten lava, we began to praise spirit, restraint, morality, and principle. The once-celebrated ivy-covered god grew cloven hooves and became the Devil.

In place of Dionysus, we came to worship Apollo – the god of reason, light, ethics, spirit, and order. "Apollo," explained Nietzsche, "represents the lord of light, the *principio individuationis*, the individuated world illuminated by the light of the sun. The Dionysian world, on the other hand, represents the thrust of time that destroys all things and brings forth all things. It is the generative power, thrust out of darkness."[31] We built a world based on lucidity, progress, rationality, and security; and the price tag of our organized worldview is the loss of Dionysus.

We can't access Dionysian energy through reason or planning. He brings a darker, more embryonic style of experiencing life. The Dionysian impulse is about the *emancipation* of unrestrained instinct, the revenge of the wild over the forces of order, breaking loose, and the energy of unbridled life force.

Today, we're encouraged to underworld in an Apollonian fashion. We contain, act reasonable, and analyze. We're taught behavioral skills to regulate emotions and given pharmaceutical pills to return stability and normalcy. Our medical goals are to relieve symptoms, bottle up and contain abnormalities, and numb suffering. We've lost the ability to let off steam without being viewed as unbalanced or insane. We've removed Dionysus from the healing equation.

Apollo never visited the underworld. It was believed he couldn't come into contact with the dead. How do we digest darkness while emulating a god who can't touch the underworld? Instead of trying to underworld with rigid principles like stability and order, we need to turn toward an energy connected to darkness, relying on catharsis, the wisdom of the body, the freedom to loosen worn-out behaviors, tap into the instinctive and wild, and reconnect with the banished parts of ourselves.

Abandoning contained and conscious ways of incorporating Dionysian energy, we worship him unconsciously through mindless consumption and addiction. By repressing the wild energy that's needed to feel alive and gratified, we've become psychologically and spiritually desiccated.

Robert Johnson called this *spiritual malnutrition*, sourcing it to our cultural preference for quick fixes over deep spiritual nutrition – a preference for Apollonian solutions over Dionysian. Johnson reasoned that we have cleansed Dionysus "out of our consciousness, denied him on moral grounds; and we are the worse for it."[32] Our hygienic mindset makes encountering Dionysus horrifyingly uncomfortable.

Without a deep-rooted sense of connection to ourselves and the natural world, we attempt to fill this void with gross materialism and emotional polydipsia. Take, for example, the psychology of addiction, which in many ways is the psyche looking to the outside for healing. If our wounds disconnect us from our inner reality, we are forced to rely on something external to free us, to give us identity and meaning, inspire passion, and find relief from feeling defective. No matter how much inner work we do, impulses to life remain inhibited, repressed, or hidden away by our defenses. When the inner world and darkness are denied and life energy, self, and meaning are found only outside us, the unconscious appears in shadow form. Is an addiction to sweets an impulse for the sweetness of life? Is alcoholism the repressed desire for freedom and spirit? To deny growth in one way is to get it in another.

Life can't be carried only by an outer object – whether a person, possession, goal, or a job. Our modern world is largely extraverted. We heal through external means – chemicals, radiation, and surgery for illness, pills for mental imbalance. We blame suffering on things outside ourselves – environmental factors for our diseases, lack of money for our stress, long work hours for exhaustion, partners for our failures. There are, of course, external ways to address life issues, but we have become disconnected from the internal ones.

"Striving to achieve that which is not authentic to us," wrote Marion Woodman, "opens the door to addiction."[33] When experiences of darkness are only rationally processed, the deep psyche is neglected and our best source of healing goes offline. Seeking to mitigate or control perhaps brings temporary stability but does not address the archetypal call beneath the addiction.

When our choices fail to satisfy us, we mistakenly believe that if we achieve more – are more perfect or more in control – we might be happier. But *more* is not the same as *enough*, and our craving can be insatiable. It's possible to repress a compassionate and loving sense of self, but impossible to destroy its energy. The unfilled parts of ourselves will make themselves known one way or another.

A client I worked with was terribly put off by anyone she perceived as dependent. Relying on another, she felt, was shameful. She was unhappy, but she wouldn't allow herself to be cared for by others, the attitude that's behind many failed relationships. When she was growing up, her mother, a single parent, worked two jobs and was exhausted when she came home. My client was forced to grow up faster than her natural developmental pace and her peers. So she came to associate neediness with causing her mother pain. The link changed her desire to be wanted, supported, and loved, to feelings of shame, and a key part of her work with me was reconnecting with the parts of herself that had never been cared for but so desperately wanted to be.

What is repressed doesn't go away. It lurks in the shadows, teeming beneath the surface. Repressing and forgetting are ways of ignoring our own reality, not telling ourselves the full story. We need to find ways of remembering, telling, speaking our truth. When we do, we reveal who we are – to others and, most importantly, to ourselves.

Dionysus is the god of inner catharsis and connection, reconnecting us to the immediate reality of our being so we can feel the intensity of the inner world. He breaks open, loosens bonds, and brings us closer to the darkness of life. Of course, the energy of excess, chaos, and release brings the potential for abuse and addiction – the shadow side of Dionysus. However, by denying Dionysian energy a seat at the table, his energy sinks into the unconscious, where it transforms into complexes, addictions, and neuroses.

When repressed, his forceful presence becomes pathological. Without consciousness his already urgent and wild energy becomes even wilder, exploding into our lives as obsessions, addictions, and madness. Passions are seen as enslavement, desire as sin, loosening as instability. Dionysus' association with compulsion, excess, imbalance, craziness, and terror make him a target for moralism. But the forest fire doesn't burn to spite the trees, the volcano doesn't erupt to spite the mountain, and lightning doesn't strike to spite the hillside. These energies are elemental and natural, not purposive – the volcano erupts because volcanoes erupt; it must release.

The repression and demonization of Dionysus led to the cultural belief that a plethora of diseases lurk in the psychic underworld. We have inhibited our ability to access a cathartic and innately human way of underworlding – screaming, feeling, moving, creating, expressing, embodying, liberating, enacting, and releasing, even simple physical discharge like jumping on a trampoline or aerobic exercise.

Dionysus may dismember, but he also brings birth and redemption through reconnection. If we want to stop trying to fill the endless void with more food, things, sex, or money, we have to return the parts of ourselves we left in the underworld. Without this, as Woodman warned, "We may find ourselves craving food that brings no nurture, drink that brings no spirit, or sex that brings no union. Our hunger is for food – but it is for soul food; we are crying out for the nourishment that will enable us to express our creative individuality."[34]

Dionysus journeyed into the underworld to reconnect with his mother, representing his roots in the world, his ancestry. No emotion or behavior can be nourishing when disconnected from its source. In today's surface-oriented society, many of us struggle to be satisfied. We long to be connected to something deeper and more meaningful than our surface selves, or masks. When we journey within to seek the source of our being, turning back to something more instinctual and rooted, we invoke Dionysus. As von Franz wrote, "If nothing else, the contact with the unconscious can become the remedy against the tortured feeling of rootlessness."[35]

Instead of Dionysus, we have a Christian interpretation of the underworld. "Between us and the underworld," argued Hillman, "stands the figure of Christ."[36] Christ's sacrifice is interpreted to mean that believers don't have to suffer their own journeys. Christ overcame darkness for the sake of the redemption of all souls. All that's needed is to believe in the Christian story. We have annulled the necessity of directly experiencing darkness. This belief system creates a moral justification for avoiding and shaming underworlding. Instead of being a teacher and way-shower, the underworld and its many inhabitants have become an evil enemy to be avoided.

In the myth, King Lycurgus and King Pentheus rejected Dionysus' divinity and were punished with madness and death. The fate of the kings reminds us that to repress Dionysus is to threaten the stability of the entire psychic kingdom. Dionysus will never sit easy in the psyche – his energy is too primal and disruptive to remain quiet and polite. The solution is not to overlay more pills or therapies on our wounds, but to return to the values Dionysus personifies – loosening, somatic awareness, freedom, theater, wildness, and passion. We heal ourselves by honoring these energies, giving them a place at the table instead of barring the door. Dionysus is a god: his energy deserves recognition, not repression.

The return of Dionysus is not a homecoming to a crazed, feral, instinctive, and limitless state of madness and disintegration. Losing one's way entirely does not serve wholeness. In Buddhist philosophy, the death of the ego bespeaks a dissolving into nonbeing, a state of enlightenment. In Jungian psychology, the death of the ego is called psychosis. We need an intact ego to face the unconscious. The Dionysian journey requires an ascent too, the *inclusion and integration* of what has been neglected and repressed.

Today, Dionysian underworlding is all but forbidden. Hysterics are locked up, the depressed, panicked, and manic are sedated, and chaotic and uncontrollable children are given Ritalin and other pharmaceutical suppressants. We've become ashamed of our impulses, guilty of our fantasies, and disconnected from body-centered intuition. In our refined world, the wild and frenzied, somatic and emotional, instinctive and raw territory of Dionysus is no longer welcomed, witnessed, or expressed. This repression intensifies the energy, forcing it to erupt into consciousness in violent and imbalanced ways.

When we think about the underworld experience, whether it's encountering the unconscious or enduring life's most difficult moments, the journey by its very nature brings suffering, destruction, dismemberment, intensity, sacrifice, and a terrifying taste of the instinctive realm. We feel the pressure of grief in our hearts, pray for relief, shake fear out of our bodies, scream, cry, beg, and almost always lose some aspect of ourselves to the darkness. To neglect the Dionysian element within underworlding is a grave mistake. The *embodied and emotional* experience of pain, splitting, and re-formation are necessary for integration and wholemaking to take place.

Reflections

Dionysus is a liberating yet terrifying god. Forgotten and unwelcome, he pertains to the horrific, chaotic, and primal psyche. He is life force unchecked – the roaring, pulsing wailings of nature, instinct, and untamed wildness. He loosens our bonds, is an energy of reconnection, and returns what has been repressed. To be in the presence of Dionysus is to be dismembered by suffering, scream, and seem mad. After everything about our lives seems to end, we are reborn – a vibrant and ceaseless form of life. To be Dionysian is to abandon order and logic and embrace what is feral, somatic, animated, and deeply alive.

Reflect on how these Dionysian qualities may be present within your experience in:

- Noticing what is repressed and neglected within you.
- Healing through connecting to the natural world.
- Your experience of the wild, animated, and instinctive parts of yourself.
- A somatic or bodily way of being with darkness.
- Catharsis and release.
- Reawakening your life force.
- Experiences of darkness that were emotionally consuming and close at hand.
- Moments when you lived in the extremes of life.
- Ecstasy as a means of standing outside yourself – dissociative experiences, both good and bad.
- Community and ritual.
- The loosening of anything that limits and binds you.
- Dismemberment – moments of being torn apart that led to rebirth.
- Theatrical or metaphorically living out your stories to feel them more closely.
- The presence of masks in your life.
- Freeing yourself from the control of the mind by turning toward instinct.

CHAPTER 11
FORGED IN DARKNESS

Our journeys into darkness are as unique as our fingerprints. Yet the archetypal experience of underworlding is not. The interviews and case examples I collected for this book make one thing became clear: *everyone* knows the underworld. At some point, to greater and lesser degrees, life will give us an underworld journey. It's a universal experience, not an anomaly or an estranged undercurrent. In fact, darkness unites us.

Underworlding means finding yourself in a place of uncertainty, often in fear, pain, blackness, and overwhelm. For such a universal human experience, it's bewildering that we treat darkness with negativity and repression. The problem is not the underworld, but our lack of an underworld perspective – our belief that only light is worthwhile, that we must discard all else. We need, in this day and age, the personal and cultural belief that there's something of absolute value in the abyss.

Those who have journeyed into darkness consciously have this underworld perspective. The dark current is so pervasive, they've had to build a relationship with it. There's really no other choice. As Victor Frankl said, when we are no longer able to change a situation, we are challenged to change ourselves.[1] One of the great questions of living is: How to affirm life in the face of the underworld?

Adopting an underworld perspective means *valuing* encounters with the dark parts of ourselves as opportunities for growth and depth. If we believe that the darkness has unfairly afflicted us, we are delusional – it affects everyone – and we spin with moral ponderings: Why is this happening? What did I do wrong? Why me? You didn't do anything wrong. This is a part of life that, for reasons explored throughout these pages, we in the modern world have turned our backs to and are inevitably surprised when we're forced to encounter them. Light and dark are two sides of the same coin. It's impossible to have a coin with just one side.

The tragedy of modern psychology is that we learn skills to distance and even try to remove the underworld. Therapy has become a tool to get over what has happened and make the dark waters dry up. But with time and suffering, we can change our relationship to darkness. We can *reimagine* our story, allow it to move in different ways, create meaning, and let it rebuild our world. One thing we can't do: we can't get rid of it.

To exclude the possibility of darkness is to exclude life itself. Each of us experiences life differently. We are all woven of different stories, experiences, expectations, and perspectives. To honor our uniqueness, we must treat underworlding with the imagination and complexity it deserves.

The difference between the psychological challenges of our age and those of our ancestors is that a mythological worldview with symbols and religious rites guided them, even through and back from the underworld. Today we face the dark alone. "Our problem as modern, 'enlightened' individuals," reasoned Joseph Campbell, is that "all gods and devils have been rationalized out of existence."[2] Are the gods truly dead? Have they abandoned us to face the great questions of being human by ourselves? Of course not; they've just been forgotten.

The Greek gods, goddesses, and heroes are not relics of a past culture far removed from our lives; they are *ways of imagining.* "It has always been the prime function of mythology," explains Campbell, "to supply the symbols that carry the human spirit forward."[3] Everything we imagine, feel, fear, and react to has already been given form in the archetypal imagination. Our lives are composed of enactments of myths.

Imagine rendering life as mythically significant. Notice how the gods, goddesses, and heroes mirror and move within your life. When overpowering the world, notice "Hercules" in your willpower. When trusting in something beyond yourself, notice "Aeneas" in your surrender. When feeling ungrounded or in between, notice "Hermes" in your meandering. When hardships repeat like the seasons, notice "Persephone" in your resilience. When life is violent and chaotic, notice "Dionysus" in your falling apart.

Amid demons and monsters, fear, and uncertainty awaits a priceless treasure that can be found only in darkness. Experiences of suffering and loss, illness and death, shame and betrayal, grief and depression will, if you let them, transform into sources of depth, authenticity, and identity. Campbell said that when we face the darkness of the inner world:

Where we had thought to find an abomination, we shall find a god; where we had thought to slay another, we shall slay ourselves; where we had thought to travel outward, we shall come to the center of our own existence; where we had thought to be alone, we shall be with all the world.[4]

The root system of darkness – the voices of suffering, all the ancestors who have walked down that long, dark corridor – is the narrative of humanity. It speaks of our desire to make meaning, our rituals and gods, our heroes and shadows. It speaks of our need to connect to each other, live meaningfully, and find wholeness. These are stories of underworlding, the voices that cannot be found in daylight.

How heartbreaking yet healing to have to be taken into darkness to know the miracle of life, to deepen and expand our beings. How bittersweet the lessons of the underworld with its passageways in which we are forced to become more than we realized. No one chooses to descend into the abyss, yet for those that have been on what Jung called "the sunset path," a time may come when they realize that who they have become was, indeed, *forged in darkness*.

NOTES

Introduction

1 Aristotle used the term *psyche* to refer to "the essence of life," and others took this to mean spirit or soul. In the 20th century, a field of inquiry called depth psychology emerged, and one of its founders, C. G. Jung, used the term "psyche" to refer to the totality of the human mind, spirit, and soul – conscious and unconscious.

2 To preserve confidentially, I have left out names and identifying information in case studies and stories, unless given approval to include biographical information. I do include names of people who have already made their stories known publicly.

3 Robert Pogue Harrison, *The Dominion of the Dead* (Chicago: University of Chicago Press, 2003), xi.

4 Victor Frankl, *Man's Search for Meaning*, Part One, trans. Ilse Lasch (New York: Pocket Books, 1946/1985), 64.

5 Joseph Campbell, *The Power of Myth*, ed. Sue Flowers (New York: Doubleday, 1988), 70.

6 Hercules is the Roman name of this hero-god. He is called Heracles in classical Greek literature. Although Greek myth predates the Roman and I use Greek names for all the other gods and heroes in this book, I call him Hercules because it's a more familiar name today.

7 Joseph Campbell, *The Hero with a Thousand Faces* (Princeton: Princeton University Press, 1949), 25.

8 Karen Armstrong, *A Short History of Myth* (New York: Canongate, 2005), 1. Emphasis added.

9 Robert A. Johnson, *Inner Gold: Understanding Psychological Projection* (Asheville: Chiron, 2008), 15.

10 C. G. Jung, *Psychology and Alchemy*, trans. R. F. C. Hull. Collected Works, Vol. 12 (Princeton: Princeton University Press, 1944/1968), 25.

11 Frankl, *Man's Search for Meaning*, 86.

12 James Hillman, *Re-Visioning Psychology* (New York: HarperCollins, 1975), 118.

13   Rainer Maria Rilke, *Duino Elegies*, trans. J. B. Leishman and Stephen Spender (New York: W. W. Norton and Company, 1939), 79.

14   Aeschylus, *Agamemnon*, in *Three Greek Plays*, trans. Edith Hamilton (New York: W. W. Norton & Company, 1937), 170.

15   Russel A. Lockhart, *Words as Eggs* (Dallas: Spring Publications, 1983), 116.

16   Maria Popova, "Ursula K. Le Guin on Suffering and Getting to the Other Side of Pain," *Pocket Worthy*, March 19, 2020. Available at: https://getpocket.com/explore/item/ursula-k-le-guin-on-suffering-and-getting-to-the-other-side-of-pain?utm_source=pocket-newtab.

17   Robert MacFarlane, *Underland* (New York: W. W. Norton & Company, Inc., 2019), 50.

18   Peter Wohlleben, *The Hidden Life of Trees*, trans. Jane Billinghurst (Vancouver, BC: Random House, 2016), 249.

19   Edward Whitmont, *The Symbolic Quest* (New Jersey: Princeton University Press, 1969), 82.

20   C. G. Jung, *The Red Book: Liber Novs*, ed. Sonu Shamdasani, trans. John Peck and Sonu Shamdasani (New York: Philemon Series & Norton, 2009), 346.

Part I: The Context

1. The Underworld

1   Walter Burkert, *Greek Religion*, trans. John Raffan (Malden, MA: Blackwell, 1977/1985), 196.

2   Ovid, *The Metamorphoses*, trans. Allen Mandelbaum (New York: Harcourt, 1993), 105.

3   Homer, *The Odyssey*, trans. Robert Fitzgerald (New York: Farrar, Straus & Giroux, 1998), 192.

4   Plato, *The Republic of Plato*, trans. Francis Macdonald Conford (New York: Oxford University Press, 1968), 351.

5   Jung, *Psychology and Alchemy*, 120.

6   Virgil, *Aeneid*, Book VII, l.312. Juno is the Roman name for Hera, queen of the gods.

7   Sigmund Freud, *New Introductory Lectures on Psychoanalysis* (New York: Norton, 1933), 105–6.

8   C. G. Jung, *Memories, Dreams, Reflections*, ed. Aniela Jaffe, trans. Richard Winston and Clara Winston (New York: Random House, 1963).

9   James Hillman, *The Dream and the Underworld* (New York: Harper and Row, 1979), 5.

10   Thomas Moore, *Care of the Soul* (New York: HarperCollins, 1992), 5.

11   Hillman, *Re-Visioning Psychology*, 31.

12   Hillman believed Jungian individuation had been coopted by Western monotheistic culture, making psychology a prisoner of the Judeo-Christian

fantasy of completeness and integration. In contrast, psychological polytheism offers archetypal containers for the inherent fragmentation and differentiation of psychological life. This is not about worshiping the gods, idolatry, hubristically identifying with them, or inflation, but about *serving* them, treating the ideas we have about our lives and selves as *perspectives*.

2. Descent and Ascent

1 Jung, *Memories, Dreams, Reflections*, 201.
2 Quoted in Mircea Eliade, *Rites and Symbols of Initiation*, trans. Willard Taske (Putnam, CT: Spring, 1994), 7.
3 Eliade, *Rites and Symbols of Initiation*, 66, 104, 107.
4 Robert Bly, *Iron John* (Boston: Da Capo Press, 1990).
5 Jung, *Memories, Dreams, Reflections*, 21–2.
6 Quoted in Eliade, *Rites and Symbols of Initiation*, 12.
7 Campbell, *The Hero with a Thousand Faces*, 16.
8 Robert Bly, *A Little Book on the Human Shadow* (San Francisco: HarperOne, 1988).
9 Jung, *Psychology and Alchemy*, 335.
10 Jung, *Psychology and Alchemy*, 159.
11 William Shakespeare, *As You Like It*, eds. Barbara Mowat and Paul Werstine. (New York: Simon & Schuster, 1997), 49.
12 Holly Williams, "The Art Hidden from Nazi Bombs 2018," *Culture*, BBC, April 16, 2018. www.bbc.com/culture/story/20180413-the-art-hidden-from-nazi-bombs.
13 Marion Woodman, "Spiralling Through the Apocalypse," in Daniela Sieff, ed., *Understanding and Healing Emotional Trauma* (New York: Routledge, 2015), 65.
14 Walter F. Otto, *The Homeric Gods: The Spiritual Significance of Greek Religion* (New York: Pantheon Books, 1954), 133.
15 Ovid, *The Metamorphoses*, 106.
16 Otto, *The Homeric Gods*, 136.
17 Campbell, *The Hero with a Thousand Faces*, 193.
18 Tim O'Brien, *The Things They Carried* (Boston: Houghton Mifflin, 1990), 89.
19 Robert Graves, *Goodbye to All That* (New York: Doubleday, 1957), 257.
20 Susan Rako and Harvey Mazer (eds.), *Semrad: The Heart of a Therapist*, (Lincoln, NE: iUniverse, 1980), 106.

3. The Evolution of the Hero

1 Burkert, *Greek Religion*, 205.
2 W. K. C. Guthrie, *Orpheus and Greek Religion: A Study of the Orphic Movement* (New York: Norton, 1966), 160.
3 Fritz Graf and Sarah Iles Johnston, *Ritual Texts for the Afterlife* (New York: Routledge, 2007), 98.

4   Richard Tarnas, *The Passion of the Western Mind: Understanding the Ideas that have Shaped Our Worldview* (New York: Harmony Books, 1991), 18.

5   Tarnas, *The Passion of the Western Mind*, 228.

6   Campbell, *The Hero with a Thousand Faces*, 387.

7   Keiron Le Grice, *The Rebirth of the Hero: Mythology as a Guide to Spiritual Transformation* (London: Muswell Hill Press, 2013), 60.

8   Nicole Fisher. "State of the States: 2020 Mental Health Rankings," *Forbes*, February 5, 2020. www.forbes.com/sites/nicolefisher/2020/02/25/state-of-the-states-2020-mental-health-rankings/#3a79a6315ae3.

9   C. G. Jung, *Modern Man in Search of a Soul* (New York: Harcourt, 1933), 238.

10   Hillman, *Re-Visioning Psychology*, 36.

11   C. G. Jung, *The Archetypes and the Collective Unconscious*. Collected Works, Vol. 9, pt. 1 (Princeton: Princeton University Press, 1959/1969), 23–4.

12   The mythological sequence common to all heroic journeys is: the call to adventure, refusal of the call, supernatural aid, crossing the first threshold, belly of the whale, road of trials, meeting with the goddess, woman as temptress, atonement with father, apotheosis, the ultimate boon, refusal of the return, the magic flight, rescue from within, the crossing of the return threshold, master of two worlds, and freedom to live. See Campbell, *The Hero with a Thousand Faces*, 36–7.

13   Campbell, *The Hero with a Thousand Faces*, 10.

14   C. G. Jung, *Mysterium Coniunctionis*. Collected Works, Vol. 14 (Princeton: Princeton University Press, 1955/1970), 531.

15   Jung, *Psychology and Alchemy*, 334.

1 C. S. Lewis. *The Problem of Pain* (New York: HarperCollins, 1940), 162.

PART II: Hero to Heroes

4. Hercules

1   Virgil, *The Aeneid*, trans. Allen Mandelbaum (New York: Bantam Classic, 2004), 197.

2   Apostolos Athanassakis and Benjamin Wolkow (trans.), *The Orphic Hymns* (Baltimore: John Hopkins University Press, 2013), 15.

3   Homer, *The Odyssey*, trans. Robert Fitzgerald (New York: Farrar, Straus & Giroux, 1998), 205.

4   Jung, *Modern Man in Search of a Soul*, 34.

5   Lewis Farnell, *Greek Hero Cults and Ideas of Immorality* (New York: Elibron Classics, 2005), 149–50.

6   Virgil, *The Aeneid*, 197.

7   "Churchill's greatest speeches," accessed January 6, 2020. www.historyextra.com/period/second-world-war/churchills-greatest-speeches/.

8 Interview with Arianna Huffington, *New York Times*, September 26, 2014. www.nytimes.com/2014/09/28/fashion/arianna-huffington-kobe-bryant-meditate.html.

9 Esther Perel, "There's You There's Me and There's Us," November 2, 2017, in *Where Should We Begin*, produced by Esther Perel, podcast.

10 Ovid, *The Metamorphoses*, 205.

11 Hillman, *Re-Visioning Psychology*, 38.

12 Apollodorus, *The Library of Greek Mythology*, trans. Robin Hard (Oxford: Oxford University Press, 1997), 84.

13 Ovid, *The Metamorphoses*, 166.

14 A complex is a core pattern of emotions, memories, perceptions, and wishes in the personal unconscious organized around a theme. These motifs can be unconscious, and most often are. However, Jung makes clear the ego is the central complex in the field of consciousness.

15 Charles Boer (trans.), *The Homeric Hymns* (Hubbardston, MA: Asphodel Press, 2006), 65.

16 Ovid, *The Metamorphoses*, 208.

17 The solar hero personifies repetitive exposure to the unconscious because the hero, like the sun, descends into darkness and ascends again at dawn. The battle for awareness runs in cycles, like the sun. Jung argued that the hero deliberately faces the dangers of the deep, suggesting that the hero is one who does not let the dragon devour him but subdues it over and over.

18 Campbell, *The Hero with a Thousand Faces*, 82, 42–3.

19 Hercules' first labor was slaying the Nemean Lion, whose golden fur was impenetrable. After attempting to shoot an arrow at it, Hercules was forced to club the beast and eventually strangle it with his bare hands. He then used one of the lion's claws to skin the pelt and wore the coat as a protective shield.

20 Dylan Thomas, "Do Not Go Gentle into That Good Night," *The Poems of Dylan Thomas*, ed. Daniel Jones (New York: New Directions, 1937), 239.

5. Orpheus

1 Thrace is a geographical and historical region in Southeast Europe, now split among Bulgaria, Greece, and Turkey, which is bounded by the Balkan Mountains to the north, the Aegean Sea to the south, and the Black Sea to the east.

2 Ovid, *The Metamorphoses*, 226.

3 Ovid, *The Metamorphoses*, 246.

4 Karl Kerényi, *The Heroes of the Greeks*, trans. Herbert Jennings Rose (New York: Thames and Hudson, 1959/1974), 279.

5 Frankl, *Man's Search for Meaning*, 81.

6 Campbell, *The Hero with a Thousand Faces*, 16.

7   *The Bible: Authorized King James Version*, Solomon's Song, 8:6, eds. Robert
    Carrol and Stephen Prickett (Oxford: Oxford University Press).

8   Ovid, *The Metamorphoses*, 226.

9   Kahlil Gibran, *The Prophet* (New York: Vintage Books, 1923), 15.

10 Cuong Lu, *Wait: A Love Letter to Those in Despair* (Boulder, CO: Shambhala
    Publications, 2021) 35–6.

11 Frankl, *Man's Search for Meaning*, 93.

12 Bruce Lloyd, "Return from Exile," in *Understanding and Healing Emotional
    Trauma*, ed. Daniela Sieff (New York: Routledge, 2015), 33.

13 Iris Murdock, "The Sublime and the Good," *Chicago Review* 13, no. 3 (1959), 51.

14 C. G. Jung, *Symbols of Transformation*. Collected Works, Vol. 5 (Princeton:
    Princeton University Press, 1952/1967), 409.

15 Ovid, *The Metamorphoses*, 226–7.

16 Ovid, *The Metamorphoses*, 246.

17 Robert Romanyshyn, *Soul in Grief* (Berkeley: North Atlantic Books, 1999), 9.

18 Campbell, *The Hero with a Thousand Faces*, 12.

19 Rafael López-Pedraza, *Hermes and His Children* (Einsiedeln, Switzerland:
    Daimon Verlag, 1989), 101.

6. Odysseus

1   Homer, *The Iliad*, trans. Caroline Alexander (New York: HarperCollins, 2015),
    180.

2   Edward Edinger, *Ego and Archetype* (New York: Penguin Books, 1972), 288.

3   Campbell, *The Hero with a Thousand Faces*, 154.

4   MacFarlane, *Underland*, 100.

5   Homer, *The Odyssey*, 189.

6   Homer, *The Odyssey*, 86, 118, 239.

7   Homer, *The Odyssey*, 192.

8   Romanyshyn, *Soul in Grief*, 4–5.

9   Homer, *The Odyssey*, 191.

10 Ibid.

11 Homer, *The Odyssey*, 192.

12 Judith Lewis Herman, *Trauma and Recovery* (New York: Basic Books, 1992), 134.

13 C. G. Jung, *Symbols of Transformation*, Collected Works, Vol. 5 (Princeton:
    Princeton University Press, 1952/1967), 356.

14 Jung, *The Archetypes and the Collective Unconscious*, 22.

7. Aeneas

1   The travels of the Aeneads are described in Virgil's *The Aeneid*. Aeneas'
    journey to the underworld in Book VI is *The Aeneid*'s most famous passage.
    This passage helped raise Virgil to the status of a Christian prophet in the
    Middle Ages. In the 14th century, the Italian poet Dante used Virgil as the
    guide for his own journey through hell in the *Inferno*.

2   Virgil, *The Aeneid*, 134–5.

3   Ovid, *The Metamorphoses*, 314.

4   Virgil, *The Aeneid*, 144.

5   Virgil, *The Aeneid*, 139.

6   Virgil, *The Aeneid*, 144.

7   C. G. Jung, *Psychology and Religion: East and West*. Collected Works, Vol. 11 (Princeton: Princeton University Press, 1948/1969), 182.

8   Virgil, *The Aeneid*, 160.

9   Virgil, *The Aeneid*, 159.

10 Virgil, *The Aeneid*, 153–4.

11 Moore, *Care of the Soul*, 35–6.

12 Moore, *Care of the Soul*, 38–9.

13 Frankl, *Man's Search for Meaning*, 133.

14 Virgil, *The Aeneid*, 139.

15 Virgil, *The Aeneid*, 233.

16 James Hollis, *Tracking the Gods: The Place of Myth in Modern Life* (Toronto, ON: Inner City Books, 1995), 121.

17 Virgil, *The Aeneid*, 266.

18 Virgil, *The Aeneid*, 8.

19 MacFarlane, *Underland*, 27.

20 Dan Schawbel, "Brené Brown: How Vulnerability Can Make Our Lives Better," *Forbes*, April 21, 2013. www.forbes.com/sites/danschawbel/2013/04/21/brene-brown-how-/#a9f24b38d68a.

21 Brené Brown, *The Gifts of Imperfection: Let Go of Who You Think You're Supposed to Be and Embrace Who You Are* (Center City, PA: Hazelden Publishing, 2010), 72.

22 Ovid, *The Metamorphoses*, 314.

23 Virgil, *The Aeneid*, 135.

1 Jung, *Symbols of Transformation*, 357.

PART III. THE GODS

8. Hermes

1   Athanassakis and Wolkow (trans.), *The Orphic Hymns*, 47.

2   Dante Alighieri, *The Divine Comedy*, trans. John Ciardi (New York: Penguin Group, 1954/2003), 16.

3   Jeanne Schul, "Frequently Asked Questions about Dreams: An Interview with Jungian Analyst Barry Williams," *Dream Network Journal* 24, no. 2 (2005), 32.

4   Homer, *The Iliad*, 521.

5   Marion Woodman, *Bone: Dying Into Life* (New York: Viking Penguin, 2000), dedication.

6   Jung, *The Red Book*, 275.
7   Woodman, *Bone*, xv.
8   Lockhart, *Words as Eggs*, 63.
9   Jung, *The Red Book*, 230.
10 Marion Woodman, "Spiraling Through the Apocalypse," in *Understanding and Healing Emotional Trauma*, ed. Daniela Sieff (New York: Routledge, 2015), 72.
11 Ovid, *The Metamorphoses*, 47.
12 Keiron Le Grice, *Archetypal Reflection* (London: Muswell Hill Press, 2016), 181.
13 Ginette Paris, *Pagan Grace*, trans. Joanna Mott (Dallas: Spring, 1990), 110.
14 Paris, *Pagan Grace*, 109.
15 James Hillman (ed.), *Puer Papers* (Dallas: Spring, 1991), 156.
16 James Hillman, *Senex & Puer*, ed. Glen Slater (Putnam, CT: Spring, 2013), 97.
17 Apostolos Athanassakis (trans.), *The Homeric Hymns* (Baltimore: John Hopkins University Press, 1976), 45.
18 Karl Kerényi, *Hermes Guide of Souls*, trans. Murray Stein (Dallas: Spring, 1976/1900), 88.
19 Donald Kalsched, "Uncovering the Secrets of the Traumatized Psyche," in *Understanding and Healing Emotional Trauma*, ed. Daniela Sieff (New York: Routledge, 2015), 17.
20 Lockhart, *Words as Eggs*, 58.
21 Romanyshyn, *Soul in Grief*, 63.
22 Kalsched, "Uncovering the Secrets of the Traumatized Psyche," 19.
23 David Kessler, *Finding Meaning: The Sixth Stage of Grief* (New York: Scribner, 2019), 71.
24 C. G. Jung, *Dream Analysis* (Zurich: C.G. Jung Institute, 1958), II, 53–4.
25 James Hillman, *Mythic Figures* (Putnam, CT: Spring, 2007), 58.
26 Jung, *Memories, Dreams, Reflections*, 117.
27 Jung, *Alchemical Studies*, 43.
28 Lockhart, *Words as Eggs*, 65. Emphasis added.
29 C. G. Jung, *The Structure and Dynamics of the Psyche*, Collected Works, Vol. 8 (Princeton: Princeton University Press, 1958/1969), 61.
30 Jung, *Alchemical Studies*, 217.
31 Jung, *Alchemical Studies*, 237.
32 Christine Downing, *Gods in Our Midst* (New Orleans: Spring Journal Books, 1993), 41.
33 Walter F. Otto. *Dionysus: Myth and Cult*, trans. Robert B. Palmer (Bloomington, IN: Indiana University Press, 1965), 9.
34 Jung, *Alchemical Studies*, 230.

9. Persephone

1   Boer, *The Homeric Hymns*, 92–3.
2   Persephone is Proserpina in Roman myth.
3   Ovid, *The Metamorphoses*, 126.

4   Hillman, *Re-Visioning Psychology,* 208.

5   Ovid, *The Metamorphoses,* 126.

6   Hesiod, *The Homeric Hymns and Homerica,* trans. Hugh Evelyn-White (Rampton: Cambridge University Press, 1914), 54.

7   Jung, *The Red Book,* 275.

8   Jalal Al'Din Rumi, "I Died as a Mineral," Consolatio, accessed September 18, 2020. www.consolatio.com/2005/04/i_died_as_a_min.html.

9   Athanassakis, *The Homeric Hymns,* 3–4.

10   Christine Downing, "Journeys to the Underworld," *Mythosphere* 9, no. 2 (1999), 192.

11   Marie Louise von Franz, *On Dreams & Death,* trans. Emmanuel Kennedy-Xipolitas (Chicago: Carus, 1986/1998), xii.

12   Ovid, *The Metamorphoses,* 126.

13   Hesiod, *The Homeric Hymns and Homerica,* 58.

14   Homer, *The Odyssey,* 206.

15   Ovid, *The Metamorphoses,* 129.

16   David Kushner, "Can Trauma Help You Grow," *The New Yorker,* March 15, 2016. www.newyorker.com/tech/annals-of-technology/can-trauma-help-you-grow?

17   Tanya Wilkinson, *Persephone Returns* (Berkeley: Pagemill Press, 1996), 27.

18   C. G. Jung, *Psychogenesis of Mental Disease.* Collected Works, Vol. 3 (Princeton: Princeton University Press, 1928/1960), 168.

19   "Persephonic," *Urban Dictionary Online,* accessed February 13, 2020. www.urbandictionary.com/define.php?term=Persephonic.

10. Dionysus

1   Steve Conner. "Children Better at Recognising Pokemon Characters Than British Wildlife." *Independent,* March 29, 2002. www.independent.co.uk/news/uk/home-news/children-better-recognising-pokemon-characters-british-wildlife-9131306.html.

2   John Burroughs, *Leaf and Tendril* (Houghton, MI: Mifflin Company, 1908), 261.

3   Steve Van Matre and Bill Weiler, *Earth Magic* (Greenville, WV: Institute for Earth Education, 1983), 3.

4   Lockhart, *Words as Eggs,* 54.

5   Lockhart, *Words as Eggs,* 57.

6   See, e.g., "Study estimates exposure to air pollution increases COVID-19 deaths by 15% worldwide," European Society of Cardiology, October 27, 2020. www.escardio.org/The-ESC/Press-Office/Press-releases/study-estimates-exposure-to-air-pollution-increases-covid-19-deaths-by-15-world. See also Robert Litman, "The Air We Share," Spirituality and Health. https://spiritualityhealth.com/articles/2020/01/04/the-air-we-share.

7   Jung, *Symbols of Transformation,* 401.

8   Athanassakis and Wolkow, *The Orphic Hymns,* 27.

9 Romanyshyn, *Soul in Grief*, 57. Emphasis added.

10 Paris, *Pagan Grace*, 5.

11 Robert A. Johnson, *Ecstasy* (San Francisco: Harper & Row, 1987), 19.

12 Calvin Hall and Veron Nordby, *A Primer in Jungian Psychology* (New York: Signet Classics, 1973), 50.

13 C. G. Jung, *Psychological Types*. Collected Works, Vol. 6 (Princeton: Princeton University Press, 1921/1971), 114.

14 Aaron Atsma, *The Theoi Project: Guide to Greek Mythology*, last modified 2019. www.theoi.com

15 Paris, *Pagan Grace*, 21.

16 Quoted in Lloyd, "Return from Exile," 42.

17 W. K. C. Guthrie, *The Greeks and their Gods* (Boston: Beacon Press, 1950), 148.

18 Johnson, *Ecstasy*, vi.

19 Paris, *Pagan Grace*, 23.

20 Campbell, *The Hero with a Thousand Faces*, 17.

21 Jung, *Psychology and Alchemy*, 89.

22 Jung, *The Red Book*, 230.

23 Roger Cotterrell, *Emile Durkheim: Law in a Moral Domain* (Edinburgh: Edinburgh University Press, 1999), 19.

24 Frankl, *Man's Search for Meaning*, 61.

25 James Hillman, *Healing Fiction* (Putnam, CT: Spring, 1994), 38.

26 C. G. Jung, *Two Essays on Analytical Psychology*. Collected Works, Vol. 7 (Princeton: Princeton University Press, 1972), 190.

27 Paris, *Pagan Grace*, 47

28 Jung, *Mysterium Coniunctionis*, 238.

29 Woodman, "Spiraling Through the Apocalypse," 68–72.

30 Woodman, "Spiraling Through the Apocalypse," 74.

31 Quoted in Joseph Campbell, *Goddess: Mysteries of the Feminine Divine*, ed. Safron Rossi (Novato, CA: New World Library, 2013), 216–17.

32 Johnson, *Ecstasy*, 21.

33 Woodman, "Spiraling Through the Apocalypse," 66.

34 Ibid.

35 Von Franz, *On Dreams & Death*, xii.

36 Hillman, *The Dream and the Underworld*, 85.

11. Forged in Darkness

1 Frankl, *Man's Search for Meaning*, 135.

2 Campbell, *The Hero with a Thousand Faces*, 104.

3 Campbell, *The Hero with a Thousand Faces*, 11.

4 Campbell, *The Hero with a Thousand Faces*, 25.

BIBLIOGRAPHY

Aeschylus. *Agamemnon*. In *Three Greek Plays*, translated by Edith Hamilton. New York: W. W. Norton & Company, 1937.

Alighieri, Dante. *The Divine Comedy*. Translated by John Ciardi. New York: Penguin Group, 1954/2003.

Apollodorus. *The Library of Greek Mythology*. Translated by Robin Hard. Oxford: Oxford University Press, 1997.

Armstrong, Karen. *A Short History of Myth*. New York: Canongate, 2005.

Athanassakis, Apostolos (trans.). *The Homeric Hymns*. Baltimore: John Hopkins University Press, 1976.

Athanassakis, Apostolos and Benjamin Wolkow (trans.). *The Orphic Hymns*. Baltimore: John Hopkins University Press, 2013.

Atsma, Aaron. *The Theoi Project: Guide to Greek Mythology*. Last modified 2019. www.theoi.com/.

Berman, Ali. "Eight Artists who Suffered from Mental Illness." Accessed February 18, 2020. https://www.mnn.com/lifestyle/arts-culture/stories/8-artists-who-suffered-mental-illness.

The Bible: Authorized King James Version. Edited by Robert Carrol and Stephen Prickett. Oxford: Oxford University Press, 2008.

Bly, Robert. *A Little Book on the Human Shadow*. San Francisco: HarperOne, 1988.
———. *Iron John*. Boston: Da Capo Press, 1990.

Boer, Charles (trans.). *The Homeric Hymns*. Hubbardston, MA: Asphodel Press, 2006.

Brown, Brené. *The Gifts of Imperfection: Let Go of Who You Think You're Supposed to Be and Embrace Who You Are*. Center City, PA: Hazelden Publishing, 2010.

Burkert, Walter. *Greek Religion*. Translated by John Raffan. Malden, MA: Blackwell, 1977/1985.

Burroughs, John. *Leaf and Tendril*. Houghton, MI: Mifflin Company, 1908.

Campbell, Joseph. *The Hero with a Thousand Faces*. Princeton: Princeton University Press, 1949.
———. *The Power of Myth*. Edited by Sue Flowers. New York: Doubleday, 1988.
———. *Goddess: Mysteries of the Feminine Divine*. Edited by Safron Rossi. Novato, CA: Joseph Campbell Foundation, 2013.

Capote, Truman. "In Cold Blood: An Unspeakable Crime in the Heartland." *The New Yorker*, September 25 to October 16, 1965.

Churchill, Winston. "Churchill's Greatest Speeches." Accessed January 6, 2020. https://www.historyextra.com/period/second-world-war/churchills-greatest-speeches/.

Conner, Steve. "Children Better at Recognising Pokémon Characters Than British Wildlife." *Independent*, March 2020.

Cotterrell, Roger. *Emile Durkheim: Law in a Moral Domain*. Edinburgh: Edinburgh University Press, 1999.

Downing, Christine. *Gods in Our Midst*. New Orleans: Spring Journal Books, 1993.

———. "Journeys to the Underworld." *Mythosphere* 9, no. 2 (1999), 175–93.

Edinger, Edward. *Ego and Archetype*. New York: Penguin Books, 1972.

Eliade, Mircea. *Rites and Symbols of Initiation*. Translated by Willard Taske. Putnam, CT: Spring, 1994.

Farnell, Lewis. *Greek Hero Cults and Ideas of Immorality*. New York: Elibron Classics, 2005.

Fisher, Nicole. "State of the States: 2020 Mental Health Rankings." *Forbes*. February 5, 2020. https://www.forbes.com/sites/nicolefisher/2020/02/25/state-of-the-states-2020-mental-health-rankings/#3a79a6315ae3.

Frankl, Victor. *Man's Search for Meaning*. Part One. Translated by Ilse Lasch. New York: Pocket Books, 1946/1985.

Freud, Sigmund. *New Introductory Lectures on Psychoanalysis*. New York: Norton, 1933.

———. *The Interpretation of Dreams*. Translated by Joyce Crick. New York: Oxford University Press, 1900/1999.

Gibran, Kahlil. *The Prophet*. New York: Vintage Books, 1923.

Graf, Fritz and Sarah Iles Johnston, *Ritual Texts for the Afterlife*. New York: Routledge, 2007.

Graves, Robert. *Goodbye to All That*. New York: Doubleday, 1957.

Greer, Patricia. *Breast Cancer: A Soul Journey*. Asheville, NC: Chiron, 2014.

Guthrie, W. K. C. *The Greeks and their Gods*. Boston: Beacon Press, 1950.

———. *Orpheus and Greek Religion: A Study of the Orphic Movement*. New York: Norton, 1966.

Hall, Calvin, and Veron Nordby. *A Primer in Jungian Psychology*. New York: Signet Classics, 1973.

Harrison, Jane Ellen. *Prolegomena to the Study of Greek Religion*. Whitstable, UK: Merlin, 1962.

Harrison, Robert Pogue. *The Dominion of the Dead*. Chicago: University of Chicago Press, 2003.

Herman, Judith Lewis. *Trauma and Recovery*. New York: Basic Books, 1992.

Hesiod. *The Homeric Hymns and Homerica*. Translated by Hugh Evelyn-White. Rampton: Cambridge University Press, 1914.

———. *The Works and Days, Theogony, the Shield of Herakles*. Translated by Richmond Lattimore. Ann Arbor: University of Michigan Press, 1959/1991.

Hillman, James. *Re-Visioning Psychology*. New York: HarperCollins, 1975.

———. *The Dream and the Underworld*. New York: Harper and Row, 1979.

——— (ed.). *Puer Papers*. Dallas: Spring, 1991.

———. *Healing Fiction*. Putnam, CT: Spring, 1994.

———. *Mythic Figures*. Putnam, CT: Spring, 2007.

———. *Senex & Puer*. Edited by Glen Slater. Putnam, CT: Spring, 2013.

Hollis, James. *Tracking the Gods: The Place of Myth in Modern Life*. Toronto, ON: Inner City Books, 1995.

Homer. *The Odyssey*. Translated by Robert Fitzgerald. New York: Farrar, Straus & Giroux, 1998.

———. *The Iliad*. Translated by Caroline Alexander. New York: HarperCollins, 2015.

Hopcke, Robert. *A Guided Tour of the Collected Works of C. G. Jung*. Boston: Shambhala, 1989.

Johnson, Robert A. *Inner Gold: Understanding Psychological Projection*. Asheville, NC: Chiron, 2008.

———. *Ecstasy*. San Francisco: Harper & Row, 1987.

Jung, C. G. *Psychological Types*. Collected Works, Vol. 6. Princeton: Princeton University Press, 1921/1971.

———. *Psychogenesis of Mental Disease*. Collected Works, Vol. 3. Princeton: Princeton University Press, 1928/1960.

———. *The Practice of Psychotherapy*. Collected Works, Vol. 16. Princeton: Princeton University Press, 1931/1966.

———. *Modern Man in Search of a Soul*. New York: Harcourt, 1933.

———. *Psychology and Alchemy*. Collected Works, Vol. 12. Princeton: Princeton University Press, 1944/1968.

———. *Psychology and Religion: East and West*. Collected Works, Vol. 11. Princeton: Princeton University Press, 1948/1969.

———. *Symbols of Transformation*. Collected Works, Vol. 5. Princeton: Princeton University Press, 1952/1967.

———. *Mysterium Coniunctionis*. Collected Works, Vol. 14. Princeton: Princeton University Press, 1955/1970.

———. *Dream Analysis*. Zurich: C.G. Jung Institute, 1958.

———. *The Structure and Dynamics of the Psyche*. Collected Works, Vol. 8. Princeton: Princeton University Press, 1958/1969.

———. *The Archetypes and the Collective Unconscious*. Collected Works, Vol. 9, pt. 1. Princeton: Princeton University Press, 1959/1969.

———. *Memories, Dreams, Reflections*. Edited by Aniela Jaffe. Translated by Richard Winston and Clara Winston. New York: Random House, 1963.

———. *Alchemical Studies*. Collected Works, Vol. 13. Princeton: Princeton University Press, 1967.

———. *Two Essays on Analytical Psychology*. Collected Works, Vol. 7. Princeton: Princeton University Press, 1972.

————. *The Red Book: Liber Novs*. Edited by Sonu Shamdasani. Translated by John Peck and Sonu Shamdasani. New York: Philemon Series & Norton, 2009.

Kalsched, Donald. *The Inner World of Trauma*. New York: Routledge, 1996.

————. "Uncovering the Secrets of the Traumatized Psyche." In *Understanding and Healing Emotional Trauma*, edited by Daniela Sieff, 11-24. New York: Routledge, 2015.

Kerényi, Karl. *The Heroes of the Greeks*. Translated by Herbert Jennings Rose. New York: Thames and Hudson, 1959/1974.

————. *Hermes Guide of Souls*. Translated by Murray Stein. Dallas: Spring, 1976/1900.

Kessler, David. *Finding Meaning: The Sixth Stage of Grief*. New York: Scribner, 2019.

Kushner, David. "Can Trauma Help You Grow?" *The New Yorker*. March 15, 2016. https://www.newyorker.com/tech/annals-of-technology/can-trauma-help-you-grow?utm_campaign=likeshopme&client_service_id=31202&utm_social_type=owned&utm_brand=tny&service_user_id=1.78e+16&utm_content=instagram-bio-link&utm_source=instagram&utm_medium=social&client_service_name=the%20new%20yorker&supported_service_name=instagram_publishing.

Le Grice, Keiron. *The Rebirth of the Hero: Mythology as a Guide to Spiritual Transformation*. London: Muswell Hill Press, 2013.

————. *Archetypal Reflections*. London: Muswell Hill Press, 2016.

Lewis, C. S. *The Problem of Pain*. New York: HarperCollins, 1940.

Litman, Robert. "The Air We Share." Spirituality and Health. https://spiritualityhealth.com/articles/2020/01/04/the-air-we-share

Lloyd, Bruce. "Return from Exile." In *Understanding and Healing Emotional Trauma*, edited by Daniela Sieff, 25-45. New York: Routledge, 2015.

Lockhart, Russel A. *Words as Eggs*. Dallas: Spring Publications, 1983.

López-Pedraza, Raphael. *Hermes and His Children*. Einsiedeln, Switzerland: Diamon Verlag, 1989.

Lu, Cuong. *Wait: A Love Letter to Those in Despair*. Boulder, CO: Shambhala Publications, 2021.

MacFarlane, Robert. *Underland*. New York: W. W. Norton & Company, 2019.

Miranda, Lin Manuel. *Hamilton: An American Musical*. Atlantic Records, 2015, MP3.

Moore, Thomas. *Care of the Soul*. New York: HarperCollins, 1992.

Murdock, Iris. "The Sublime and the Good." *Chicago Review* 13, no. 3 (1959), 51.

Neumann, Erich. *The Origin and History of Consciousness*. Translated by R. F. C. Hull. Princeton: Princeton University Press, 1954.

O'Brien, Tim. *The Things They Carried*. Boston: Houghton Mifflin, 1990.

Odier, Charles. *Anxiety and Magic Thinking*. Translated by Marie Louise Schoelly and Mary Sherfey. New York: International University Press, 1956.

Oliver, Mary. *Dream Work*. New York: Atlantic Monthly Press, 1986.

Otto, Walter F. *The Homeric Gods: The Spiritual Significance of Greek Religion*. New York: Pantheon Books, 1954.

————. *Dionysus: Myth and Cult*. Translated by Robert B. Palmer. Bloomington, IN: Indiana University Press, 1965.

Ovid. *The Metamorphoses*. Translated by Allen Mandelbaum. New York: Harcourt, 1993.

Paris, Ginette. *Pagan Grace*. Translated by Joanna Mott. Dallas: Spring, 1990.

Perel, Esther. "There's You There's Me and There's Us." *Where Should We Begin*. November 2, 2017. Produced by Esther Perel. Podcast.

"Persephonic." *Urban Dictionary Online*. Accessed February 13, 2020. https://www.urbandictionary.com/define.php?term=Persephonic.

Plato. *The Republic of Plato*. Translated by Francis Macdonald Conford. New York: Oxford University Press, 1968.

Popova, Maria. "Ursula K. Le Guin on Suffering and Getting to the Other Side of Pain." *Pocket Worthy*. March 19, 2020. https://getpocket.com/explore/item/ursula-k-le-guin-on-suffering-and-getting-to-the-other-side-of-pain?utm_source=pocket-newtab.

Rako, Susan and Harvey Mazer (eds.). *Semrad: The Heart of a Therapist*. Lincoln, NE: iUniverse, 1980.

Rilke, Rainer Maria. *Duino Elegies*. Translated by J. B. Leishman and Stephen Spender. New York: W. W. Norton and Company, 1939.

————. *The Unknown Rilke: Expanded Edition*. Translated by Franz Wright. Oberlin, OH: Oberlin College Press, 1983.

Romanyshyn, Robert. *Soul in Grief*. Berkeley: North Atlantic Books, 1999.

Rumi, Jalal Al'Din. "I Died as a Mineral." Consolatio. Accessed September 18, 2020. https://www.consolatio.com/2005/04/i_died_as_a_min.html.

Schawbel, Dan. "Brené Brown: How Vulnerability Can Make Our Lives Better." *Forbes*. April 21, 2013. https://www.forbes.com/sites/danschawbel/2013/04/21/brene-brown-how-vulnerability-can-make-our-lives-better/#7a32378936c7.

Schul, Jeanne. "Frequently Asked Questions about Dreams: An Interview with Jungian Analyst Barry Williams." *Dream Network Journal* 24, no. 2 (2005), 21–33.

Shakespeare, William. *As You Like It*. Edited by Barbara Mowat and Paul Werstine. New York: Simon & Schuster, 1997.

Tarnas, Richard. *The Passion of the Western Mind: Understanding the Ideas that have Shaped Our Worldview*. New York: Harmony Books, 1991.

Thomas, Dylan. *The Poems of Dylan Thomas*. Edited by Daniel Jones. New York, NY: New Directions, 1937.

Van Matre, Steve, and Bill Weiler. *Earth Magic*. Greenville, WV: Institute for Earth Education, 1983.

Virgil. *The Aeneid*. Translated by Allen Mandelbaum. New York: Bantam Classic, 2004.

Von Franz, Marie Louise. *The Feminine in Fairytales*. New York: Spring Publications, 1972.

————. *On Dreams & Death*. Translated by Emmanuel Kennedy-Xipolitas. Chicago: Carus, 1986/1998.

Whitmont, Edward. *The Symbolic Quest*. Princeton: Princeton University Press, 1969.

Wilkinson, Tanya. *Persephone Returns*. Berkeley: Pagemill Press, 1996.

Williams, Holly. "The Art Hidden from Nazi Bombs 2018." *Culture*. BBC, April 16, 2018. www.bbc.com/culture/story/20180413-the-art-hidden-from-nazi-bombs.

Wohlleben, Peter. *The Hidden Life of Trees*. Translated by Jane Billinghurst. Vancouver, BC: Random House, 2016.

Woodman, Marion. *Bone: Dying Into Life*. New York: Viking Penguin, 2000.

————. "Spiraling Through the Apocalypse." In *Understanding and Healing Emotional Trauma*, edited by Daniela Sieff, 64–87. New York: Routledge, 2015.

INDEX